'If this was a thriller, people would say it was unlikely. Unhappily, it's true' *Irish Times*

'Remarkable for its lack of bitterness . . . Begg's narrative in *Enemy Combatant* is calm and reflective, but running through it is the underlying sorrow of a man still haunted and in shock from the nightmare that befell him' *Glasgow Herald*

'What is impressive about the account in this book is the sympathy with which he describes some of his captors' Stephen Fidler, *Financial Times*

'The first authoritative version of conditions in Guantánamo . . . His account is utterly plausible and very disturbing . . . Written without rancour' *Spectator*

'Compellingly simple' *Amnesty*

'This is fascinating and disturbing stuff' *Sunday Herald*

ENEMY COMBATANT

A British Muslim's Journey to
Guantánamo and Back

MOAZZAM BEGG

with VICTORIA BRITTAIN

POCKET
BOOKS

LONDON • SYDNEY • NEW YORK • TORONTO

First published in Great Britain by The Free Press in 2006
This edition published by Pocket Books in 2007
An imprint of Simon & Schuster UK Ltd
A CBS COMPANY

1 3 5 7 9 10 8 6 4 2

Simon & Schuster UK Ltd
Africa House
64–78 Kingsway
London WC2B 6AH

www.simonsays.co.uk

Simon & Schuster Australia
Sydney

A CIP catalogue record for this book
is available from the British Library.

ISBN 10: 1-4165-2265-4
ISBN 13: 978-1-4165-2265-2

Typeset in Palatino by M Rules
Printed and bound in Great Britain by
Cox & Wyman Ltd, Reading, Berks

بسم الله الرحمن الرحيم

For Dad, Zaynab, and my children

Contents

Acknowledgements

In the Name of Allah Most Compassionate Most Merciful

When I first returned from Guantánamo I was anxious enough, and naive enough, to think that I could complete this task on my own. I soon realized though that I wasn't even sure about how to start. I was very fortunate, however, to meet Victoria Brittain within the first couple of weeks and was pleasantly surprised to discover that she was actively involved in the lives of the families of the Guantánamo prisoners. She is one of those people who care.

News of her work on the play *Guantanamo: Honor Bound to Defend Freedom* had already reached me in custody. So when I was looking for someone to help me write my story I'm glad I didn't have to look too far.

I am particularly grateful also to Feroz Abbassi (who suggested the title, back in Guantánamo), Abu Bakr, Andrew Gordon, Clive Stafford Smith, Gareth Peirce, Pat Kavanagh, John Gittings and my father, Azmat Begg, for their invaluable revisions, suggestions and corrections. Also I would like to thank Seema Ahmed, Edwina Barstow, Hannah Corbett, Tim Otty, Tariq Sadiq, Michael Ratner, Helen and

Mike Oldfield, Ronan Bennett, Sheila Joshua, and Mary, Guy, and Yvette (the Typing Pool, Wales), and from America, Joshua Dratel, Major Dan Mori, Neal Katyal and David Remes.

At times I have worked obsessively to complete this book, and I could not have done it without the patience and support of my wife, Zaynab. My eldest children, Umamah and Abdur-Rahman, despite their tender ages, have always taken a keen interest in my progress and often read parts of the book for themselves. They have been a great source of encouragement for me.

Author's Note

The source for the dialogue used in this book is primarily my own memory. However, extensive notes taken by lawyers or by me, and the recollections of those people with whom I was able to confirm the content of our conversation have been of immense value. Although a little of the dialogue in this book is almost verbatim, particularly the more recent, the majority has been reconstructed.

I have always understood that the names given to me by intelligence agents and law enforcement officers were assumed, and not real, so I have kept them. Some of the other names used in this book have been changed for legal reasons, and because of the sensitive nature of the issues.

Whilst it is almost impossible to accurately Romanize many Eastern languages that have their own distinct letters and sounds, I have preferred to use words that are phonetically closer to the original language when transliterating names, places or general speech and terminology. This method is now commonplace in English literature that has been translated from Arabic. For example, since there is no corresponding 'e' vowel in Arabic, and feminine nouns end with a light 'h' sound, I have used 'Makkah' and 'Madinah', instead of the more common 'Mecca' and 'Medina', and 'al-Qa'idah', instead of 'al-Qaeda'.

Prologue

The concertina wire is ingrained deepest in my memory. As we strolled meaninglessly around the enclosure, cameras surmounted with machine guns, and guards in military uniform followed our every move. The situation was hopeless – without a foreseeable end. The dismal monotony of daily existence was becoming unbearable. The uncertainty of the future compounded the atmosphere of apprehension and fear.

I whispered to a fellow detainee, 'How much more of this can we take? It's becoming impossible. If we don't make a stand now we'll lose our self-respect, in addition to our freedom.' My companion sedately replied, 'Patience, my brother, we must have patience.'

And then it began. The firing was indiscriminate; rounds whistled overhead, the bodies fell around me. Turning back towards my confidant I began to spurt out muffled words about running, but he was already on the ground like the others, dead. Everyone was getting shot – except me. I felt unable to do a thing, but then I did. I called the *athaan* as loud as possible, for the world to hear. It did hear – eventually.

I had known all along that my wife was expecting a baby, and I still had some hope of being present for its birth. But when I heard someone yell across the wire that the child was about to enter this world – with its father captive amongst coils of razor wire – I knew that even if I survived this massacre, it would be a long while before I was reunited with my family. At this thought I became oblivious of the surrounding carnage. I raised my hands, in the traditional Muslim way, towards the sky, and began to weep. Voices in my head whispered to me to seek help from Allah and beseech His mercy. My hands rose, and continued to do so, passing the clouds. And still I wept.

That was how I woke up, next to my wife. She was woken by the sounds of my sobbing and asked me in her gentlest voice why I was so upset. I told her about the nightmare. But it was 1995. It would be another seven years before I learned its true meaning.

Oddly enough, the suggestion to begin any book that I intended to write with this dream came from an American soldier to whom I had told it in the winter of 2002, at the US Bagram Air Base Detention Centre, Afghanistan, where I was held for over ten months. I told her about the uncanny similarity between what I had seen in my dream and the scenes that had confronted me in Kandahar and Bagram.

The idea of writing a book about my life – growing up in Birmingham, and visiting Afghanistan and Bosnia – was something I considered as early as 1999. By that time I had already had some extraordinary experiences, which would ultimately lead to the most profound and difficult period in my life to date.

Enemy Combatant, however, found its origins in Camp Echo, Guantánamo Bay, Cuba, during my time in solitary confinement, after I penned some skeleton notes for an autobiography. I found my interrogators – CIA, FBI, and MI5 agents – as well as alleged al-Qa'idah members, with whom I had been held, all encouraged me to write a book when I eventually returned.

One of the more ambitious aims of this book is to find some common ground between people on opposing sides of this new war, to introduce the voice of reason, which is so frequently drowned by the roar of hatred and intolerance.

I have made a few momentous decisions in my life – some with great joy and others with regret, but all worth writing about. If those choices and their consequences can portray a world very different from that of most readers and create some understanding in the process, then I think some good has been achieved. And if it doesn't . . . then it was still worth the effort.

Moazzam Begg

Attacks from the air on September eleven
Kindled once more sweet vengeance's flame:
Never forgotten or ever forgiven,
Those uninvolved must carry the blame

Like prisoners of conscience, raised to new heights,
Few are made present by merit alone.
Confined to a cage, deprived any rights,
Laws are rewritten and oppression condoned

—*from 'The Dagger's Hilt',*
January 2004, Guantánamo

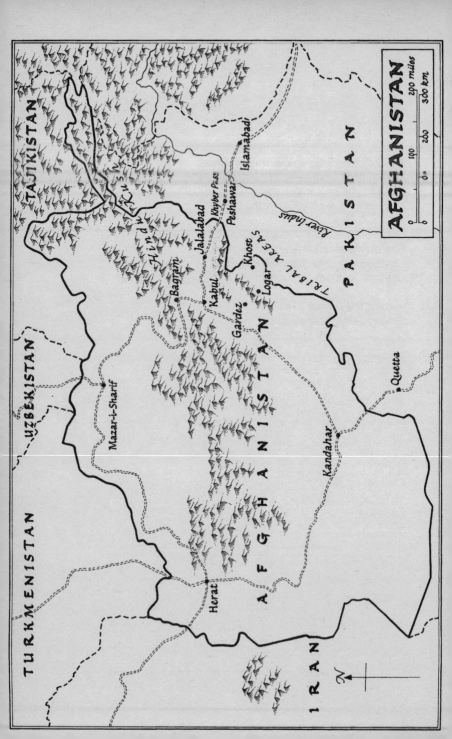

1
ILLEGALLY DETAINED

Midnight. Islamabad, 31 January 2002

The house was silent. Zaynab and the children were all asleep. It had been a long day for them: a friend from Kabul and her two children were staying over for a visit. They were in bed too by now. I was still awake, at my computer, writing a letter, then playing a game. I checked my watch at the sound of the doorbell. My first thought was that someone had got the wrong door, or that there was an emergency with the neighbours.

I didn't feel worried, although it seemed a little strange because of the time. I opened the door, and stood there in my socks, stunned. I saw a group of people standing in front of me, and the first thing I knew was a gun at my head. I was pushed right back, through the forecourt, through the open front door, into the living room where my peaceful evening had just ended in shock and rising fear. I was made to kneel. In front of me was a baffling group of people, not dressed as policemen, but in local Pakistani and Western clothes.

They didn't say a word. They didn't even ask me who I was. I could have been anybody. As I knelt there, I saw from the corner of my eye that some of them were walking in towards the rooms in the back where my wife and the other family were. With an instant reflex to protect them, I said, 'That's my family in there, don't go in there.' Then I couldn't see anything more, as they put a cloth hood over my head. They pulled my hands behind my back, handcuffed me, and fastened flexicuffs (a disposable plastic shackling device) tightly around my ankles. I was physically picked up and carried into the vehicle, which they had parked in my driveway. If any neighbours had been awake they would not have known that anything was wrong. The house was detached, and the walls and gates high.

I was dropped in the back of a 4×4, lying flat. Within seconds, as we started to move, somebody pulled up my hood just enough so that I could see. Instantly a camera flashed in my face. Behind it, I saw a very badly disguised American, dressed to look like a Pakistani. He had a cloth wrapped round his head in a style that attempted to be but was obviously not Pakistani. My first reaction, despite the terrifying position I was in, was laughter. He looked ridiculous. He didn't say a word, but just took a photograph. Then the person on the other side of me, also an American but dressed a little better with an Afghani cap, produced a pair of handcuffs. I was cuffed behind my back already, but he waved these at me, and he said, 'Do you know where I've gotten these handcuffs from?'

'I've no idea, how would I know where you got your handcuffs from?'

'I was given these by the wife of a victim of the September 11th attacks.'

I was calm enough to tell him that she would think he was really stupid, having caught the wrong person. Then he put them on top of the ones I already had on. I was incredulous. Could this scene really be happening?

I tried to plead with the Pakistanis, speaking to them in Urdu as a local, someone familiar to them, as the Americans obviously were not. I told them, 'Look, if I've done something wrong, then do this the proper way, get me access to the British Consul, or get me a lawyer, and let me have some contact with my family, let me phone to see if they are all right.' I went on trying to plead with them as we drove along. I couldn't believe they were ignoring me, but in only about ten minutes we stopped.

At first, in front of the Americans, the Pakistanis wouldn't say any-thing – they just wouldn't react at all. They kept themselves very hard and rigid. I spoke to them, in the Urdu way, as you do to somebody who is older than you, who you call 'uncle', but they were cold and unresponsive, which was so uncharacteristic of how things usually were between people in Pakistan. But this was a secret world, and I'd been kidnapped with full government approval. It was obvious to me, because they didn't react, and from the whole strange, tense, atmos-phere, that they were under some severe pressure.

They carried me out of the car and I assumed the Americans had left (after taking back their handcuffs); I never saw them again. I found myself in what I imagined was an intelligence service facility of some sort, and I was expecting to be put in a cell. In fact the Pakistanis put me into a fairly decent room with a sofa, a chair, a mat on the floor, and a quilt, a pillow, even a window. But they soon covered the window up with masking tape, so that I could not look outside, and then for about forty-five minutes the man I had been calling 'uncle' sat down next to me, alone, and asked some formal details such as my name, address, places I'd visited, what I was doing here in Pakistan, no more than ten questions. He had a blank sheet of A4 paper, and he wrote all this down as though these were normal formalities and there was nothing exceptional about what was happening. But I could really see the strain in his face, and the struggle he was having with himself about having picked me up in that way from my house and my family. He was very uncomfortable.

The first thing he said to me was, 'Look, son, I don't know what you've done or why the Americans want you so desperately, but you can see that I've put you in a room here and not a cell. You've done nothing wrong in Pakistan that I know about and I feel bad at having come to your house in the middle of the night. I've seen how your house is; I've seen how your family are. You just don't seem to be the type of person that would cause any sort of trouble.' He went on, 'The only reason we're doing this is because of the Americans.'

I asked him, 'Why are you doing this for them, if you think that I haven't done anything, which I haven't? Why are you doing this to me, why are you bending over backwards to please the Americans?'

'If we don't, we'll be hit so hard by the Americans, by President Bush's army. You know that statement of theirs, "You're either with us or against us"? Well, we've had to take a position.' I had assumed by now these men were the Inter Service Intelligence (ISI) – Pakistani intelligence. Who else had the capability to kidnap me like this, with full American support?

One of the guards had already taken the handcuffs off and cut off the flexicuffs, which took some time as he only had a very blunt pair of scissors. There were some building repairs going on in the room, there was a little hole in the wall where some bricks were missing, and I could see through to the outside. When we had finished talking, the guard shackled my hand to a chair for the night. Although he didn't say anything, it was quite obvious why. However, the shackle was so big that my hand could slide right through it. Once he'd gone, I took it out for the rest of the night, and just slid it back in again when anyone came into the room. I really expected this ordeal to be over within hours, if not days, that it was some mistake, so I didn't think of escaping. Not yet.

I stretched back in the chair, and touched my pocket. I felt the outline of my mobile phone. It had been in my pocket, as usual, when I was on the computer, and they had never physically searched me. I had forgotten about the phone, but now it felt like a real lifeline. The first thing I did was phone a friend who lived fairly close by. It was about two in the morning. When he picked up the phone his voice was very sleepy. I whispered down the phone, and, strangely, he whispered back to me. I told him what had happened, and asked him if he could first go and check my house to see if everybody was all right, and then see if he could get in contact with some of my uncles and aunts and other family members who lived in Pakistan. Then I phoned my father in Birmingham. I couldn't believe my luck that I could make an international call from this prison room. Again I whispered down the phone to him. I told him what had happened, and also that all I knew was that Americans were there when they took me, and that it was on their orders that I was held. I asked him to tell my solicitor, Gareth Peirce, and also to contact some of the family here in Pakistan, and also to get Zaynab and the kids to a safe place. I felt terrible about how worried he would be, especially because I knew he'd just had a heart-bypass operation. But I didn't know what else to do.

It was obvious Dad was in complete and utter shock, though he too was whispering back down the phone, so it was difficult to tell from his tone how he really was. Then the battery began to die. There was one ring of a call, and it must have been international, as no number came up, but as I answered it, the battery went dead. There were plug points in the room, and I lifted the carpet up and found wires. In sheer desperation, feeling such longing for those outside contacts in my real world, I tried to connect them to the electricity and then to the mobile phone, but of course, as there was no adaptor to change the current, it couldn't possibly have worked, and it probably broke the mobile.

Then I tried to sleep. I lay on the floor on the mat, with the quilt, but I just couldn't sleep, my mind was racing. I was really afraid about what was going to happen, but at the same time I was holding onto logic, and telling myself that in the end justice would prevail. I told myself, 'You know you haven't done anything wrong, you shouldn't feel worried about being prosecuted, or held to account for something that you haven't done.'

I woke from a half-sleep full of all these thoughts when a different man came into the room. It was morning and he brought me tea, and a paratha (fried bread), and a battered pair of slippers. He told me that whenever I wanted anything I could just bang on the door and the guard would come. They came, but I soon found they knew nothing, so I kept asking for an officer.

On the second day they took me out of the room, but they hooded and handcuffed me first, so I knew this was not just a trip to the toilet. I saw an armed guard with a Kalashnikov rifle waiting by the door as they put the hood on. He walked along with me, and I was helped into the back seat of a vehicle. We drove a fairly long way, but it was obvious from the sounds of the cars and the fact that we had not been on a motorway that we were still in Islamabad. I could even very vaguely make some things out through the car's tinted windows, because the hood was just cloth.

I overheard one of the Pakistani officers speaking to somebody in English, and as Pakistanis don't generally speak English amongst themselves, I assumed he was speaking to Americans or British. I heard him mention 'G10'– the name of the district in Islamabad where one of my friends lived. The house where I was taken was very grand, typical of the G10 style.

All four of my interrogations were held in this house, though not always in the same room. It was obviously in use as a normal house, and it was the home of a fairly wealthy person – big sofas, big television screens. I saw much of it, as they put me in various places to wait, even in a bedroom once, and in the huge main living room. Sometimes I needed to use the bathroom, so I saw those too. Sadly, the Pakistanis went about in the servile way that often typifies the inferiority complex of many people in the Indian subcontinent towards Westerners. They made a show of trying to make things as comfortable as possible for their friends, serving exotic dishes and drinks with towels draped over their forearms, like waiters in some Victorian-style restaurant.

At the first meeting there were two Americans, both in civilian casual clothes, older men, perhaps in their late fifties. They didn't identify themselves or their organization. We were in the dining room, sitting at the dining table. I was on one side, in my handcuffs, and they were on the other side. There was an armed Pakistani guard just outside the room. I was baffled. What was this all about? I hadn't heard about this kind of kidnapping happening in Pakistan, although while I had been in Islamabad I had heard about many round-ups in Afghanistan since the Americans arrived. Later I heard from many detainees how they too had been picked up in similar raids in Pakistan, or worse, picked up from the streets.

I had been held now for over twenty-four hours since my abduction. One of the Americans produced my wife's purse with her driving licence in it, and her mobile phone. When they brought out my wife's personal things I became really afraid. Why would they have her things? Where was she? Had something bad happened to her?

Already they had found my psychological weakness: acute anxiety I could not hide whenever I thought about my wife and children. I was looking for logic then, but later I understood that all these questions were just part of a huge fishing trip. I found out too that they had taken other things from the house, including my computer, and about £8,000, our savings and money my family and friends had sent from England.

They asked me what I was doing in Pakistan, and whether I had been in Afghanistan, but I refused to answer, saying I must be allowed to speak to a lawyer or to the British Consul. They said, 'We can't help you with that at all.' They then made some subtle threats, suggesting, 'You might be sent somewhere worse.'

The next day they brought me back again, but this time there were different people in the room. There was a woman who asked me where our British passports were. I had left the passports at somebody else's house, where I had stayed for a few days until I got my own house. Some of my personal belongings were still there. This American woman was really keen to know where our passports were. I told her, 'Never you mind, they're in a safe place.'

They had taken my Pakistani passport, which I did have at home with me, and at the first interrogation, the previous day, they had produced it and said, 'We notice that you have dual nationality.' I tried to understand what they really meant by drawing attention to this, but there were no clues. The Pakistani passport was just a one-year document, which I had got in Birmingham, thinking that when I was in Afghanistan, if I needed to travel into Pakistan and back it would probably be easier to use that instead of a British passport.

That day, one of the two Americans from the day before was there again, and there were also two British intelligence officers, who identified themselves as from MI5. One was a young woman, the other told me his name was Ian. In fact, I had heard about him. A few days before I was abducted, I had spoken to a friend in Birmingham, Shakeel, who told me that a person called Ian from MI5 had come to visit our Islamic bookshop, and said that he was really interested in speaking to me and he was coming to Pakistan to try and meet me. I had told Shakeel to give him my telephone number, and say that when he got to Pakistan he could give me a call and we could meet up. Shakeel had described him as a 'fat bloke with glasses'. It was a perfect description, and I had recognized him before he even said his name.

This was now the third time in my life that MI5 wanted to speak to me, so I wasn't particularly alarmed. Perhaps I was naive in thinking that he'd just come over for tea, in the way that his colleague had done before, to air some concerns, and hopefully, I'd dispel them. I'd done nothing illegal; I wasn't hiding from anyone. When I saw him it was very different from the antipathy and tension that I felt with the Americans. In fact I felt some relief to see him, knowing that he was British; that he was from England. I began, 'Look, can I speak to you by myself, away from these other people?'

'No, you can't.' That was the first indication that the Americans and the British were completely intertwined in this business.

'OK, can you give me access to the British Consulate if you're not going to take that kind of responsibility for me . . . if that's not your job here.'

'I can't help you there, I'm not a social worker.'

'Well, from one Briton to another, at least can you tell me, or reassure me, that my family are OK? Just give me information about that.'

Again he said, 'I'm sorry, I'm not in a position to do that, I'm not here for that.'

I was taken aback that he obviously had no reciprocal feelings about me being British, even after I told him the harrowing story about my evacuation from Kabul, and tearful reunion with my family. 'So, what do you want me to do, why are you here?' I asked.

'Well. It seems like you've got another chance. How often does anyone get a second chance? All you have to do is cooperate with the Americans. That would be the best thing for you.'

Ian asked me a few questions. First of all he wanted me to tell him why I was in Afghanistan, what I was doing there, and who I had met. Then he asked me all about Bosnia and my visits there, and my trip to Turkey back in 1999. I told him exactly what I was in Afghanistan for, what I did there, what made me go there. Then I answered all the other questions he asked me. I was still thinking that I had nothing to hide, and therefore nothing really to fear.

I noticed that the Americans were taking some notes, and at one point one of them got up, went to the corner, and made a phone call. I didn't hear all of it, but I heard one part, and it stuck in my mind: 'We have another one for Kandahar.' I looked at the woman officer, and I had a sudden feeling of complete hopelessness. She looked back at me, and just turned away. Ian and the other MI5 officer then got up, and went, just as abruptly as they had come in. This was a side of Britain that I'd never seen, not like this. 'He's just a Paki,' they probably thought. That's what I thought too. 'Why should they care? I'm just a Paki to them.' I never saw either of them again.

Back in my room, alone with my thoughts, I had stabs of guilt for what I had put the family through by underestimating the seriousness of the situation. I just had not understood what September 11 was going to mean for Afghanistan. I stopped going over what might be in the future, and hurt myself going back into the past, and letting my guilt well up. I hadn't got over the terrifying experiences of the last two months when the US bombing had forced us to flee from our new, exciting home and work in Kabul.

The next interrogation was just with Americans. One of them, Paul, seemed upset that I had spoken to the British, but not to him. He said, 'It takes your own people for you to talk. You've clearly shown that. But the British have washed their hands of you; you're not going to see them any more. So your only opportunity is to cooperate with us. We've released people in the past . . .' There was a long pause, then, 'We can make life easy for you, or we can make life difficult. You can answer our questions here, or you can do it in Kandahar and Guantánamo.'

Again I asked him to get me reassurance that my family were all right. It was obvious that the British were not going to do it, so I had nobody else to ask. But the Americans too were uninterested, and just said, 'Uh-huh, there's nothing we can do about that.' We left the G10 house.

Later, back in my cell-room, I pleaded with the Pakistani guards, although Uncle, who I felt I had a bit of a relationship with, was not there that day. I begged them, 'Please, please, at least go to the house and find out how they are, what they are doing, and ask my wife if she can write me a letter.'

One of the Pakistani officers agreed. 'I'll go to your house, and I'll find out if everything's OK, and I'll try and bring you a change of clothes, and get you some things from home.' Later he told me, 'I did go to the house, and I found there was a padlock on the door, and the neighbours told me the family had left two or three days after you were taken.'

I felt totally confused, more than ever on my own, and I tried to put out of my mind what might have happened to Zaynab and the children, and where they might have gone.

Meanwhile, days went by, and sometimes nothing at all happened. Lunch and dinner were always chapattis and curry, and I got into a routine of optionally fasting on Mondays and Thursdays, the supererogatory fasts that Muslims often do; ISI officers would buy me food to break the fasts. During these days, in fact, I increased my practice of Islam and hoped for Divine mercy more than ever before. Just as my fasting and Quranic recitation increased, so did my prayers and supplications.

Normally the only people I spoke to were the guards. And the guards really knew nothing. I continually asked for one of the officers in charge. I bugged the guard every ten minutes, every fifteen minutes, knocking on the door and saying, 'Look, I need to know what's going on, I need to have contact with my family.' The guards made it clear they felt very sorry. They were very apologetic and very sympathetic because they didn't know what I was there for. They were used to people who had committed murder, rape, robbery, and even acts of terrorism. But they really didn't know why I was there. I did eventually speak to a senior officer, a man who spoke fluent English and was obviously quite high up the scale. He just said, as Uncle had said on the very first night, 'You are here because of the Americans.' None of them would tell me their name, and when I asked, they said, 'It's better that you don't know.' They would not even tell me if they were ISI.

Any time I needed anything I just knocked on the door, and eventually somebody came. Sometimes no one came, and I just knocked louder and harder. But eventually somebody always came and asked me what I wanted. If I wanted water they filled up a bottle and left it for me. If I needed to go to the toilet they brought a towel, put it over my head, and escorted me across the corridor into another part of the building where the cells were. The bathroom was really dark and filthy. It had running water, but there was no soap. The toilet was a hole in the floor, Middle Eastern style. There was a small hole near the ceiling, which allowed in a thin ray of light, during the day. That was when I saw the cells.

As I approached the toilet I could hear voices speaking in Arabic. I asked the guard, 'Please, would you let me speak to these people?'

'I'll close the door, but you must speak to everyone quickly.' He gave me five minutes with them. I went to each of those cells, and my heart sank when I saw the state of them. There was no natural light at all. They were dripping with damp. Some of the men had been in there for three or four months. All of them were Arabs; three were Libyan students from Islamabad University. They were desperately trying to get somebody from their embassy to come and speak to the authorities. But at least they could speak to one another and pray together.

After the meetings with the Americans, the talk about going to Kandahar and Guantánamo, the refusal of lawyers, having no access to my family, and then the British washing their hands of me, I began to think about escape. I thought about all sorts of things, from trying to attack one of the guards, grabbing his weapon and just fighting my way out, to sneaking out, or climbing out. My thoughts got desperate when I went over in my mind what was happening to my family. I thought that if anything happened to my family, I would hold America responsible for the rest of my life.

The window in the room, which they covered with masking tape, was left uncovered at the last few inches from the top. If I wanted to look out, I had to stand on top of the sofa and peer over, then I could actually see over the wall slightly, and I could see cars going past on the other side. Once, as I was doing that, I looked at the metal bars screwed across the window and they seemed like normal, rather flimsy, screws. I had a belt buckle, which, with a yank, I pulled off. It had a little protruding part that I got to work as a screwdriver. Over several days I undid these screws two by two until there were none left and the grille was movable. And every time I went to the bathroom, I threw them down the toilet. It was a sliding window, which I slid open.

My plan was to move at night, after around eleven when the guards stopped coming into the room and the lights went off. There was a guard outside by the guard shack, near the entrance, where the cars came in; I could see the shack, and I could see when he had fallen asleep. The most dangerous part would be getting out of the window and over to the wall. But I thought I could do it, with a strong leap. There was no barbed wire or anything like that on top, and I could see the road on the other side, a main road.

One problem was that I had no money, and no shoes, because they removed my slippers at night. I would have to run into the middle of the street, jump into a taxi barefoot, and then – where would I go? Home was the only place I really knew well (we'd only been in Pakistan since November), but would that be bringing more trouble on my family? Anyway they were not there any more. One possible friend's house – the one I had phoned on that first night – I would have recognized, but I did not know exactly how to get there. Ideas ran through my mind, like, getting a taxi driver to take me to near his place, and when the time came to pay for the taxi, I would just run off, and run down the streets barefoot.

But I was put out of my misery the next day. A guard came in the room, walked up to the windows, looked around it, and shortly afterwards I was taken and put into another room. Nobody said a word. Perhaps they were going to use the room for something else anyway, or perhaps that guard knew what had happened with the screws but didn't want to get me into trouble. That was the end of my escape plan.

I kept asking for someone to speak to. Eventually they did bring somebody else into the room – an Afghan refugee who spoke some Urdu, so we could communicate. We used to talk, and he told me about the times when he had fought against the Russians. I built up a rather good impression of him. But then I found that he was held for an unrelated reason. He was supposed to have been collecting money from hajj groups, and arranging their visas through the Saudi Embassy in Pakistan, because the embassy in Kabul had been closed. He told me that he arranged a deal with some officials at the Saudi Embassy to issue visas for the Afghans. But apparently one of these officials had made off, and left the country with $90,000 in visa money. This prisoner was accused of having had a hand in it. But he always maintained that he didn't do it, and that anyway the sum was only $45,000.

This is when I learned first hand something about what Pakistani security officials could really do, and it jolted me out of some of my naivety. At night, I used to hear a banging noise, dull thuds. I thought it was workmen. And then one night they came and took my cellmate, and I heard the banging again. When they brought him back I realized what had happened. The banging was not workmen; it was torturers. It went on every single night. They had used a long, thick rubber pipe to whack him, he told me. He had bruises and lacerations all over his back. They also put him on sleep deprivation, and guards came in and out to keep him awake. They also said he could not sit. He had to stand up the entire time, and they made sure he did. He had to stand all night because they wanted him to admit that it was $90,000. He didn't. The next day they brought him a doctor to treat his wounds and put on some sort of balm. But then he was taken again the following night, and they did exactly the same thing again. He came back, and he was still forcibly kept awake.

Once I gathered up the courage to complain to one of the guards, 'Look, this is wrong, why are you doing this to him?'

The guard replied, 'If you don't watch your mouth, you'll be getting the same treatment.'

It was rare for the guards to speak to me like that, because in Pakistan if you speak good English it means you are well educated, and therefore from a fairly wealthy or powerful background. Whenever they would start getting a little bit cheeky with me, I'd speak some English with great certainty, although they would not understand a word. In fact one of my small comforts was that I knew they would never have dared do anything to me.

Another time one of his interrogators, an ISI man, came in. He shook my hand, and said, 'How are you doing? I think things will go better, things will go well for you, I think we are coming to a conclusion soon for you.'

I was really happy. But then his tone changed entirely when he turned and faced the Afghan, who was still on sleep deprivation, and he spoke to him in Urdu. He walked up to him face-to-face, almost nose-to-nose, and he said, 'Have you got your tongue yet?'

The Afghan pleaded with him, 'Please, you don't understand, I'm telling you the truth, I've been telling you the truth all this time. I don't know why you're—'

All of a sudden the Pakistani intelligence officer punched him in the face. Then he did it again, and again . . . I was just transfixed. He turned around and looked at me, as if to say, 'Don't even think about it.'

Then he grabbed the Afghan by the shoulder, pulled him down and kneed him repeatedly in the groin.

The last words the officer said to him were, 'Listen, if you haven't got your tongue by the time I get back, I'll teach you how to speak languages you've never even heard of.'

I could tell that the truth didn't matter to him, the prisoner just had to say what he was told. This was my introduction to what physical torture can make a person do. Nothing matters any more after a certain amount of punishment. That man took a lot of punishment before he admitted the amount was in fact $90,000. Eventually he did, and I saw him sign the statement. Other people came into my room too at various times; every one of them had been beaten.

But the agents were offering them all the chance to go home for Eid, as though nothing had happened. Eid was going to be in the next few days, and suddenly I felt hopeful. A few days later the other prisoners were gone. I was still there. I asked, 'Am I going home for Eid?'

The officer who had been so optimistic with me said, 'No, probably not for Eid, but, you know, maybe a bit later, a little later than that. Not to worry, everything will be OK.'

The Pakistanis were always like that with me, 'Everything will be OK, things are going your way, no problem, it's just a few technical hitches that need to be sorted out, everything's fine.'

In fact, up until the moment I was handed over to the Americans, they maintained that everything would be fine, nothing would happen. But despite all the reassurance, I had my first anxiety attack there in my room, two days before the handover. Nothing like that attack had ever happened to me before. I'm a very calm person and I can normally deal with difficult situations quite easily. But what was destroying me in there was worrying about my family. Thinking about them having to go through something like my disappearance, after suffering the US bombings in Afghanistan, and just not knowing what they were actually going through, was really killing me. I couldn't control myself. I went crazy. I started ripping up the quilt and throwing things around, whatever there was to throw around, and eventually a guard came and tried to comfort me. I slapped him in the face. To his credit he didn't retaliate, he didn't try to hit me back, or anything. I was trying to plead with him, 'Please, how can you do this to me when you know I don't know what's happening to my family, and you're holding me here without any charge and without any legal recourse.'

About two hours later a doctor came to see me, to see if I was all right. He gave me a complete physical check-up. Then, about two hours after that, the person that I used to call Uncle came along. He said, 'Uh, you've got to go. They want to see you.'

I wondered if perhaps it was because of what had just happened. Maybe they had realized that this had all gone a bit too far? They took me back to the house in G10. The officer in charge was someone who I later got to know, because I met him in Guantánamo – an FBI agent, Mike.

That day we sat as usual in the dining room – me with the hand-cuffs on and him across the table. There was a Pakistani officer in there too for the first time, but he said little. Mike had a very short message for me. He gave me the impression that he didn't really like what was going on, but he was doing his duty.

'I'm here to inform you that we've decided to send you to Kandahar, and then to Cuba. It's going to be a military environment and it'll be a lot harsher than this. Now, if you continue not to co-operate with us you will be spending a very long time there. And if you don't speak the truth, regardless of whether you cooperate or not, you are still going to be spending a long time out there.'

I'd seen images of Guantánamo Bay. I just looked at him; I had tears in my eyes. 'Is it going to be . . . going to be years?'

'Oh no, just a few months.'

I thought this just couldn't be happening, but I had the presence of mind to ask if I could at least write a letter to my wife before I left. He said yes, and gave me some paper and a pen. It was a terribly difficult letter to write, as I was trying to say, 'I don't know if or when we'll ever meet again.' I wanted to ask her to forgive me for anything I might ever have done to hurt her, and I wanted to give her some parting advice, for her life, for our children. Mike said, 'We're not social workers, but I'll get it to them.' When I asked if he was sure he could find them, he said, 'Well, we got to you, didn't we?' Zaynab never did get the letter.

The meeting ended with me pleading in Urdu to the Pakistani officer to help me. I appealed to his conscience, to his national pride, this was not even an extradition, how could he let this happen to me. He leant forward, poured some water into a cup and gave it to me, saying, 'All I can offer you is this.' I felt like picking it up and throwing it in his face.

'Moazzam,' one of the Pakistani officers said on the way to what I discovered was the airport, 'you know, my friend, I have sold both this life and the next for what I am about to do." . . . And there falls not a leaf but He knows it, nor a grain in the darkness of the earth . . ."' he quoted from the Quran.

I said nothing.

'I will have to answer for it one day.'

As the vehicle came to a stop he said, 'Everything will be all right, don't worry. My journey ends here, but yours is about to begin.'

2

THE LYNX

My earliest childhood memories are mostly of my father, Azmat, and my brother Azam, who is a year and seven months older than me. But they are also haunted by my mother, Shakila, who died when I was six. I remember very little about her, except being with her on our first trip abroad visiting her relatives in Delhi, her birthplace. We boys found India a strange new world, so different to Birmingham, where we were born. The crowds, the dust, the smells, and the obvious visible poverty in Delhi, Bombay, and my father's birthplace, Agra – with its massive and magnificent Taj Mahal – were my first glimpses of our Eastern heritage, and they stuck in my imagination.

The other thing I remember about my mother is the last time I saw her. She was lying, looking very peaceful, in a hospital bed, with her face pale and yellow, and most of her hair gone. She put her arms around each of us and kissed me for the last time. Dad had braced us for the impending tragedy some time before she died. Since she had been in hospital for so long, we knew in a way what was coming.

On the day when she finally died from breast cancer, my father took us to the park and told us, 'Your mother is no more; she's gone to Allah.' We all cried. My father explained that we were all like passengers, waiting to embark on a train journey that took us to the next destination. She had boarded that train earlier than people usually did, but someday, we would all have to get on board. He added that we had been the dearest things in her life, and her last wish was for her sons to grow into men respected and well known in the world.

As time passed, memories of my mother, only present in photo albums and her dust-covered psychology books, slowly began to fade. We visited her grave often to say a prayer and lay flowers, but she was mentioned very little at home. My mother's mother was the only living reminder of her in our lives. Apa, as we knew her, was a religious woman who frequently performed the hajj. She often bought expensive presents, and showed us fascinating pictures straight from the heartland of Islam. She outlived my mother by nearly ten years, after which we buried her too. The few thousand pounds she left behind was argued over between my dad and brother. I just asked my father to donate it for the famine in Ethiopia. (The *zakah*, 'poor due', is the third pillar of Islam; it is a fixed yearly percentage that must be paid by all adults after a certain amount of capital has been in hand for over a year. *Sadaqah* – general charity – was something I began to practise as soon as I was earning money, in my mid-teens, even though I was exempt from *zakah*.) This notion of charity was to become an important feature of my adult life.

For a while it was just the three of us in Birmingham – my father, my brother and me. My aunts and other family friends all helped to take care of us, especially since my father was often in London, Zurich, or Luxembourg, managing banks, but whenever he was home, it would be just the three of us again. My father would tell us bedtime stories, sometimes from the Quran and early Islamic history, or from the *Arabian Nights* or accounts of life under the British Raj. They gave me a glimpse into another world that stretched to India, and beyond. He told us about our Indian Muslim heritage, even suggesting that the priceless diamond, the Koh-i-noor, in the Tower of London, was really ours, as the British had stolen it from our forefathers. 'The name "Begg" means leader, or chief,' he told us, 'it's found in surnames from China to Yugoslavia. The Mongols, who ruled over the largest empire in history, used it. We are the descendents of Tatars, Mongols who settled in Central Asia and established the Great Mughal Empire in India.' Even the names of Tamerlane and Genghis Khan were mentioned with a certain reverence in our house, and sometimes my father called me 'Temujin', the Great Khan's real name. Many years later, I watched my father complete the ethnic-origin section of the census form. Finding no suitable option, he crossed them all out and wrote in 'Mongol'.

My father often told me about his childhood and how he had been among the best athletes at school. He told me that he had had his fair share of fights at that age too, but that he always used his strength and agility to defend the weaker boys against bullies. He instilled in me a sense of justice and a desire to help others that became guiding principles for the rest of my life.

From an early age my father enrolled us both at a Jewish primary school. His seemingly odd choice was entirely pragmatic. King David, with its high standards of education and emphasis on religious and moral ethics, coupled with kosher dietary laws similar to our own, was the ideal option for him. But the choice also demonstrated my father's liberalism, his desire to take what was best from all cultures. It laid the foundations for the kind of religious teaching that I became so very interested in as I grew older. I loved the mirrored stories that we heard from the Torah at school and the Quran at home. Some of the Jewish stories that I heard from our teachers were indelible, like the heroic rebellion led by Judah Maccabee, who 'would never bow before any man'. That could have been from my father's tales of the Islamic world.

I enjoyed taking part in plays celebrating Jewish history during the festivals of Hanukkah, Pesach, Purim and Yom Kippur. Sometimes, wearing a *kippah* (yarmulke) on my head, I recited prayers on stage, just like my Jewish friends, in Hebrew. One of them, Mischa Moselle, gave me the nickname Mozambique.

My favourite subject then was geography; by the time I was ten I had memorized the name of every country in the world and its capital city. I hoped someday to visit some of them.

My school uniform bore the Mogan Dovid, the Star of David emblem, on my cap and blazer, which I wore to school each day with the pride of a small schoolboy. On holidays I'd wave the Israeli flag around, just like the other children. And in the afternoon, after school, I went for my Quranic reading lessons.

Religion was not generally something any of us kids got too passionate about, but once I argued with my best friend, Mischa, that Islam was superior to other religions because of its emphasis on charity.

Our classroom door had a poster on it depicting a rolled fist, and some words I didn't understand. One of them was 'Zionist'. It was almost ten years later that I discovered what it meant.

My father's bookshelves were filled with books on banking and finance, as well as on law and history. He had many English classics too. Dad was hardly the quintessential Englishman, but he did enjoy British history and literature, and often took us to Shakespeare's birthplace in Stratford-upon-Avon, or to Wordsworth's home, the Lake District. We were regularly treated to visits to Warwick Castle and Blenheim Palace. His own father had strongly disapproved of going to the cinema when he was a child, but my father used to take us very often. His favourites included *Cleopatra, Where Eagles Dare*, and *A Bridge Too Far*. He also enjoyed telling us his favourite anecdote from Bernard Shaw's *Arms and the Man*, about 'the chocolate cream soldier' and how it helped deter him from the family tradition of join-ing the army.

Despite his integration in the British way of life, in an almost Tory style, he always had a sense of keeping to the Islamic faith – however loosely, which was usually confined to halal food, no alcohol, and the odd Friday and funeral prayers. He endorsed the old Victorian values, which were quite similar to his own Islamic ones. Respect for parents and teachers was drilled into our heads almost daily. 'You are behaving just how English people have started to,' he would say if we were dis-obedient or answered him back. Our punishments – swift and harsh – stemmed directly from how he was brought up by his own father. We had to stand against the wall, hearing the orders, 'Eyes shut, mouth shut, head up, back straight, chest out, hands by the sides, feet together, don't move . . .' If we moved, we got hit – sometimes with a belt, or worse. My brother got more than I did, but often, if he got hit, I did too. Perhaps so I wouldn't feel left out.

Dad was also President of the Society for the Advancement of Urdu, and was himself a keen poet in Urdu. He was committed to the preservation of this part of his own heritage. At various functions we used to meet his friends, who were mostly doctors, professors, and businessmen. Most of them were Muslims of Indo-Pak origin – like us. But his close friends also included Hindus, Sikhs, and indigenous English people.

After my mother died, my father, as a bank manager, became an eli-gible widower, beset by suitors. I thought one of them was destined to become our stepmother. Josephine, or Jo, as we called her, came from a very English family. She collected Azam and me from school every Friday, which finished early for the Sabbath, and took us out for the afternoon. We usually stayed over at her house for the night. For us it was a vision of another, very English world, with formal manners, and customs quite different from Passover or Eid, like Christmas stockings full of presents, and Christmas pudding with silver sixpences, or the introduction of watercress in our salad. Jo introduced us to things that we had no idea about, like collecting flowers from our trips with her to the Cotswolds or the Malvern Hills, and pressing them into albums. She read us bedtime stories too, from classical English literature, or the Brothers Grimm and Hans Christian Andersen, which I loved almost as much as my father's tales of India. Jo was very genuinely caring towards us, and we looked forward to each weekend with her.

My father's brother and sister were very important to us in this period too. My uncle, Ghazanfar, came over from Pakistan when we were about eight, and stayed with us before he got married and moved on. He put huge emphasis on our education, giving us extra maths and science lessons in our spare time, while he was studying for his PhD. He held on to a lot of the older Eastern values that my father had left behind, and arranged Quranic reading lessons for us, when he found to his dismay that neither of us could read Arabic. I used to go reluctantly, as I didn't really like it, although the woman teacher never used violence or harsh words to us, as a lot of mosque teachers would. But I was conscious that we were learning Arabic the Pakistani way, with Urdu pronunciations of Arabic words that didn't even sound right. I resolved someday to learn Arabic and understand the Quran I was reading.

When my father did remarry, though, it was not to Josephine, but to someone he met in his bank. Gulbahar, or Aunty Gul, as we called her then, came from a large Asian family and was born in the UK. We thought that his final decision was based on his desire for a traditional upbringing for us. Initially, after the novelty of a new person in our household had worn off, and as we grew older, we began to give our stepmother a hard time. We got even worse in our teens. But she always reacted in the most patient, accommodating manner, without ever resorting to violence. In fact she was magnanimous, ignoring our rudeness – washing, cooking, and cleaning for us as much as any mother. I tried to remain independent from the start, though, organizing what I could in my own way. I ironed my own clothes, cleaned up after myself, and kept my room tidy. Over time she won us over with her patience and perseverance.

I was about eleven when my sister, Uzma, was born and we boys became very attached to her. But one morning, when she was still a baby, my father came into our room, looking shaken, and said,'Uzma's finished.' She'd contracted bronchiolitis that very morning. Just like that. I jumped out of bed, and threw myself on the ground crying. Then I went into my father's bedroom, and there she was in the cot. She was dead. That took a very heavy toll on my stepmother. A couple of years later, her second child, Asad, was born.

After King David, Azam and I went to a local school. In my year, there were about twenty Asian children, about ten black and over a hundred and fifty white children. So my friends were mostly Muslim, Hindu, Sikh, and Christian, but hardly any were Jewish.

Moseley Secondary School was built in the early nineteenth century, with Gothic architecture and desks with inkwells. It was a large grammar school that had become a comprehensive. Plaques in the west wing celebrated the contribution of old boys who had died serving in two world wars. Several teachers still wore black robes, and administered 'the pump' (a gym shoe) for misbehaviour. We had Assembly every morning, which included readings from the Gideon Bible and hymn-singing. It was my first real exposure to Christianity, clearly an intrinsic part of the school's identity. I found no difficulty reading, or accepting supplications like 'the Lord's Prayer', or songs that praised God alone. But anything that attributed divinity to man I could never say. The concentric points of the Islamic and Jewish faiths were the unity of God. He was not human, animal, idol, or statue. He was One, and had no partners. Jesus for me was a very distinguished prophet, able to perform miracles when he walked the earth. However, he was not God on earth, or his son. I believed he was not killed or crucified; instead, God raised him to the heavens, to return him to earth before the Last Day.

I remember once speaking up in RE class when we were studying the nativity. The teacher insisted that Jesus was the Son of God because of the Miraculous Conception and the Virgin Birth. I asked her, 'Jesus at least had a mother, who did Adam have? He had neither mother nor father, so surely his conception was even more miraculous?' She was quite upset with my question, and quickly moved on to a different subject.

Part of the lingering old traditions of Moseley school included subjects like classical studies (CS) and Latin. In the second year, after excelling in class, I chose Latin, which, with history and CS, was my favourite subject.

Things began to change by my mid-teens. My brother had already got involved with a local street gang, mostly young Pakistanis, from traditional families, not particularly practising of Islam, but steeped in strict Kashmiri customs and tradition. In revolt, many played truant from school, had girlfriends, drank, smoked, and took drugs. There were fights, petty robberies, and car thefts for joy riding. I managed to stay away from most of the criminal side of things, except for the occasional gang fight. South Asians in Britain back then tended to be studious and academic, but submissive even in the face of blatant aggression.

The British Movement and National Front had strong support in some Birmingham areas. Many of us had been told 'Paki go home' at some point in our lives, and others had been beaten up for no other apparent reason. My step-uncle had been attacked by a group of skinheads on the way back from school. They had broken his jaw and he wasn't able to eat for weeks. Skinheads had attacked even my dad, when I was just a child, but he'd managed to fight them off. Worse still were the attacks on Asian women. They have always been an easy target because of how they look – hijab, shalwar kameez, sari – and a generally non-confrontational nature.

It was not uncommon in the eighties to find racist graffiti on the walls in Birmingham, or indeed to see the tattoos of hate on skinheads' arms, necks, and foreheads. The ones I remember include 'APL' (Anti Paki League), NF (National Front), 'Pakis out', and 'Wogs out' (I was amused to discover that 'wog' had originally stood for 'Worthy Oriental Gentleman').

The idea of belonging to a gang that did not take a meek stance against racism, attracted me. Although I was younger, about fifteen, I was soon in the gang too. It was called the Lynx. Our members and friends were English, Arab, Irish, Indian, and Afro-Caribbean, but the majority were Kashmiris.

Around this time my stepmother bought me a series of books called *The Heroes of Islam*, which, with Homer's *Iliad* and *Odyssey*, became my favourites. That was the first time I had actually read for myself about the Prophet Muhammad and his companions. But it was the Anthony Quinn film about Islam, *The Message*, that really captured my imagination. I felt emotionally drawn to the characters portrayed in this epic story, and a sense of pride that these were *my* people, that it was *my* history. These people were courteous, brave, disciplined, principled, and victorious. But they were Arab Muslims, not the Christian Knights of Albion, who I'd been taught – through school and television – had the monopoly on chivalry.

Although I'd never been there, I decided one day to embroider a flag of Pakistan on the right arm of my ex-Italian army combat jacket. It caused some problems in school. The year head told me to remove it, saying that school was not the place for symbolism. But I'd spent so much time and effort on it that I decided to leave it on, and the teacher soon seemed to forget about it. For me though, it was also an assertion of a sense of identity, although in fact my father and mother were originally from India. Most of the Lynx were from Pakistani Kashmir, and spoke an absolutely different language from Urdu. I couldn't relate to the country they would often talk about, when they'd return after a visit. My Pakistan was different. My Pakistan was my father's poetic, intelligent, educated, and military Pakistan.

I was in one of the top classes for my year, and everybody in it – mostly girls – was very studious. But my grades were slipping, and I wasn't doing as well as I should have. This was due to my own truancy and involvement in the gang. I spent hours of school days hanging around the Shillelagh cafe, playing Space Invaders, pinball, or pool, listening to Michael Jackson's 'Beat It' on the jukebox.

I liked the sense of belonging that I felt there, the sense of an association with people who had something in common with me. And yet, it was not a natural progression: my first friends had been Jewish, most of whom were then at grammar schools, and even at Moseley, a Polish boy, Andrew, had been my first best friend. Later, and for my remaining school life, a Kenyan Asian boy, Anjum, took that place, but he was far removed from any gang connections.

Most of the Lynx went to schools in the more disadvantaged areas of Birmingham, and they had little to do with mine. Their experiences of racism were worse than anything I'd yet known. Most of them had been beaten up by racists at some point, and even hospitalized. It had begun with bullying by some of the older white kids who looked on the influx of younger black and Asian pupils with disdain. But the violence continued even after the older boys had left school. They often waited outside the gates to get in a bit of 'Paki-bashing'. Sometimes the skinheads came in coachloads. The local Asian youth had had enough, and they formed the Lynx.

Only once did my two worlds collide. I was only fifteen, a fourth year, but I had seen the start of things getting nasty. Fights were rarely one-on-one, but there was plenty of brutal ganging up on one person. If somebody was having a fight, his friends came round and 'laid the boot in', kicking the person until his face looked deformed. That happened to quite a few people, including my brother. He was beaten up very badly, just outside school, he ended up in hospital, and was off school for a couple of weeks. The boys who did it were predominantly white, some of them mixed-race. They probably knew that out of school my brother was in a gang. A Paki gang. The lines had been drawn, and the battle cry was, 'Let's go Paki-bashing . . .'

Once, as I was about to leave the toilets, five of them who had been stalking me around school walked in. One of them came over and grabbed my hand. 'You think you're fucking hard, don't you, with your Paki jacket and your Paki Lynx gang? We're going to fuck you up, just like your brother.' My heart was racing, thinking, 'How do I get out of this?' as I looked around at the others. I was never so glad to see the teacher who walked in just then, and I made good my escape. But there was no backup for me in school. I would have to look over my shoulder all the time unless I challenged them. Nobody at school was willing to help me, except Anjum. Still, I was confident that I could bring in the boys from the Lynx.

The following day, as I was walking out of school, I saw the fifth-formers stripping apart a fence, taking the posts out, ready for a fight.

They had seen the Lynx waiting outside. Bones, Chico, Blob, Budda, Hack, Khan, Sam, and Sigi were standing in a line, facing the Springfield Road entrance, where all the fights happened. They were all wearing the same jacket as me: ex-Italian army combat, with a red eagle patched on the left arm, our uniform and symbol of defiance.

The Lynx were all armed with concealable weapons including chains, baseball bats, iron bars, and nunchaku. I came out early and lined up with them. Only eight had turned up. But somehow, word had spread around the whole of the fifth form that people from outside the school were coming for a fight. For them it was a school-pride issue. Soon about fifty or so had gathered in an unorganized mass, facing us. I realized I had made a terrible mistake. Shouting and arguing began, and my voice got drowned out.

One of our boys, a German Pakistani called Sigi, very charismatic and brave, took control. He was ready to fight the whole lot of them. The rest remained stern-faced and brandished their weapons, though they were clearly worried. But one of the school kids I knew came up to me and said, 'Look, things are going to get very nasty if you don't stop it. Do some talking.' He was right, and Sigi rose to the challenge.

'Listen, if you want to go for it now, we're ready to kick the fuck out of you, but we'll all end up in the shit,' he said, as he stood in front. 'Why don't you pussies meet us on Saturday night at Sparkhill Park instead? Bring all your boys. There'll be no teachers, no young kids, and no pigs to worry about.'

They agreed. Everyone was worried about a full-blown fight in public view. Sigi not only saved our necks, but our reputation too. The challenge was accepted, but I knew the school kids had no fixed gang structure outside, and they never turned up. It was a psychological victory for me; my street credibility rocketed, and in school people knew I had backing. I was never troubled again.

For me, this one was the forerunner of other, more serious, gang fights. Sometimes it became fighting for its own sake, with people recounting slightly exaggerated stories to friends about what happened. It was about the 'being there', even though I seldom did any fighting, as I was the youngest and the smallest.

The most memorable gang fight of that time happened in the style of the cult-classic film *Quadrophenia*. A gang of mods, arriving on Lambretta motorbikes, stormed into Hack's family shop and trashed it. When Hack threw down a challenge, telling them to come back and settle the score like men, they answered, 'OK, you Paki bastard. We'll be back tonight – outside the Mermaid.' At Sigi's house, a place where we often met, Hack told us about the incident, and that they were coming back that evening.

Late that afternoon, we all gathered in the car park at the back of the Mermaid pub. Word of the fight had spread, and soon other Asian gangs like the Sparkhill Warriors and the Dragons converged on the place for a piece of the action. But it was understood: the area was ours, the fight was ours, and the plan was ours. Three of us – Sigi, Sam, and me – were going to entice them away from the Mermaid, and lure them into a trap. Everyone else got into position, hidden behind the car-park walls with their sticks and bricks. The mods didn't come on Lambrettas this time; they came in vans, surveying the empty-looking car park as they passed us. As soon as they saw us, the bait, we began taunting them, and started to run back to the car park. They parked their vehicles on a side road, near the pub. As they jumped out, ready to chase us three, our boys came rushing around the corner, and hit them with a shower of bricks. And then the fight began. It was pandemonium. Hockey sticks, baseball bats, and iron bars took over. I was trying to hit one of the mods, but I ended up hitting one of the Dragons by mistake in the frenzy. The thuds of the strikes were quickly followed by yells of pain. Within minutes, the mods who had not run away were not even standing either – except one.

Boot, the huge martial-artist, squared off with the last mod standing and pulverized him with a broken hockey stick. And then the police arrived. We all scattered into the streets and alleyways we knew so well. Many of the mods were arrested.

It was a complete victory for us. The news spread all around Birmingham to all the gangs, black, white, and Asian. This was one of the incidents that helped establish the reputation of the Lynx as a powerful gang that meted out its own kind of street justice.

Some of that reputation was lost in one really big confrontation soon after, in Birmingham city centre. It even sounded like more than we could handle from the start. There was to be a huge march by the National Front and to us that meant skinheads. Various gangs from around the city gathered near one of our haunts, the Central Library, to confront them. There was a police presence, mounted and foot patrols, and the usual crowds of people on a Saturday afternoon. We were more or less lined up, a few Lynx, Panthers, Sparkhill Warriors, and some Trojans (most of whom were black). Some of the gangs had even fought one another at various times, but then we were united: to confront the neo-Nazis.

We heard banging, getting louder and louder. As they came up the hill we could see that they were carrying metal dustbin lids and base-ball bats, and banging them in unison. It was the closest I ever got to know how men must have felt before battle in medieval times. It seemed as though hundreds of them were marching in rank and file. They all stopped and raised their right hands in the Nazi salute, while the shouts of 'Sieg Heil!' roared through the air. Then they charged.

I saw them coming closer, less than fifty yards . . . the police couldn't or wouldn't interfere. I turned around for a final look of reassurance at all our people, but there were hardly any left. There was a muscular black guy next to me swinging a chain, and my friend Sam on the other side. I looked at him, hoping he had a quick answer. 'Run, Moz,' he shouted, 'run for it. Now.' That day we escaped unharmed. But the next time I wasn't so lucky.

One night I was walking with some friends past the Mermaid, where skinheads and punk-rockers had gathered to drink, opposite Shillelagh's. We were not particularly in the mood for a fight, and certainly not dressed for one. Then I saw one of my friends arguing with one of the punks outside the pub. Suddenly, he struck the punk in the head. My friend had hit him with a stick with a large nail protruding from it, which got embedded in the man's head. He ran into the pub screaming. Within seconds a dozen or more of his friends came out, with beer glasses and Guinness bottles in their hands. All of us just ran for it, past the mosque and away down the road. But one stayed behind. It was Boot. He stood there, alone.

As I was running, I turned round and saw him firing out machine-gun kicks. But then they covered him. He was on the ground, and they were 'laying the boot in'.

I made a lightning decision: I stopped running, and turned round. Then I ran back into the middle of all of those punks and skins to get them off him. I did manage to get them all off him – because they started on me instead. I felt the steel-toecapped boots and beer bottles in my head, my back, my groin, my legs, and my face. It just didn't seem to stop. Part of my tongue was cut when they kicked me in the chin. Blood was pouring into my throat. I really felt that I was about to die. In those split seconds, I thought, What's the last thing a Muslim says when he dies? *'Laa ilaha ill-Allah, Muhammad ar-Rasool Ullah,'* There are no gods but Allah, Muhammad is His messenger, I screamed out. At least I was going to die outside a mosque, I thought. Suddenly the whole thing ended. The kicking stopped, the pain eased, and my attackers disappeared. I thought it was because of what I had said. But then I saw a police car had come around the corner and parked in front of me.

There was just one policeman inside. He looked at me, and told me to get into the vehicle. 'I'm going to take you down to the station because there's been a reported disturbance of the peace.' He talked into his radio. As he was about to drive off, the punks returned. They didn't do anything much, but lurked around the car, thinking perhaps he might just let me out, and they could get me again. I deliberately started taunting them. They surrounded the car and started banging on it. The policeman must have got scared, and he drove down to the bottom of the road, and told me to get out. I was drenched in blood and my face was all bruised and battered, but I was extremely glad I wasn't under arrest.

When I got home it was about ten o'clock. My father answered the door, but I turned my back to him, pretending to tie my shoelaces up. He waited for me to come inside the house, but I said, 'Dad, go in, I'm coming in a minute.' I turned around, and he saw my state. He was terribly shocked.

'What happened?' he asked.

'Nothing, Dad,' I mumbled, 'I'm fine. Go inside.'

'Don't talk rubbish. We're going to the Accident Hospital, now.'

When we got to the hospital, the same punks and skins were there already, including the one who had had the nail embedded in his head, and another with a broken nose. They started swearing as soon as they saw me, and rushed towards my father and me, 'That's the one, the Paki bastard . . .' I saw a reflex tester and picked it up, ready to defend myself. Then the police arrived.

My poor father was totally shocked. I was taken away, in handcuffs, just like the punks and skins. At the police station they charged me with wounding with intent. They thought I had tried to kill that person by embedding the nail in his head. I told them what had really happened, but I wouldn't tell them the person who did it. So the case against me went to court.

I turned up for all the court appearances, but the punks almost never came. And when they did turn up the magistrate seemed unimpressed by their outfits. The case was eventually thrown out.

My father had not known much about my life in this period. I was making a hard transition from school, where I had scraped by with a few O-levels, but my grades were poor. I had no one to blame but myself.

Dad was generally easygoing with me during my teens and didn't exert the kind of pressure on us two that many of his peers did on their children. Dad wanted us to achieve high educational standards, but he was also very liberal in what we were allowed to do. We took advantage.

Despite the occasional walloping – which faded with time – my father and I often sat and discussed things in depth, including his past. Sometimes, it was the typical 'when *I* were a lad' comparison between his teenage years and mine. But his youth had been so profoundly different to mine.

In an effort to get to me to appreciate just how good I had it, he told me how, as a child in India, he studied under a streetlight when they couldn't afford kerosene for the night-lamp. He told me too the story of his migration from his home in southern India to a new and uncertain life in Pakistan, a Muslim homeland. He recalled the notorious death carriages: trains loaded with Muslim passengers passing through Hindu areas that arrived at their destinations with everyone on board murdered, and how the violence was returned to Hindus in Muslim areas. In Pakistan, his community became known as

Muhajirs – the migrants. Migration to a Muslim land was also going to feature in my life, although I didn't know it then.

After school I studied computing at college, and then began work with my father at Begg & Sons Co. Ltd, Estate Agents and Building Society, which he set up after leaving the bank in 1984. It was some years before I went back to study A-level law. The Lynx thing slowly tapered off as people got older. After the neo-Nazis disappeared from our streets, the Lynx began fighting other groups – most of them Asian. First it was against the local Asian gangs, then it moved on to groups in other areas. The sense of justice I felt in taking on the neo-Nazis was gone since the raison d'être for the Lynx had ceased to exist.

Several of them settled down to family life and business. Some spent a lot of time in borstals, detention centres, prisons, and drug-rehab centres. Others died in fights, or from alcohol and drug abuse. And some began to practise Islam.

The Lynx period of my life lasted for about three years and I was not particularly proud of it, especially since I had wasted some important opportunities for advancing my education. And I didn't like what some of the gang had become. My dad knew it too, and we often argued about that. It was not easy in the Asian community to earn the respect of the elders, particularly for youths like us, who were accused of behaving like *gorey* (whites) because we pubbed, clubbed, and dated. But when it became known that we came to the rescue of *their* sons, daughters, and wives, the attitude changed. I suppose we played some part in clearing the streets of racists, a reputation the Lynx holds to this day in Sparkhill.

But it wasn't always working-class Asians that I found myself rushing to protect. Once, I heard a loud noise from over the road and looked out of my bedroom window. I saw some people forcing their way into a house across the road from me, where an old Scottish widow lived. I ran out of my house and into hers. They were at the top of the stairs when I arrived. I could hear her frightened voice, pleading with them to leave her alone. 'Hey! What the hell do you think you're doing?' I shouted. The would-be robbers froze for an instant, then ran back down and pushed me out of the way, and were out of the house. I chased them down the road, and caught up with one. He turned around – brandishing a knife.

I recognized him, and clearly he'd recognized me: he was the younger brother of a former Lynx member. 'Put that thing away, you fool,' I said. 'Don't worry; I'm not going to do anything . . . now.'

He began stuttering some excuses, saying he didn't know there was someone in the house.

I went to the woman's house and helped to fix her broken door. Then she invited me for a cup of tea. She showed me pictures of her husband as a soldier during the Second World War, and talked about how things used to be. After that, I visited her often, until she decided to sell her house and leave for Scotland. I couldn't help thinking that this defenceless old woman had left because of what happened, and probably resented Asians. But she wasn't like that. She asked me to visit her in Scotland. Before leaving she gave me a gift that I've always kept: an old English pound note.

The police later asked me to make a statement against the would-be robber. I told them I'd rather not. In fact I'd already been to see his brother and told him about the whole thing. He said he'd take care of it. When I saw the boy next his face was battered and bruised. Perhaps his brother had 'taken care of it'.

Even during the Lynx period I still worked closely with Dad. Our relationship was good and he entrusted me with everything from overseeing staff to buying and selling houses and arranging mortgages. I remained at the estate agents with Dad for four years, until he stopped the business in 1989, and opened the Sultan, an Indian restaurant. I remained there also, managing, waiting, washing, and cooking until we had all had enough and my father decided to retire, in 1991. I was thinking seriously about what to do with myself. My father planned other business ventures, but I needed something different.

The army had always appealed to me, largely because my father had told me so often that his generation was the only one of our family that had never enlisted. He told me how our ancestors had fought in sixteenth-century campaigns launched from Kabul under Babur, the founder of the Great Mughal Empire. Our family tree notes that in the seventeenth century, 'Raheem Begg was an officer in the military service of Aurangzeb, the last Mughal Emperor.' Since that time, our ancestors had been officers in the British Indian Army. Between them, my grandfather and his father and grandfather had seen action in the Indian Mutiny (though I don't know on which side), the Boer War, and the two World Wars. One of my father's uncles had been a POW in Europe, while another was killed fighting bandits near the Afghan border. We had a very strong military tradition as a family, and I was inspired by it. I used to look at my grandfather's medals from the Second World War in awe. So I thought I would resume the tradition, in contrast to the doctors, teachers, and bankers, of my dad's generation.

I spoke to my father about my plans, but he explained why, after toying with the idea of the Pakistani air force as a youth, he was dissuaded by his own father. 'Wars are not fought with honour or courage anymore,' his father had said. 'Any coward can drop a bomb from thousands of feet, and kill thousands of people – soldiers or civilians.

Where's the bravery in that?' My grandfather's early training had included horsemanship and sword fighting, which he taught my father, and my father taught me.

I was a little scared of joining the army, in fact. This wasn't going to be the British Indian Army; it was the British army in England. I knew I would have to face racist taunts or worse. I wanted to join the elite Royal Marines or the Parachute Regiment. But then I came across the Gurkhas – crack mountain fighters from Nepal. I thought, 'These guys aren't white; they actually resemble me a little. They might even accept me.' I went to the army careers office and passed a simple aptitude test. But when they asked me if I had a criminal record, I told them about the pending skinhead case in court. I was asked to return when the case had been resolved.

During this time there was a much-publicized incident of a teenage Sikh who committed suicide after being subjected to racist abuse in the army. Fears of racism finally deterred me from enlisting, and I never returned to the army careers office. Years later I thought about joining the army again, but it didn't get past thoughts. The First Gulf War had begun, and I couldn't see myself joining an army at war with an Islamic country.

3

UNDERDOGS

My first real taste of the world beyond Birmingham – aside from a school skiing trip to Italy – was in my late teens, when my father arranged for me to go with my stepmother and her father to Saudi Arabia, for the lesser pilgrimage, the umrah. From there I was to go on alone to Pakistan, to spend a couple of months with my father's sisters, one in Karachi and the other in the Punjab. It was a kind of reward for my helping out at the estate agency. I'd wanted to travel and gained a fascination for foreign countries and cultures as a child.

We arrived in Saudi Arabia with no previous experience of a pilgrimage, or any ideas of what the rituals were, and none of us spoke any Arabic. But I had been reading up on the history, and so I became our guide on the trip, surprising the others.

I was immediately entranced by the place, which was so different from everything I knew. I saw a melting pot of the Muslim world far beyond my experience, with people from places as diverse as China, Ghana, Malaysia, South Africa, and Turkey, as well as Arab countries, all united by a common faith. I even met some white Muslims from Britain. But I also noticed a tremendous class-consciousness in how people treated each other, with the Saudis at the top of the pecking order, and black Africans at the bottom – just below people from the Indian subcontinent. Often I saw Saudi officials speaking to foreigners in the rudest, most conceited way, which I knew wasn't the way it was supposed to be in Islam.

Madinah, the historic seat of the early Caliphate, and burial place of the Prophet Muhammad, gave me a lot to absorb. I was literally moved to tears at the thought of what happened here 1,400 years ago: the first migration, the Hijrah – which dates the beginning of the Islamic calendar – ended here. Then there were the sites of al-Quba, the first mosque of Islam; Badr and Uhud, the most decisive battles in Islamic history; and the Prophet's Mosque, with its dazzling green dome – the second most sacred placed in Islam.

The place was magnetic. Visiting the city of Makkah, where I first saw the Ka'ba, the sacred house built by Abraham and his son Ishmael, I felt an immense spiritual nostalgia, thinking about its past, and what it meant for Muslims. For the first time in my life I sensed a clear feeling of identity with my religion, deeply rooted right in this place.

When I left Saudi Arabia and arrived in Karachi to meet my auntie, it was another culture shock. First, at the airport, I wondered how I would recognize her amongst the throngs of people, but it was instant recognition by both of us, and we had a very emotional embrace. The last time she saw me was just after my mother died. I stayed with her for a few weeks, after which I went to stay with my doctor auntie in the Punjab.

Najeeb, my aunt's son, arranged to take me on a two-week trip along the Karakoram Highway – part of the ancient Silk Route that stretched to the Chinese border. It was one of the most memorable journeys of my entire life. The countryside was absolutely stunning. We were so remote from ordinary life, up among the mountains. As we went along, the buses we took got smaller as the roads got narrower; often we were just inches from the ravine, with a thin blue vein of the river running through below, and the occasional carcass of a vehicle that had fallen off.

At one point the whole road was blocked by a huge rock-and-snow avalanche, so we had to either risk running in front of it, or turn back. We decided to take the risk and ran across, one by one, each photographing the other, and got to a minibus waiting on the other side. After Gilgit we went on to the mountain villages of Hunza and Karimabad, near the border with Xinkiang Province in China. The people seemed to be from another world, speaking a language called Brushuski. And the Hindu Kush Mountains ahead of us were simply breathtaking. We snapped away with our cameras, photographing the world's third tallest mountain, Nanga Parbat (the Naked Peak), ancient Buddhist carvings etched on sheer cliff faces, villages built into the mountain rocks . . . It was a holiday I felt I just couldn't get enough of.

As the journey came to an end, I asked my cousin about visiting Afghanistan. I had been curious for a long time to see what was happening in the jihad against the Soviets, but he told me it was too dangerous. The closest I got was my uncle's relatives, in Peshawar.

My Urdu was ten times more fluent when I finally returned to Birmingham, with the memories fresh in my mind of my two journeys. My aunts had teased me that I would never wear Pakistani national dress, shalwar kameez, on the streets of England, when I returned. They were right, initially. But many years later I proved them wrong.

Back home in Birmingham, I began to feel that in all the confusion of speaking both English and Urdu, with my father and his poetry society and insistence on being a Mongol, the one thing that was coherent, and made my origins irrelevant, was my religion.

When my father opened the restaurant, and made me an active partner, the work hours were long and unsociable, but a girl I was seeing and wanted to marry helped to counter that. She was a Shiite, which made little difference to me, or to my parents, even though we are Sunni. But it was an issue to her: she didn't want to hurt her parents by defying their wishes for the future husband they had chosen for her. So, after about a year she broke it off. I took it quite hard, and for a while I felt very dejected and confused.

Then I had another profound shock. My friend Sigi had been living happily with his girlfriend on the second floor above our restaurant. But he discovered that she had been unfaithful, which absolutely devastated him. He decided to go on a little holiday with a friend to Majorca, and consider his future. He never returned. One night, drowning his sorrows, he got drunk and choked on his own vomit.

It was a terrible loss for his family, and all his friends – many of them from the Lynx. I went with his family to collect the body from the airport. Seeing his face was terrible. Sigi had been very good-looking, but his face had bloated out to several times its normal size, purple everywhere, with lacerations and bruises. That face, and the whole story, left a deep impression on me. The enormity of his death became a pivotal factor to many of us. Everyone had loved Sigi. I did not just feel that I had lost a dear friend; I could not stop thinking, 'Where is he now? Where does the soul go after death?' Life was fleeting, I had learned, and death guaranteed. There had to be some greater purpose to it than the routine existence of daily life.

Not long after we sold the restaurant, I got a job in the Department of Social Security. At the same time I began studying law part-time at university. It was the time of the First Gulf War and I began to feel a lot more politically conscious, because of what was happening to Muslims in Iraq. I bought a Palestinian scarf, and wore it round my neck, ostentatiously, to show my solidarity with the best-known Muslim issue.

My favourite film of all time is probably *Braveheart*. I have always had a tendency to back the underdog, or under-supported: I backed the Pakistan cricket team when it played in England, but I wanted the English to win when they played in Pakistan. I sympathized with the Native Americans even as a child, when the Western epics depicted them as savages, before *Dances With Wolves* made them fashionable. When I read extensively about the Vietnam War I found myself supporting Ho Chi Minh. I felt more empathy for Fidel Castro than I did for his American enemies. Mandela had my full support against his apartheid oppressors. And I openly backed the Palestinian struggle for freedom from Israeli occupation. I didn't know that much about Saddam's Iraq in 1991, but I did know the odds were stacked against him. And my dad felt exactly the same.

There wasn't anyone I knew in the Asian community who supported Operation Desert Storm. Some of the Sikhs and Hindus at work were more vociferously opposed to it than I was. At home it was the same: my father and I felt it was a demonstration of a particular kind of hypocrisy that seemed so typical of certain Western nations, vis-à-vis their own interests. And now, for the first time, I was being asked to choose between conscience and country. My conscience won every time.

Neither of us liked the Iraqi occupation of Kuwait, which would have been the underdog. But Kuwait was never the issue. Several UN resolutions had clearly designated Palestine, Kashmir and South Lebanon as occupied territories, and yet there was no concerted US action for liberating them. In fact, Israel's occupation of Palestine was wholeheartedly supported by the US. Iraq's forces had been bolstered by weapons supplied by the US, UK and France in an attempt to check the spread of Iranian-style Islamic revolutions in the Arab world. What had the West done when Iraq invaded the Shatt al-Arab waterway in

Iran? Supplied chemical weapons to Saddam. The images of massa-cred Iranians were fresh in my mind. In 1988, I recalled, a US warship in the Persian Gulf downed an Iranian Airbus loaded with nearly three hundred civilians. The Iranians just received a,'whoops, we thought it was an F14 coming for us' from the US. I was sickened. If Iran had made the same mistake with a US passenger jet, what would have happened? The First Gulf War?

At work, I was often called upon to arrange dance parties because I had musician friends with PA systems. I hadn't been to a mosque in years. My political views were not formed listening to radical Islamist clerics or jihadists. I liked listening to UB40, Gloria Estefan, and Simply Red. The media, and the events it reported, had shaped my outlook on the world.

One of the girls at work had asked me if I could help her with an Arab-type fancy dress. I offered her my Palestinian scarf, and a little headdress holder from Saudi Arabia. I hadn't realized though that she was planning to go to the pub dressed as an Arab, to celebrate the Iraqi defeat. I felt sick that I had not said anything to her before about my opinions. After that, I made a point of airing my views at work, although most people didn't even know where Kuwait or Iraq were, or even what actions British troops had been involved in over there. It didn't really matter. The victory celebration was just another excuse to get smashed on a Friday night.

About a year later I began to hear about Bosnia in the media, and then through the Central Mosque, which I had started visiting spo-radically. I always felt a little nervous about mosques in England, mostly because of the stern old men with long beards who could hardly speak English. But I put aside my inhibitions when I heard about Bosnian refugees who had just arrived, and were sheltering in the mosque. I was very curious about these European Muslims. I bought some blankets and a few boxes full of groceries, and went to the mosque to hand them over personally. When I got there, the refugees just looked like poor white people. They didn't look Muslim to me. The women weren't in hijab, and the men looked like Irish labourers. A couple of them, in fact, were Catholic Croats. I tried to communicate with them, and picked up a few words of Serbo-Croat.

I soon met others, including some who had no place to stay, so I asked my father if he would give them a room in a house he usually rented out to students. He did, of course.

One of the Bosnian refugees invited me to visit him once, and I met several others there. They were all young, and I couldn't help thinking, 'Why are you here? Why aren't you fighting for your people?'

During a conversation with one, Edin, I asked if he was going back to fight. He lifted up his shirt and said, 'I fight in Bosna, many dead, many hurt. This is reason I no fight in Bosna now.' I could see only a small scar, the entry point, which he indicated. 'Bullet still inside, first have to get out.'

As we were talking I found it fascinating to hear about their concept of Islam, which was quite different to mine. While we spoke, another Bosnian, Samir, who was sitting next to me, started fidgeting, then rolled up his trousers and pulled his leg off. He did the same with the other leg, expressing some relief, and continued talking. I was stunned, sitting there with my mouth open, not knowing what to say about his prosthetic legs.

He spoke before I did. 'I lost them both to a tank shell . . . It's strange, watching the shrapnel whiz over your head – even after your legs are gone, and you still think, "It's not going to hit me."' Samir's English was quite good. He'd graduated from Sarajevo University.

Samir told me something about the history of Yugoslavia under Marshal Tito during the communist era. Over a decade after his death,

Slovenia and Croatia had broken away from Serbia, and the Bosnians had followed suit. There were three main groups in Bosnia – all Slavs, but with three major religions: Orthodox Serbs, Catholic Croats, and Bosnian Muslims. They had all reasserted their religious and national identity after the disintegration of communist Yugoslavia. At that time, he said, they used to be very close to the Serbs and Croats. 'Me, especially,' he said. 'I had Serb neighbours. We used to date their girls and they used to date ours.'

But when the war began, everything changed.

The Serbs and Croats in Bosnia, he said, both had the independent neighbouring states of Serbia and Croatia for military and logistical support. The Bosnians had no such useful neighbour, and the only sympathy they had was from a silent, impotent, and ignorant Muslim world.

It seemed to me that a lot of people were talking about Bosnia, but far less were doing anything. I heard about the aid effort in the news, but it was criticized for being 'too little too late' – exactly what I thought.

My increasing visits to the mosque meant that I was unavoidably there during some of the five daily prayers – which were not too difficult to perform in congregation, but I found very hard to do alone at home. So I didn't. Not until I began to feel that Islam was being attacked. That feeling grew as I began to learn more about the wider Muslim world and the turmoil it had started to face.

During the Christmas holidays in 1993 I decided I needed a break, and went, with some friends, to visit our families in Pakistan.

In Karachi, we met some members of Jamaat-e-Islami (Pakistan's largest Islamic organization, and its third largest political party), who invited us to their centre in Lahore. It sounded very interesting; we thought they were keen to show off their place to us because we were British. They told us it had a university, a hospital, schools, residential buildings, a theatre, a library, and a karate dojo (gym), an idea I found particularly impressive. The martial arts were not popular in Pakistan like they were in the West, so this seemed like a pioneering step. In my early teens I studied wing chun, and later obtained a blue belt in tae kwon-do and a green in jujitsu. Self-defence in the UK was increasingly adopted by many first-generation British Asians to combat the realities of racist threat. Some of the practitioners even developed their own styles, with a cultural or religious tint, much as martial arts that were imbued with Buddhist philosophy had often been. The Five Tenets of Tae Kwon-do, Courtesy, Integrity, Self-control, Perseverance, and the Indomitable Spirit, were, as well as the physical aspect of it, to become a great source of strength for me in the years to come.

The Jamat's centre, Mansura, was almost cordoned off from the rest of the city, a mini-city within a city. It had guards on the doors, and was walled like a medieval town. At the mosque we saw people from all sorts of backgrounds, mostly Pakistani, but many from Indian Kashmir and the Central Asian republics. The hospital was primarily for those wounded in Kashmir and Afghanistan. Some had even been in Bosnia.

And as we entered the hospital I saw photographs on the walls of some of the appalling injuries. I was very afraid of what the real thing would look like. The first person I saw had been shot in his eye and part of his face had been shattered. He told us, 'I was fighting against the Indian army in Kashmir, and they shot my eye out. I'm just back here for it to heal, and then I can go back again.'

When he heard that we were from Britain he was so pleased and very hospitable, getting out of bed and offering us his food. I felt very moved by him, but also a bit inadequate.

Later, we met some of the old veterans who had fought against the Soviets; one man told me how he'd seen his son killed in front of him. Others spoke of miracles they had experienced, like water spurting from a bone-dry mountain crevice, in the middle of nowhere, when they had been marching for days with only their AK47s, and thought they were about to die of thirst. Others still told even more fantastic stories of seeing angel-like swordsmen, in flowing white robes, descend from the skies on the enemy in the midst of battle. All of them were always re-emphasizing that it was faith that kept them going.

I had just less than two weeks left before I was due back in Britain. I was faced with the choice of visiting my uncle in the Punjab as I had planned, or taking an offer of our new friends: to visit their training camps in Afghanistan. I had vivid pictures in my mind of Sandy Gall on ITN with the mujahideen, and I saw them as he had depicted them, a heroic people who had taken on the mighty Soviet Empire, against all odds, and defeated it. I had always wanted to go there, and here was my opportunity.

I told my family in Pakistan about my intentions; they were worried, but it was fairly common in those days – tens of thousands of Pakistanis had been. We went to Peshawar, and from there to the border of Pakistan. I imagined it was going to be an easy ride, and that we were just going to drive to our destination. We Brits had our English clothes on, our boots and rucksacks and suitcases. But when we reached a border guesthouse the locals just laughed at us. They gave us old tattered shalwar kameez, an Afghani cap and a carrier bag, saying, 'This isn't a backpacking holiday; you can't carry more than this. And you can't look too English.'

We walked for hours through mountains and dust. Nothing was growing; there was hardly any vegetation. But the view had a rugged beauty that excited me when we finally crossed into Afghanistan. Each time we stopped by a stream we drank greedily. Our guide told us stories of battles here against the Soviets. He showed us what looked like a pile of rocks, but was actually a graveyard of *shuhada*, martyrs who had fallen here. There were burnt-out tanks, and broken down armoured vehicles, spent ammunition and unexploded ordnance.

It was all so far away from anything I'd ever experienced. I saw an occasional Afghan walking along, with his Kalashnikov slung over his shoulder, descending from a summit, and climbing another. I thought, 'God knows where he came from and God knows where he's going.' I was in the middle of nowhere, with a sense of total remoteness. I was entirely disconnected from the world I had known. Some of the people with us were actually going to train in the camp, and I was filled with curiosity about them, and respect.

As we approached what appeared to be our destination I began hearing heavy gunfire and explosions. I turned around and looked at the others, wondering if we all thought the same. Their expressions said it all: 'I didn't come here to fight. I'm just a visitor. I don't want to step into the middle of a civil war.' My legs were carrying me forward, but my brain was telling me to stop.

As we got closer to the sounds of shelling and gunfire, I saw little white arrows painted on the rock, for directions at night. We passed an outpost, which had several plants neatly arrayed outside – in empty artillery shells. Eventually we looked down at the camp, known as al-Fajr, with its houses made of mud and straw, and a mountain stream running through it. We took a quick drink from it, and then went to meet the emir of the camp.

We sat down and we were introduced as 'the people from Britain – our special guests'. And that was how it always was for us in this place. We were very aware that we were definitely getting special treatment. They wanted us to get up and talk to everybody, but none of us knew what to say, we'd just come to visit out of curiosity, and initially we didn't even know what questions to ask.

When it started to get dark we sat down with everybody to eat. We all sat on the floor on a mat made out of straw. The overwhelming majority were either Pakistani or Kashmiris from India. We were served one bowl of lentil soup between four, and some pieces of bread. Because we were visitors, we got an extra half-slice each. The bread was old and cold. Then they passed round a jug of water, refreshingly ice-cold. Everybody drank from the jug. Finally we were served green tea – in individual cups. It was all a huge culture shock. These people lived on a handful of peanuts, lentils, and chickpeas, and mouldy bread and tea. I found it very impressive to see how simply they lived. I assumed it was all part of the general conditioning and training for mountain warfare, where food is scarce and people have to learn to share.

Although it was winter, the days were very hot, but during the night we shivered with cold. The call to prayer, echoing through the mountains, was our wake-up call. I stumbled my way down the dark mountain ledge to where others had gathered at a frozen stream, to wash. I had to crack the ice to get at the water. As the day went on I saw the camp routine come alive: morning prayer, Quranic recitation, a parade, a run and exercise. There were various classes of theory, and then practical classes, with weapons. I saw punishments meted out against those who failed to follow camp rules. These included hundreds of press-ups, a climb to three mountain peaks, jumping fully clothed into the freezing pond, or outright expulsion from the camp.

The emir was a busy man, but very hospitable to us. He had a permanent smile, even when he spoke about the most serious issues. He was also very frank about his mission.

'To me jihad is like a drug I'm allowed to take, and I always come back for more. I feel I have fulfilled my purpose in life when I come to the defence of the oppressed,' he explained carefully. 'As long as Muslim lands are occupied I have vowed to fight for their liberation. It is my duty as a Muslim, as a Pakistani and as a human. Death in this path does not frighten me – I welcome it, with open arms. One of our brothers, martyred years ago, in these very mountains against Rūs [Russia], said something I will never forget: "Much of mankind has chosen life as a path to death, but I have chosen death as a path to life."'

He went on to talk about the history of al-Fajr. 'Hundreds of mujahideen trained and fought in this camp during the Soviet occupation, but in the early days, most of them had had very little fighting experience. One night it was raided by just a handful of Spetznaz, who killed almost everyone in the camp. Then they poisoned the streams and wells. Eventually though, the camp was functioning again and we learned to counter their tricks. We began placing scouts around the mountains to inform us about enemy movements. When they came a second time, the Spetznaz were taken by surprise. We had emptied the camp before they arrived, and then we surrounded it. This time they were slaughtered, or captured. A few converted to Islam and joined the fight against their former employers – you might have seen them in Mansura. And some are still held prisoner in these mountains, under Hikmatyar.' (He was referring to one of the seven foremost Afghan guerrilla leaders and his organization during the war.)*

'Even all these years after the war?' I asked.

'The Russians, my brother, are still meddling in our affairs.'

---

* Gulubuddin Hekmatyar is still fighting a guerrilla war against the new Afghan government.

During their free time – in the evenings – we talked with some of the Indians, many of whom had come from Srinagar. Their stories were very harrowing, but not worse than the Bosnians' I thought. I noticed most of them were older men, with grey hair, in contrast to all the young Pakistanis. One of the Kashmiris told me how men had been forced to watch the rape of their own daughters by Indian troops; one man had even been forced to lie with his own daughter. Another told me how Indian soldiers would tear up the Quran and urinate on it during house-to-house searches. Naturally, he told us, the incensed population resisted, and the graveyards and Indian prisons were filling up with Kashmiri youth. The older men were increasingly forced into keeping up the resistance. I understood that for them this place was a symbol of that resistance.

In the distance we could see other camps. I was told that some were Tajik, some were Arab, and others were from various Pakistani groups. The whole region seemed to be dotted with camps, and we asked if we could visit one of them. The emir said he'd have to go over and have a chat first. 'We don't have any working relationships with one another. People are quite suspicious, especially the Arabs. They've got their own agenda, and we have ours. Some of the groups don't even like each other.'

Eventually we did get permission to go with the emir, and visit the Arab camp. There appeared only to be a dozen or so men in this camp, compared to the hundred and fifty in ours. Their set-up seemed more permanent, with some solid brick buildings, and several vehicles, including a tank.

They invited us to eat with them, and we had a tempting Arab meal of delicious soup, cooked meat, and chicken, followed by fruit. In comparison the Pakistanis were running a boot camp, and ate like peasants.

I didn't understand Arabic then, but I picked up references to Palestine, Kashmir, and Bosnia. And I found myself almost nodding in agreement with what their emir was saying, although I hadn't a clue what it was really. When we left, with typical Arab hospitality, they said, 'Take whatever you want, help yourself.' We Brits left there with bananas and apples in our pockets.

I was only in the Pakistani camp for a few days, but I saw a good deal of their training, which seemed quite basic, and not too glamorous. They used to run round the mountains firing blank rounds at each other most of the time. However, there was an instructor, known as Tahir al-Inqilabi (the revolutionary), who was in charge of the armoury and the weapons classes. Sometimes I saw him teaching classes on AK47 rifles, sniper rifles, RPG7s, and anti-aircraft guns. Most of the weapons were Russian, except for one American M16, which had no rounds, and an old Lee Enfield .303, from the days of the British Raj. 'These are very old,' said Tahir, as he showed us a selection of weapons from his armoury, 'antique weapons that you could sell in the West for thousands of rupees . . . I mean pounds.'

Tahir went back into the armoury and brought out a large wooden box. He opened it and took out an old plastic doll, a butterfly shaped pillbox, and an Action Man. 'Rūs used to leave these presents for our children,' he said, removing the doll's head, 'with a detonator inside, and packed with C4 explosives.'

One night there was an alert in the camp that there was going to be an attack, and we three were issued with weapons, even though we didn't know how to use them. The attacks were expected from local nomadic tribes, *kuchees*, who would raid and then just disappear. Many of them had sided with the Soviets during the war, and were not trusted. But the cause of this alert was one of the Brits. His bag had been stolen. The people in the camp sent out search parties to try and find out who had taken it, and eventually they came back with some-one. He was tied up, looking very wretched and scared. I really felt sorry for him and worried about what was going to happen, since the instructor standing next to him was holding a sword.

The alert was because the nomad's people were expected to retali-ate in revenge for his capture. We were all told to sleep outside because the huts could be set alight. But the next day a *jirga* came over to the camp. It was a tribal council, which we were told, was held to solve the problem between the two groups. After hours of talks – which we were not permitted to attend – there was a decision. The people at the camp had to make redress to the tribe for hitting the man, and he in turn had to hand the bag back, and promise never to come to the camp again. It was a long way from Birmingham magistrates' courts, and it wasn't exactly Islamic law, but it just seemed to me very fair.

My time at the camp had come to an end, but the last night I spent there I woke to the sounds of multiple explosions and screaming. We were under attack; it must have been the nomads. Someone ran into our room and shouted, 'Get up, get up. It's an attack from the *kuchees*. Gather at the assembly area, and get your weapons.' I was too stunned to be scared; I just did as I was told. I staggered around in the dark to find my shoes, and ran out of the room. I was met with the sight of red and green tracer rounds whizzing over my head, and flashing RPGs slamming into the mountainside with a deafening crash. 'Keep your head down,' someone yelled, 'crawl on your bellies if you have to, but keep moving.' I got down on my stomach, just like those around me. Others were running around panicking and screaming. One man sat on the ground sobbing. 'Oh, Mother, please forgive me. I should have listened to you and never come here.' Another's face was being bandaged as he cried, 'Oh God . . . my face, my face.' Then I was scared.

As I crawled along, I began to think, 'Why tell us all to assemble in one place if we're under attack? That's suicide.' Surely a handful of people could gather and distribute the weapons. Something didn't sound right to me. But then an old Russian ambulance came from somewhere, blurting out a siren that sounded like it was about to die. By now I'd reached the assembly point. The firing and explosions stopped. The ambulance halted and out came some people covered in bandages, and the emir. All eyes were on him, as he began to undo the bandages. Then he turned facing us on the ground and said, 'Most of you have reacted well. Some of you I'm ashamed of and you do not deserve to stay here any longer. This was a simulated exercise, no one was hurt, but it will teach you a lesson you'll never forget.'

By the time of my return I considered myself a practising Muslim. The Afghan visit was a life-changing experience for me. No few days had ever affected me like that. I had met men who seemed to me exemplary, in their faith and self-sacrifice, and seen a world that awed and inspired me.

4

MERCY MISSION

Back home in Birmingham, I decided it was time for me to get married. My father had already told me I should be thinking about it, and had arranged for me to meet various girls and their families. I met a few, but his method wasn't working for me. So I asked a friend if he could help me find a wife. He introduced me to my future brother-in-law, a very easy-going British Palestinian, recently graduated from Cambridge. He invited me over to his house to meet his sister.

'This can't be the place,' I thought when I arrived outside the enormous house; 'he seemed such a modest person.' Hesitantly I knocked on the door, thinking that I should just turn away and drive off. Inside it was very grand, and I felt a little intimidated, but Samir made me very comfortable. We ate lunch together and talked for a while. Then Zaynab came in. Samir was conducting things in the correct Islamic way, not in the way of traditional Asian marriages. So Zaynab was not in hijab when I met her. I was attracted to her from the very first moment. She sat down, and we talked for a while. Samir went off into the corner of the room and just left us. After a while, it was clear that we liked each other, but I still felt intimidated by the surroundings. I wanted to talk to her on my own ground.

We arranged to meet again at her friend's house. I also knew the friend's husband, so it was familiar ground for both of us. We were left to speak freely to one another, over a lunch that lasted for some time. Over the next couple of months we phoned one another and met a few times.

One of the things I explained to her was my passion to go to Bosnia. I had to try to explain to her that something might happen to me there and ask whether she understood the implications. I don't think she was really aware of the risks involved; she just wanted to get married. She had already met various possible husbands, but it was me she had decided on. So we agreed to get married. It was a very simple Islamic contract that we did in her lounge. Samir and I called my father, my brother, and a friend as a witness, and an imam to conduct the ceremony.

For the first month of our married life we stayed in my parents' house, and I was so pleased at how they received her: she was like the daughter they never had. She became part of the family from then on. Then Zaynab's parents bought her a house as a wedding gift. We moved into it and spent our first years there. Marriage had totally changed my life; I felt ecstatic having someone of my choice to share it with me. But I could not ignore the injustice I saw reported on the television screens every day, or the stories I heard from the victims.

I had asked my Bosnian friend, Edin, about Bosnian cuisine once, and he invited me for a traditional meal at his friend's house. The friend was a young Bosnian Muslim woman who had come to live in Birmingham as a refugee. As she couldn't speak English too well, Edin translated some of the little that she said. Her face looked worn, and her eyes distant. After we left Edin told me her story. It was beyond anything I had ever heard, or imagined. Serb soldiers had raided her house and raped her in front of her husband. The gang rape continued over the screams of their three-month-old baby. As long as the child cried at least she'd known it was alive. When the crying stopped she begged the soldiers, 'Where's my baby? What have you done to him?' A soldier came in carrying the child's head and placed it on a table next to her, before he raped her again. In England, she was receiving psychiatric care, but also her community were trying to find her a husband. Hers had been killed, just after they had raped her.

I didn't need much convincing about helping the Bosnians, but I got one last prod. An amateur British filmmaker had gone to Bosnia and made a film entitled *Massacres in Bosnia and Croatia*. It was the most horrific live-footage I'd ever seen. It showed charred body remains strewn all over cities and villages, macabre against the magnificent Bosnian countryside. The commentary said that bets were placed between soldiers carrying bayonets whether pregnant women were carrying a male or female child, followed by scenes of a dead woman and her carved-out foetus beside her. The film also showed a young boy, perhaps six years old, who had had his throat slit, because the Serbs were conserving rounds. An old Bosnian woman interviewed for the film said, 'Why do you send us only food? So the Serbs can slaughter us like fattened sheep? Arm our people so we can fight back.' I resolved then to find a way to go to Bosnia.

News of camps used by Serb soldiers systematically to rape thousands of Muslim women outraged me. I saw the genocide of Bosnians, and 'ethnic cleansing' happening in front of Europe. But the choices I had were limited to donating money to organizations that operated out of Croatia – not Bosnia – and helping the refugees once they were in England. For many people even that would have been too much. But I knew that simply feeding and clothing people facing extermination was not enough.

I began by donating regularly to various charities, starting with a weekly percentage of my income, and a gold ring I had had for many years. But that was nothing – people were getting butchered. I went to conferences around the country about proposals for a solution, and became terribly upset that the EU, including Britain, had agreed an arms embargo against all parties in the conflict. The Serbs and Croats all had weapons coming from their neighbouring states. The Bosnians had nothing. One of the very few influential voices publicly calling for arming the Bosnians as far as I knew, oddly, was Baroness Thatcher's.

Ever since my last trip to Pakistan and Afghanistan I had been thinking obsessively both about Bosnia, because it was so close, and about what I had seen of resistance in Afghanistan. I had met people there who had actually gone out and done something practical about injustice, rather than sit at home. Finally, I found someone who was not just talking about helping the Bosnians – except mercenaries. I read reports and saw televised interviews with former British soldiers, mercenaries, who were fighting in the Balkans, though not always for the Bosnians. But that type of rented help without conviction was not what they needed.

I had heard about an organization called Convoy of Mercy, which delivered aid to Bosnia from Britain. The organizer was a British Pakistani, Asif. I went to meet him and he told me, 'I take aid to the needy in Bosnia. Anybody who goes with me has to work very hard and obey the rules. It's no joy ride; it's not a holiday. You come with me, you listen to what I say, and you work. As far as you going off and joining the Bosnian army, you can . . . that's up to you. I can't encourage you and I can't stop you. My work is not just one single outpouring of compassion; it's continuous: I take a convoy every two weeks. If you are coming, you're going to have to put some commitment into it.'

I told my manager at the Department of Social Security that I'd like to take a couple of months' unpaid leave. I wanted him to keep my job open for me to come back to, but if he wouldn't, I was still going, I told him. And to their credit, they supported me, and promised to keep my job. They didn't know, of course, that I wanted to join the Bosnian army – although I hadn't entirely made up my mind just then.

I was incredibly excited, and anxious. My dad was worried, and although he supported the general idea of helping in Bosnia, he really did not want me to go.

When I got to Asif's place in North London at the start of the trip, I saw at once how very English in style he was, a bit like Dad. He even had a British flag flying on his vehicle. The first thing he said to me was, 'Right, come with me to the warehouse and start loading up.' We loaded for five hours: goods from all around the country, crates of tinned food, cartons of long-life drinks, bags of clothes and blankets, and boxes of medicine and medical equipment. We filled up two vans.

The vans were all in bad order, and we were going to drive for 1,500 miles. They broke down in almost every country we crossed: France, Luxembourg, Germany, Austria, Slovenia, Croatia, and Bosnia. There were two people in one van, and the rest of us four in the other, all men, some Muslim and some not. Asif drove the van that I was in.

Suddenly, late at night, somewhere in the middle of the Black Forest, on a road covered in snow, he stopped the vehicle and told me to take over. He was going to sleep. This was not what I was expecting. I was the lead vehicle, and it was the first time in my life I'd ever driven a van, or driven on the right-hand side of the road. And I didn't know the way. All I had was a piece of paper detailing which towns and villages we had to pass.

Asif didn't believe in stopping at hotels because he said we had been entrusted with public money, every penny of which he was accountable for. 'If you want to stop at hotels,' he said, 'it's at your own expense. But I will not wait. I sleep in the van, and eat on the road. I'll buy you all a pizza in Ljubljana.' When we stopped for fuel or any-thing, he said, 'We're not waiting for anyone, if you get out and don't join the convoy in time, you will be left behind. I did that to someone in Croatia on the last convoy, who thought he was here on holiday.' I have never worked with anyone like Asif – before or after.

After Slovenia, we got closer to the war zones. Once we entered Croatia I could feel the tension. They wanted to see more documenta-tion, and searched the vans. Asif was amazing at the borders. He was a stiff-upper-lip British type, often threatening troublesome border guards with diplomatic action. He had been shot at, captured, and beaten by Croats on earlier trips, but nothing deterred him, he was unstoppable. He knew enough of the language now to be fluent and very assertive when he was speaking to the guards. I learnt from this, for some of my own journeys later on.

Eventually we arrived in Split on the Dalmatian coast, another fan-tastically beautiful place. We stopped and went for a swim in the sea. Soon we started seeing white UN vehicles, adding to the sense of entering a war zone. We continued down the coast to Makarska, where the Pakistani UN contingent was based. Asif had a fairly good rapport with them, I saw. They had previously helped to carry some excess food that he'd had when one of the vehicles had got damaged. We stayed with them for a while and I found it quite odd to see Pakistanis there, in such a different context. Yet I was very unimpressed by them, because just like other UN contingents, they were letting the atrocities against Muslims continue.

As soon as we crossed the border, Asif said, 'You're now in Bosnia, we have to be careful. There are areas here that keep changing hands, just as the alliances do. At present there is a Muslim–Croat Federation, but they have fought vicious wars against each other in the past.' He told us to lie down and draw the curtains as we went through Bosnian

Croat territory. The ride was very bumpy now, as the roads were filled with bomb craters.

Mostar was the first city we saw. It was devastated. I couldn't see a single house or building that hadn't been bombed. The historic bridge over the beautiful river had fallen into it. Along the road to Mostar, Asif pointed out a cathedral that had a large cross on its steeple. 'They cru cified one of the Arab volunteers up there a few months ago. This is the type of place you've come to.'

For miles on end I saw bombed-out homes, with all the roofs destroyed. I noticed that almost every inch of every house had a bullet hole. Even the road signs hadn't escaped the frenzy of destruction. Of the few people I did see around, most looked like ghosts, with blank expressions, hardly bothering to look as we drove past. The other thing I noticed was the graveyards. They were every-where.

One of our passengers on the convoy was Bosnian. Mustafa had fled with his daughter to Britain, and had been there for almost a year. Now he had returned to join the army and fight against the Serbs. We all felt a huge amount of admiration for this old man. We dropped him off in one of the desolate little villages, and I never saw him again until the following year, when he told me all about his bat-tles. He had also grown a very long beard.

After Mostar we arrived in Jablanica where people immediately flocked around the convoy. The Bosnians here were so happy to see us. *'Merhaba*, Asif, *kako ste vi?'* they shouted. *'Merhaba brac, kako ste vi?'* ('Welcome, brothers, how are you?')

'Dobro, aka bogda. Malo novi brac.' ('Well, by God's will. Some new brothers here.')

Asif was strict with us, the workers, but the Bosnians saw another side of him, and they loved him. He was often invited to their houses for coffee, or for meals, and we went along with him and saw how the Bosnians lived. Their lives were so miserable and difficult; I was not surprised that so many of them had fled to Western Europe.

We soon discovered that Asif had a hand in all sorts of projects: chicken farms, rehabilitation centres, hospitals, and schools. Just out of Jablanica we came to a village called Ostražac, where Asif had his main centre. The centre was overlooking a beautiful lake – where I swam, on my second visit in the summer – with snow-capped mountains all around. Everywhere there was the same warm welcome for us. Whenever they saw us driving past, the children would raise their right index finger in the air, as Muslims do during the prayer. It meant *shahada*, the testament of faith.

When we first arrived there was so much work that needed to be done that we didn't get a chance to rest, or to look properly at the place. After unloading, and chopping some firewood, Asif had me digging out grooves for a drainage pipe in the cellar.

After almost two weeks working in that centre distributing food to the refugees I felt a sense of accomplishment. But I was filled with guilt when I looked at their faces, knowing I had come from a life that was luxurious in comparison to what they had, and I would return to it. Turning up with a tin of beans was not enough.

I learned a bit of the language, and I heard lots of people's stories. One day we visited a unit of the Bosnian army run by Mu'allim (teacher), who had been trained in Islamic theology in Egypt. He seemed to be well organized, and respected for fighting the Serbs. I heard some of the soldiers' harrowing stories, such as how they had fought in the snow, with temperatures down to −25, and some had lost limbs from frostbite.

En route to Zenica we stopped in Travnik, up in the mountains to the west, using snow-chains on our wheels. We got closer to the war zone, passing bombed-out vehicles, destroyed houses, and miserable-looking refugees. We heard stories of how a handful of Bosnian and Arab mujahideen had fought off a whole enemy battalion and managed to save the city.

Travnik was beautiful, with plenty of Ottoman architecture in the myriad mosques and madrasas. The Turkish-style minarets protruding from the mountainside did look a bit like the Scud missiles the *Sun* had once claimed they were, disguised by the Bosnians as minarets. In the city we met some Arabs, including a doctor who had been living and working there for many years, even before the war. But we met others too who had joined the various units of the Bosnian forces. I was still thinking of doing that myself, but as we neared the war zone, thoughts about how committed I was began to waver. I was not really sure what to do. I thought about Zaynab and our first child she was expecting, and knew that it was unfair to be going off on something as dangerous as joining an army.

Three of us Brits had asked Asif if we could go to Zenica, where the Bosnian army's foreign legion was based. We had heard about the foreigners from all over the Muslim world who had converged on this place and given their allegiance to III Korpus, Armija Bosanska, or Kateebatul Mujahideen (as they were known in Bosnian and Arabic) under the leadership of Alija Izetbegović, President of Bosnia and Herzegovina. We had also heard they had been fighting daring battles against the Serbs.

Asif said, 'OK, I'll drop you off at Zenica, if you want to go there. But then you have to make your own way back. You can come back to the centre when you're finished, but you've got to work until the convoy returns to England.'

I went to Zenica with the other Brits, all of us excited because we had heard so much about it, but also very nervous. We had arrived at the headquarters of the Bosnian army's 3rd Corps, or the Kateebah (Battalion) as the Arabs called it.

We were sent to speak to the man responsible for new recruits. He was an Egyptian, and not immediately friendly.

'What have you come here for?'

'I just came to see how—'

'Are you a reporter or something?'

'No,' I said, feeling defensive, 'I'm just a person that's concerned, and wanted to see how I could help.'

'The people who come here are foreign volunteers, mujahideen, who stay six months to a year at a time. They commit themselves to get trained, and then to go on to the various front lines. Some return, some are wounded and others are *shaheed* [martyred]. Are you ready for that?'

I had asked myself these questions many times. 'Do I think I'm ready to kill for this cause, am I ready to die for it too?'

Before I answered, he said, 'Look, we are in the middle of winter now, so there is not much fighting anyway. You can stay here for a couple of weeks, if you want, and see how we are unique and different to the other parts of the army. You can go to our camp as a visitor, stay with the brothers. But I can't let you go to the front line unless you are properly trained.'

One of the other Brits decided it was not for him, and he left within two days. 'This is much harder than I thought,' he said to me. 'I'm not prepared for this, physically or mentally. I miss my wife too much.' He caught a coach to Croatia and never returned. The other joined up and stayed for six months.

I ended up spending three weeks there, mostly in Zenica at the base camp. There were people from all over the world there, all seeming completely at ease with each other. I even came across a Serb who'd converted to Islam and decided to join this side. But he was never sent to the front.

At the army-training centre in Oracus I saw they had a very European approach to training, in contrast to what I had seen in Afghanistan. Here the trainers seemed more professional, and I saw that precision, efficiency, and punctuality were considered important. In Afghanistan they were more relaxed; they seemed to fire a shot, have a sip of tea, relax, and fire again. Here soldiers were fully kitted out with winter and summer combat gear; they ate on chairs at tables with silverware and had an organized rank structure, and were put through a rigorous physical training. Most of the weapons were from Eastern Europe, but one of the soldiers showed me a rifle he said he'd bought from a Croat arms dealer. It was the first and only time I saw and touched a British SA80 assault rifle. He said the British had given hundreds of them to the Croats.

I found it interesting that most of the people in charge were Arabs. But there were Turks, Gambians, Pakistanis, French, Filipinos, and Malaysians, as well as Bosnians, and a strong influence from Saudi Arabia. In fact several Gulf States had aid agencies and education centres dotted around the country associated with the Kateebah. The people in charge seemed to be mostly Egyptians, many of whom were Bosnian nationals, married to local women. They told me about operations they had conducted against the Serbs, and I could see this was not guerrilla war like in Afghanistan; it was conventional front-line action. They had trenches dug, and they had heavy artillery.

Obviously they liked talking about their victories. But there were losses too. Many foreigners had been killed. At least five were British. A battle had recently taken place, in which they'd lost over twenty men, but they'd captured the objective. I visited some of the injured in hospital and was surprised to find a British man there who had been terribly wounded. He had lost his eye, and a chunk of his shoulder. I asked him about his motivation, and about the injury. He told me, 'If you are committed to it, then you'll think it's a sacrifice worth making.'

After my time was up I went back to Travnik, where I stayed for a couple of days with a friend I'd made in Zenica. I didn't return to the centre, but instead took a coach to Munich, and from there, back to England.

Soon after I got back to Britain I went and talked to Asif. I felt a debt to him for taking me to Bosnia, which had been my dream for so long, and I could tell that he had been impressed by something about me. Maybe it was that I had picked up more Bosnian than his volunteers usually did, or maybe it was because I was one of the few who listened to him without argument.

After I returned from Bosnia I packed in my job at the DSS. How could I be sitting quietly in an office all day after what I had seen? Since I began practising Islam, I had stopped going to the pub after work. I stopped going to nightclubs. Initially, I was always involved in social activities with my colleagues; slowly but surely many of these things stopped. I felt myself moving into an entirely different world, of my own making in many ways, but a world that already existed, and was somehow waiting for me.

During the next two and a half years I went to Bosnia eight or nine times with the Convoy of Mercy. I visited the barracks of the Kateebah once again, but I had lost any illusions about joining the Bosnian army. Many of the people I'd met there had been killed.

In Britain I worked voluntarily for the Convoy of Mercy often, helping in various fund-raising projects and collecting goods for the convoys. We kept on going even after the war had officially ended in 1995, with the Dayton Peace Accord, which stipulated the expulsion of all foreign fighters. By the time of my last visit, in 1997, most of the leadership of the Kateebah had been assassinated, killed in an ambush, well after the Peace Accord.

In early 1995 Zaynab and I moved into our new house, close to the Birmingham City football ground. On 5 May that year, our first child was born. We named her Umamah (Young Mother), but my father wanted Marium, so she became Marium Umamah. Zaynab and I were overjoyed. She was like a baby doll. It was the first girl in the Begg family since my sister Uzma died. I was to be there to help my wife through each of her next three pregnancies, but one; I would be there for the years of infancy for each of them, but one.

The following summer I got the first jolt about my new responsibilities, and vulnerabilities. I came home one afternoon to find Zaynab terribly frightened and upset.

She told me she had been walking home after shopping, with Umamah in the pushchair, when a car full of white youths drove past her slowly. They wound down the windows and started swearing at her, hurling racist abuse like 'raghead' (because of the hijab she wore). Then they drove off. She ignored them and carried on walking. As she approached the turning to the main road the car came back from behind her, half of it driving on the pavement. As soon as she realized the car was just a few yards behind, she ran with the pushchair. When she reached the main road she turned and saw the car had stopped and one of the youths had jumped out and was coming towards her. She kept running until she got home. I was livid when I heard; how could they be so hostile to a woman with a baby? I went out and drove up and down that road looking for the louts, knowing that the chances of finding them were slim. And even if I did, what was I going to do by myself? The Lynx, I thought, would never have tolerated this, never have let it pass without retribution.

In the summer of 1997, I went with Zaynab and Umamah for the hajj. The experience was not as emotionally enthralling as my first visit had been as a teenager. Worse, it was the year of the great fire in Arafat, the vast plateau near Makkah, where more than 1,500 people died. We had had to flee from the human stampede trying to escape the searing heat of the flames, made worse by intense summer heat.

Millions of people had come for the pilgrimage, but what we saw of the arrogance and rudeness of officials left us very disappointed and happy to leave. On the return trip we stayed with Zaynab's uncle for a few days in Damascus, her birthplace. One day, strolling through the ancient Byzantine courts and the Umayyad Mosque with Zaynab and Umamah, we saw what was said to be the grave of John the Baptist. Then I stumbled upon the grave of one of the most revered men in Islam, and the subject of one of my childhood fascinations, Salah ad-Deen Ibn al-Ayyub – Saladin.

Our second child, Abdur-Rahman (Servant of the Merciful), was born on 27 June 1997, soon after we returned to the UK. But my father preferred Umar, after the Second Caliph of Islam, so he became Umar Abdur-Rahman, my first son.

Zaynab and I had been thinking for a while about moving to a Muslim country. We wanted our children to grow up in Islamic surroundings where we did not stand out so much, and people were similar to ourselves. I wanted the children to have a good grounding in their roots, their culture, and their religion. And for me it was also part of the personal search again.

I considered various places in the Middle East, but the most familiar place to me was Pakistan. I was learning classical Arabic, but it would have been obvious to the first person I spoke to in any Arab country that I was a foreigner. In Birmingham I met people who had emigrated to Pakistan and built homes there. I decided we would go and stay with one of them. I knew a Palestinian, Khalid, who was getting married to a girl in Peshawar, and was living there. There was a small Palestinian community in Peshawar and I thought it would be easier for Zaynab to adjust there, amongst them. So in early 1998 we let our house and left England.

We rented a house with Khalid. We all really loved it there in Peshawar and ended up staying nearly five months. This was the first experience of actually living somewhere apart from Birmingham. Zaynab settled in very easily with the Arab community, better than I did in the Pakistani community. The two groups never really mixed much, which surprised me. Khalid's friends used to come round to the house a lot, all Arabic speakers, so I found myself the odd one out in cultural as well as linguistic terms. But Zaynab was naturally comfortable with the Arabs.

Khalid had plenty of friends, both Arab and Pashtun, who had fought in Afghanistan against the Soviets. Among them were some Kurds who came over one day. They talked about how they had gone back to Iraq and begun an uprising against Saddam Hussein, after the war with the Soviets was over. One of them, Mohammad, told me about the terrible atrocities that they had suffered: mass arrests, torture, and murder. This was the first time I'd heard at first hand about what Saddam Hussein was like. Until then I thought he was the underdog, attacked by the West, and so he naturally had my support. But Mohammad told me that several members of his own family were killed by the chemical-weapons attack at Halabja in 1988. He described to me how all inhabitants of the town were found lying on the ground with their faces contorted with pain. He had taken to the mountains and begun fighting Saddam's forces. Later on he fled with his family to Afghanistan and joined some Kurds who had had their own camp near Jalalabad since the Soviet days.

I got on very well with him, and another, Abdullah al-Kurdi, who asked me if I would like to visit Afghanistan with him. (I was to owe this man and his family an enormous debt of gratitude three years later when he helped save my family after the US bombing of Afghanistan.) Their camp was just over the border and through the Khyber Pass, only about a two-hour journey from Peshawar. He told me it was on the banks of a huge lake, surrounded by mountains. It sounded beautiful, and full of the history of the mujahideen struggle against the Soviets. I decided to accept his offer. It was the first time I had been through the Khyber Pass, and I couldn't help thinking about the Pashtun tribes here defending themselves against the British all those years ago. It was quite extraordinary to feel I was in this lawless area where anybody could get kidnapped, mugged, or killed, and where everyone was carrying guns.

Abdullah gave me a modest meal in his small hut before we went to see their camp. Here again there were several other camps that we were not allowed to visit. The Kurds had three small buildings that they used for weapons training; similar to the Kashmiris I had visited before, but on a much smaller scale.

Swimming in the lake was a daily pastime for many people, but when the dam – used to generate hydroelectric power – was opened it produced a very powerful and dangerous current. Once, when I was in the lake, the Taliban started shelling from their checkpost overlooking the lake. I thought they were actually aiming at me, since the mortar shells landed in the water, and I could see the explosions getting closer. The Kurds started shouting at them, 'What are you doing? We have people in the water.' The Taliban shouted an apology, saying they were just firing a few rounds off out of boredom.

Like many of their countrymen, I felt, these Kurds could easily have chosen the safety of the West, as refugees, and been content with saving themselves and pursuing worldly goals. Instead they had decided to challenge Saddam, choosing a life of exile that would probably end in prison or death. I asked Mohammad once, 'Why don't you seek help from the Americans? You have a common enemy now.'

'One lesson we've learned from our history,' Mohammad answered, 'is that we can never trust outsiders, even if they come to our aid against domestic enemies. Like us, Salah ad-Deen was a Kurd, and he saved the Muslim world by defeating his homegrown enemies, as well as the Crusaders. Others before him lost their lands and honour by accepting external help against their own – even if they were tyrants. The Americans did help us when they invaded Iraq, but *we* were not the reason they came – there's no oil in our part of Iraq. More importantly, when Saddam gassed our people, America sat by and watched – just like the others. In fact who do you think supplied him with the weapons in the first place? France, the UK, and the USA. Saddam is an evil we must destroy ourselves, but at least we understand the source of his evil. What would happen if a greater evil took his place – one that we can't even understand?'

That visit was near the end of our time in Pakistan, and we were sorry to leave. Zaynab had got used to living there, enjoying the company and the environment. We used to go out often in the evenings, visiting friends, or to a park where they made tasty kebabs. Sometimes we'd visit my aunt in Karachi or my cousin in Lahore; they all liked Zaynab very much. My children were too young for school at the time, but I was very interested in a specialist Arabic-language school I visited near our house, and promised them financial help, intending to return there when my children were older.

One thing I never got used to was the poverty. When people

discovered we were from England, they often wanted to become our friends, but for the wrong reasons.

After almost five months we returned to Britain. I had a project in mind to set up a bookshop, and hoped that if it prospered we could spend longer periods abroad, eventually buying property and settling in Pakistan.

Back in Birmingham my work with Convoy had finished, so, for a while I was unemployed, but I used the time to gain some IT qualifications. It took many months for my friend, Shakeel, and I to get the bookshop organized. Our ambitions were to make enough money to support our families, to give some of the profits to charity, and to educate people about Islam.

First we found premises to rent, which we redesigned and renovated. We wanted the shop to look very modern, but with an Islamic theme in the decoration. It took several months before we were ready to contact suppliers for our first orders. Our shop primarily sold Islamic and educational books, but we also sold a wide range of other products like traditional Muslim clothing for men and women, perfumes and incense oils, craftwork, audio-visual lectures, and films – all from various parts of the Islamic world. I used my contacts in Pakistan to send over books, clothes, and honey. The latter was to cause me some problems the following year.

As things progressed we produced some of our own publications, usually translated from Arabic, which is something I quite enjoyed doing. I also designed a large poster for children that taught Arabic letters for non-Arabic speakers, and which proved very popular. Our books were in various sections that included the Quran and related sciences, faith, jurisprudence, history, biography, women, sects, politics, jihad, inter-faith dialogue, languages, and children. We also had separate Arabic and Urdu sections. However, the most popular book, by far, was in the hereafter section. It attracted Muslim and non-Muslim readers alike and was a translation of a thirteenth-century treatise entitled *Signs Before the Day of Judgement*.

I enjoyed working in the shop, which, in the early days, consumed a great deal of my family time. By now I had passed various courses in Arabic and was fluent in it. As my own Islamic knowledge also increased, I introduced weekly study circles at the shop. I hadn't been a particularly spiritual person before, but studying Islam challenged me to question myself at all times.

I felt that correct Islamic education – grounded on hard scriptural evidence and not on culture and superstition – would create a healthy environment of inquisitiveness and learning for those around me. It was not only an opportunity to disseminate my own knowledge, but also a platform to open up discussions on a variety of significant issues.

I enjoyed debating with the many Muslims who had distinctly different views to my own, and I began to understand the complexities and sensitivities of their beliefs. But the most invigorating conversations I had were with people of different faiths, particularly Jehovah's Witnesses and Christian Evangelists. I usually had the advantage of knowing my religion well enough, and a sound knowledge of the Bible and various Christian doctrines to counter their arguments.

I found too there were many people that were struggling to fill the spiritual vacuum that existed, and yet shunned what they knew of organized religion. Despite that rejection, Islam was attracting thousands of indigenous Britons, some of whom converted right in front of me in the bookshop. People of Muslim origin were also returning to their faith in droves; the woman's hijab was one of the fastest-selling items. And, nearly ten years after our gang disbanded, former members of the Lynx – and other gangs – also came to our bookshop to learn about Islam.

Many young people were becoming interested in Islam, rather as I had in the early nineties, often airing their frustrations about the state of the Muslims and their increasing demonization and humiliation in the world. A good proportion of the Pakistanis in Britain come from Azad (Free) Kashmir, in Pakistan. A few of the border towns had training camps for Kashmiri fighters, operating with the blessing of the Pakistani government, military, and intelligence services. Some of these young men went off to the training camps to learn how to fight. Some of them participated in the various jihads around the world. Some of them never returned home and are buried in unmarked graves. And some of them are probably still fighting.

5

SPOOKS

In winter 1998 I had my first experience of MI5. I heard a knock on my door one morning, at about five o'clock. I opened it and saw three people – one woman and two men. I was completely baffled when one said he was from the Immigration Department, and the other, from MI5. The latter, identifying himself as Andrew, was to haunt me for the next five years. The woman didn't speak. Perhaps they'd thought they'd woken me, but I was already awake; I'd just finished my *fajr* (dawn) prayer. I asked them to come in, and remove their shoes before they entered the lounge. I didn't have any sofas, just cushions on the floor, the old Arabic way. I told them to take a seat, and that I would be down in a minute with my glasses.

'No, we'd rather stand,' said one of them. I thought it quite funny that he probably felt embarrassed at not knowing how to sit cross-legged and hide the holes in his socks at the same time. When I came back down I saw they had actually sat down, looking quite uncomfortable, except the MI5 man. He was relaxed.

They produced some pictures and they asked me about someone who they told me had been arrested in Dubai on accusations of terrorism. He was a Tunisian, Adam, who I'd met in Britain about six months before.

They told me what I already knew: that he went from Britain to

Saudi Arabia on the umrah, and from there, to Pakistan. There he was arrested on a false passport. And then he was sent to Dubai, though I did not understand why. In Dubai he escaped from custody at the airport, lived on the streets, and was eventually captured again, and then escaped a second time. While he was still free, he phoned me in Britain, to say he was sending some documents to my address. They included his police arrest sheet, and a handwritten letter. He wrote, 'I am writing to you as a last resort . . . I was arrested in Pakistan and handed over to the Dubai authorities so they could torture a confession out of me . . . It says I am "a member of the GIA" [Armed Islamic Group] . . . I am part of bin Ladin's group . . . they have done bad things to me . . . they used *falaqa* on me [beating the soles of the feet] . . . I am very hurt and tired, please get me a lawyer . . . please, please help me . . .'

I had taken the papers to Gareth Peirce. I had spoken to a lawyer friend of mine in Birmingham about it, who knew Gareth, and recommended her as the most principled solicitor in Britain, and one who had taken up many cases of Muslims. That was the first time I had met Gareth, who was to become such an important person in my life. She said that there was not much that she could do about a case in Dubai, but that she would see if there was a lawyer there who she could contact. But I heard no more from Adam until Andrew told me he was recaptured in Dubai.

The security people wanted to know how I met Adam, why he contacted me, and if I sent him any money. I told them where I had met him, and that I had in fact sent him some money, by Western Union, when he told me he was sleeping in the streets. I told them about the letter I had received from him, but they didn't seem interested. Perhaps they'd already read it. They said they believed he was a member of the Algerian GIA, but I told them he was a Tunisian. They said he was a very dangerous man, and they were glad that he was not coming back to the UK.

'But what has he done?' I kept asking, though I never got an answer. After about half an hour they all got up to leave. I offered them a cup of tea, but they declined. Before he left, Andrew said,'If you hear anything, please let us know. This is your country, after all.'

I was left with a strange feeling after the visit. They weren't police, didn't really threaten me with anything – only asked for information. Was Adam really someone dangerous enough for them to question me about him, at five in the morning? And what had he done?

That same day I told my family and friends about the visit. In fact, I felt a bit excited: the world-famous MI5 had come to see me. But they'd also been to see one of Adam's closer friends in London. Zaid was a Tunisian, and he was still trying to get leave to remain in the UK. Unlike me, he had been really worried by the visit.

On 17 July 1999, my second daughter, Nusaybah, was born. We named her after one of the aunts of the Prophet Muhammad. But because the other two children had second names, and my father didn't object, we chose Zaynab for her second name.

One of the hottest topics of debate at the bookshop was the concept of jihad in Islam: was it an individual Muslim duty, like praying and fasting; how, when and where was it applied; what were its rewards; what were its rules; what were the differing opinions? I had become familiar with the hundreds of Quranic verses, prophetic sayings and legal rulings regarding it over the past few years.

Linguistically jihad means 'struggle', the word that some scholars had attempted to confine its meaning to. They said that it was restricted only to the struggle within, the *nafs*, the inner self. Whilst that was partly true, I learned that throughout history – from the time of the Prophet, and the first Caliphates – up until modern times, the majority of Muslims (and the non-Muslims they used it on) always understood jihad as warfare.

The most popular book we sold on this subject was Sheikh Abduallah Azzam's *Defence of the Muslim Lands*, written during the Soviet occupation of Afghanistan, which argued that jihad was an individual Muslim obligation, just like prayer and fasting, if Muslim territory had been forcibly occupied. The ruling was based on the fatwa of the classical scholar Ibn Taymiyyah during the thirteenth century, when Mongol hordes were devastating the lands of Islam: 'And [regarding] the aggressive enemy, who destroys religion and life: nothing is more incumbent, after faith, than repelling him.'

But one of the most powerful arguments I read was that even if jihad had been emphatically prohibited in the Quran, it would have become permissible by necessity – just as pork does for Muslims, if there's nothing else to eat. Who needed a fatwa to defend his own family? Self-defence was a right that everyone had.

The problems arose when senseless acts of murder were carried out by desperate mujahideen – or in their name – that tainted the very causes they were fighting for. The beheading and machine-gunning of tourists in Kashmir and Egypt or the rape and slaughter of civilians in Algeria all blurred the oppression that had led to such madness.

And of course there was the issue of bin Ladin. I had spoken about him to Sheikh Abdul-Majeed, a Palestinian friend and scholar I referred to for Islamic issues. He had studied and lived in Pakistan in the 1980s and early '90s, and fought against the Soviets in Afghanistan. He talked about *hijrah*, migration from a non-Muslim land to a Muslim one. He had come to study in London for a few years, but he planned to return to Pakistan and Afghanistan with his family.

Abdul-Majeed said that bin Ladin was unnecessarily courting

trouble with the US, at the expense of the occupied Muslim states, as well as of those people who were fighting oppression in their own countries. Although Abdul-Majeed had no love for America, the real problem, he said, was 'our own' Muslim countries that had betrayed Islam and its people.

Abdul-Majeed was balanced in his approach to practical life. Once he was asked if Muslims were allowed to join the British army. He said that it was not permissible, particularly if it would involve fighting fellow Muslims. But he also said that it would be permissible, obligatory in fact, to fight alongside British forces against a foreign invader – if Britain were attacked. I forgot to ask what would happen if the invader was Muslim.

All of us spoke of the jihad against the Soviets with a certain pride. I heard the stirring speeches of the assassinated Palestinian scholar Sheikh Abdullah Azzam, who had revived jihad in the 1980s in Afghanistan. In Bosnia I had watched footage of frontline assaults, transfixed to the screen. I visited several websites that documented the plight of the Chechen people, and their resistance to occupation. I had seen films about Russia's 'mass killings of peaceful civilians' in Chechnya reported in documentaries like *Babitsky's War*.* I saw live footage of the mujahideen under the legendary commander in Chechnya, Ibn al-Khattab, who was regarded in awe throughout the Muslim world for his daring assaults on the Russian forces. I had heard about people from Britain who had gone to join the Chechen struggle.

So in the winter of 1999 I planned a trip. The route was going to take us from Turkey, through Georgia and on to Chechnya. My friend

---

* Andrei Babitsky: Russian Radio Liberty correspondent, who was arrested by the Russian authorities, accused of supporting Chechen rebels.

Amir knew people in Turkey who would arrange it for us. I was not sure exactly what I wanted to do there, just as in Bosnia. All I knew was that the people were crying out for help, and I felt I had to go. I was ready to help in whatever way I could, fight if I had to, despite my lack of training. This time, just as I had thought before going to Bosnia, there was a possibility that I might not return alive. From the news I gathered from the Internet and documentary films, Chechnya's struggle was more intense than Bosnia's, and even the UN had turned a blind eye. Zaynab was very upset at the thought of losing me, and I was torn between her and the kids and my sense of outrage at the plight of the Chechens. I assured her that despite the potential danger, I would come home.

In the end we decided to coordinate our efforts with an aid convoy some people in Birmingham were taking. We would meet them there and help in the distribution.

There was great sympathy for the Chechens among the Muslim community. When people heard about my intentions to go there they gave freely. Even non-Muslims donated money, as the struggle had been highlighted on various websites, and translated into dozens of languages.

I believed it was always best to deliver money and aid by hand, rather than through intermediaries – something I had learned from Asif. Also, I wanted to buy Turkish Islamic artefacts for the shop, if I returned.

When I passed immigration at Birmingham airport I was stopped by an official. 'We've got somebody who wants to talk to you, Mr Begg. If you'll just follow me,' he said. I was very angry, thinking they had stopped me just because I was the only Asian around.

They took me into a completely isolated room and after a few initial questions about where I was going, who I was going to see and what I had in my baggage, they left. MI5 Andrew walked in. Oddly enough I was quite pleased to see him. 'Better the devil you know,' I thought. Of the three people who had come to my house at five in the morning, I had found Andrew the easiest to get along with.

'As you can see, Mr Begg, I've grown my beard since I saw you last,' he began.

'You'll have to do a lot more than that to infiltrate the Muslim community,' I said, half-seriously. This time it seemed as though he just wanted to have a general conversation, asking about my views on Fidel Castro and Gerry Adams, as well as on the state of the Islamic world. Or perhaps he was delaying me intentionally. I kept on checking my watch, increasingly anxious that my flight was going to leave. 'If I've done something, tell me and let's go to the police station. If I haven't, let me go. I have a plane to catch.'

'I just want to know about why you're going to Turkey, and what you're planning on doing there. You know Turkey has a very poor human-rights record. I'm sure you've seen the film *Midnight Express* and . . .'

'I have, but I'm not running drugs or weapons – I'm sure you've checked my luggage already. I'm just going for a holiday to Turkey and Georgia. I don't know why you would jump to the conclusion that I'm going to do something wrong.'

Andrew was certainly well read and informed on the issues that were important to me, and we talked for about an hour. 'I always enjoy my conversations with you, Mr Begg, but I have to tell you that if you do something in Turkey, there is nothing this government can do to help you.'

'Thank you for your concern, and those reassuring words, Andrew. I'll bear that in mind next time I go to Turkey with a case of heroin strapped to my chest.'

I'd missed the flight, of course, but they did arrange for me to be put on the next flight, with all my baggage re-checked.

When I arrived in Istanbul, I was extremely surprised when Amir told me to quickly get in the car, which soon sped off. All through the flight I had had the feeling I was being watched, but I thought it was paranoia, after the meeting with Andrew. In the car Amir told me we were going to a Turkish friend's house. As we drove off, he said, 'We've got a tail, there's a car behind us.' He was absolutely right, there was a car following us everywhere we went. Our driver weaved through traffic, racing up and down steep streets, turning left and right, and still the car was always behind us.

Eventually we lost our tail, and we spent the night at Amir's friend's house. Next day we decided to leave, finding a hotel in the Sultan Ahmet area, right across from the magnificent Blue Mosque, and the Hagia Sofia. I spent a few days just sightseeing, visiting the underground Roman cistern, the Topkapi Palace and museum that overlook the Bosphorus. Amir stayed in the hotel playing video games; he'd seen it all before.

Wherever we went together, Amir always maintained that somebody was behind us. I really thought he was paranoid, until he pointed out a chubby man with grey hair, and told me to watch, I'd see him again. We took a taxi to Fateh and ate at a traditional Kurdish restaurant. After a while, as we were leaving, Amir pointed at someone across the road holding a newspaper. 'Look, I told you, there he is.' It was the same grey-haired fat man. After that I noticed him all over the place, and he seemed to make less effort to be inconspicuous.

We decided to change hotels, and moved to an area called Aksary. The hotel we stayed at seemed to be filled with foreigners – most of them Arab. Many of them had tried to enter Georgia, but had been refused entry at the border, despite having valid visas. One of them, a doctor from Madinah, was part of a Saudi charity building hospitals in Georgia for Chechen refugees. He was buying medical equipment in Istanbul, and was going to fly it to Tbilisi. Others included the Chechen Foreign Minister, Movladi Udugov,* who had come to evacuate his family, and a friend of his who ran a Chechen-resistance website.

After a few days we decided to take a coach from Istanbul to the Georgian border. The coach was filled with Georgians and a few Turks; we were the only others. When we got on, Amir looked out of the window, and said, 'Wait, I've got to do something.' He had seen the car that had been following us. He went out and bought a tray of snacks and took them over to their car. I saw him knocking on the window. They wound it down; he said something to them and passed over the tray. He waved to them, and they waved back. When he came back I asked, 'What happened? What did you say?'

'I said, "Why are you spying on us? If we've done something wrong, tell us. If we haven't, then I don't understand the need to stress yourselves. All I can do is offer you my condolences, and hospitality. I know you've been working hard all day, without much of a break. You probably haven't eaten very much either, since we keep seeing you around." You should have seen the looks on their faces when they took the goodies.'

'You're insane,' I said, unable to control my laughter, 'I can't believe you just did that.'

The journey to the border of Georgia lasted over sixteen hours. The Turkish guards let everybody through – except for Amir and me. 'We've been expecting you two,' they said. 'They weren't sure why you were

---

* Movladi Udugov: considered one of the main ideologues of Chechen independence.

here, but now it's clear. Best of luck, go ahead, but in our experience you'll be back here in the next ten minutes . . .' We looked at one another in astonishment. The Turks were very supportive of the Chechen struggle.

We walked up to the Georgian border, and tried every way to persuade them to let us in. Amir had become so friendly with one of the Georgians during the journey that he actually invited us to his house. So we even had a legitimate address to go to. But the guard was under strict instructions not to let foreigners through. I offered him a few hundred dollars, but he just turned his nose up at it. We walked back, and the Turkish border guard said, 'I told you you'd be back.'

We took a coach back to Istanbul, pretty disappointed that we were not going to see Chechnya after all.

We went back to the hotel in Aksaray, where I gave the Chechen minister all the money I had collected for his people. Then I went to the old covered marketplace in Bayazid and stocked up with books, trinkets and artefacts to take back to Birmingham for the shop.

Before I left Turkey I thought I finally understood what the British and Turkish intelligence services had been worried about: there was a summit meeting between the Presidents of the Central Asian Republics, Boris Yeltsin and Bill Clinton – right there in Istanbul.

Some time in late 1999 I had a visit from the police, simultaneously with raids at the bookshop and a friend's house. Strangely, the police knocked on my door and very politely said, 'We have a warrant to search your premises. If you'd like to get your family ready we can take them to a hotel or wherever else they like. We'll wait outside and give you a few minutes. Just let us know when you're ready.'

A policewoman took Zaynab and the children to my parents' house, and the others let me stay and watch the search.

There were so many police officers in the house that day, but I had no idea what they were looking for. I don't think they had either. Eventually, after many hours, they found an old pepper spray that I'd bought a long time ago and forgotten about. I'd meant it as a protection for Zaynab to keep in her handbag, though she never did. They arrested me and took away some papers and my computer. I was taken to the police station, charged with an offence under the firearms act and released that same evening. I didn't particularly link it to the MI5 encounters, so I was not as worried as I should have been.

Shortly after the raid, Shakeel travelled to Pakistan. I thought it was probably not a good idea, but he wanted to buy some things for the bookshop, visit his family, and bring his wife and children back to Birmingham.

Before he even boarded the plane he was stopped at the airport by MI5, questioned, and released. During the transit between Manama and Karachi, four security officials approached and took him to a room and interrogated him. They took all his money and the presents he'd bought for his children. Then he was stripped and beaten with a stick. Eventually they put him on another plane, with his clothes all torn. He emailed me from Islamabad, and told me he couldn't believe the humiliation he had suffered, and that he was still bleeding. He added that the Pakistanis had also threatened him. They showed him a file they'd received from the British, with pictures of him and me in it. There was a picture of me outside the bookshop handing him a box – a box of books. The Pakistanis told him that this was nothing to do with them. 'It's your government that's doing this.' Shakeel told me that he was tailed by Pakistani intelligence all the way to his small village, and everywhere else he went. Finally he moved with his family out of the village, and stayed in a hotel in Islamabad until he managed to get a flight back. He told the Pakistani authorities that he was leaving, and they made a point of telling him to take a direct flight to Britain, which he did.

I went to speak to Gareth in London about all this, and she tried to get some official explanation, but there was never any response. When I told her later that I also planned to travel she advised me that it was not the best time. The intelligence services, in her experience, were likely to misconstrue almost anything. 'I'm sorry,' she said, 'it was the Irish first and now it's the Muslims. Things are probably going to get worse before they get better.'

About two months later the police asked me to return to the station with my friend who had been raided at the same time. He'd just gone through a cancer operation. When we got to the police station, to our utter amazement, they told us that we were under arrest under the Prevention of Terrorism Act. The wording used included 'support, commission and instigation of acts of terrorism' and 'extremist Islamic groups'.

Up until this time I had thought it was all just a silly mistake or a fishing trip, but now I knew it was going too far. 'Tell me what act I'm supposed to have committed and I'll answer your questions,' I kept saying to them.

Instead they asked me about my visits to Bosnia and Pakistan, about various people who I had met in Birmingham and elsewhere. They questioned me about the bookshop: who visited, were there many foreigners, who financed us, whether we had meetings there. They also asked about my ideology and my views on jihad. They even asked me about 'the honey connection', and wasn't that really a code for explosives?

In one of the letters they seized from my house a friend from Pakistan had mentioned Masood, the Northern Alliance commander, and his fight with the Taliban. But the interrogating officer read it as

'Mossad' and actually thought it was referring to the Israeli secret service. I wanted to laugh out loud, but I had maintained that I would remain silent unless they specified the allegations. Then, as if on cue, the officer produced an Explanation Order, a document obtained from the court demanding that I answer their questions, under threat of imprisonment. We challenged the legality of the order. My friend and I were released the same day.

The police had got the keys to the bookshop from Shakeel and searched it. They didn't take very much, except £300, which we always kept under the till for the weekly rent. We made an official complaint to the police authority about that, and they replied that they were investigating the matter. Perhaps they still are – we never got the money back.

A few weeks later Gareth came to Birmingham and we successfully challenged the Explanation Order and won our case. But this series of incidents gave me some ideas about what was changing in 1990s Britain, and I started to get a little uncomfortable, and worry about what they would do next. My close friends were constantly being visited by MI5. They used to ask them to inform on me, but I was quite open with everyone about my plans. I didn't have anything to hide. In the bookshop I used to hear a lot about Afghanistan from people who were going back and forth regularly, and one of them told me about a school project that he had initiated in Kabul. He was a Palestinian, Rami, based in Britain. He asked whether I was willing to help.

I was very impressed by the photos he showed me and the detail he gave me. I asked him to leave the photographs and the information so that I could approach friends and relatives about it. He mentioned that he had a girls' school planned, despite the popular view that the Taliban prohibited women's education. I thought that this was a case illustrating how the Taliban's bad press was probably exaggerated.

I talked to Zaynab about it; she was particularly interested in the idea of supporting a girls' school and Rami's project was for both boys and girls. We managed to raise a few thousand pounds amongst ourselves, and Rami gave us regular updates. The headmaster of the schools even phoned me from Kabul to thank me. I began to feel that this was something I really wanted to get involved in.

Rami also told me that the water shortage in drought-stricken parts of the country was dire. As well as larger, and more expensive irrigation pumps, he had begun a project to install hand-pump wells in the worst affected areas. He had employed a Pakistani contractor – already working for various aid agencies in Afghanistan – who had the right drilling equipment. Each well and hand-pump cost two hundred dollars. Rami left me with photographs of the ones already completed, and asked me to get other people involved in sponsoring them. He said they'd even put up a plaque with the sponsor's name outside the well.

In a short while I had gathered enough for ten wells, and sent the money to Rami. Within a few weeks Rami sent me the pictures of the wells – three of them with the names Umamah, Abdur-Rahman, and Zaynab on the plaques.

There seemed little attempt by the world at large to really understand the relative ease with which the Taliban swept to power in the mid-1990s. I had heard that Mullah Omar actually led a group of about thirty Quranic students who gave an ultimatum to a local warlord who had kidnapped a group of children as sex slaves. When the student militia freed the children it was not surprising that the locals began admiring the Taliban.

The simple fact of the cost of living there weighed with me too. Many people told us that we could live in the best areas of Kabul for less than £100 a month, and gradually, the idea of uprooting the family and going there to live took hold of me, and, as I talked about it, it seemed quite possible.

So, in mid-2001, with the shop going fairly well, and my friend Shaker also wanting to join us there with his family and share a house, Zaynab and I made the big decision to go. We arranged for our house to be let and that was to be our income for Afghanistan.

We left in late June, but after what had happened to Shakeel, I did not want to go through Pakistan. There were no direct flights to Afghanistan, so we decided to go through Iran. When we got on the flight at Heathrow I was really excited, thinking, 'This is it, we're actually going.' At the same time I was worried that at any moment MI5 was going to turn up again. But they didn't.

At Tehran airport there was a lot of bureaucracy but the people were very friendly. One man I'd met on the plane actually invited us to his house in Tehran.

We toured around the capital for a few days, enjoying it very much. Then we took a flight to Mashhad, a holy place for Shiites, near the Afghan border.

I had no idea exactly how I would get into Afghanistan. I knew once I was in Kabul it would be fine, as I knew people who I hoped were expecting me. Rami had told me that from Mashhad I could get a taxi to the border, then to Herat, and from there take a plane to Kabul. So that was my plan.

There weren't too many people doing the border trip, especially not with family, but I found a taxi driver who I spoke to in a mixture of Urdu and Arabic that got close enough to Farsi for him to understand. We set off with him very early in the morning.

The Iranian border post was a very bleak place in the middle of nowhere and there was hardly anybody there. Doubts started creeping into my mind, and I asked myself, 'What the hell are you doing in this place with your family? There's nobody else here, and even the Iranians think you're stupid.'

I could see some broken-down tattered buses, with overweight sleepy-looking drivers, and I approached them to help me carry our massive load of baggage across the border. Eventually they drove us to the Afghan border post where an old Afghan turned up with a creaky old trolley, and we put our luggage on it and walked across.

We were in Afghanistan, and it felt utterly different from Iran. It was a complete shock. I'd only seen the camps, and part of Jalalabad, but this was very different indeed and not what I had imagined for our arrival. They were using the tops of disused armoured vehicles as offices. These little rusty boxes on the ground were immigration and customs for the Taliban.

They were even more surprised by me, in my Western clothes, but obviously Asian, with a wife and kids. They all stared at us for a while, and then they asked me what we'd come for, and where I planned to go, and did I know who I was going to see?

Zaynab sat by herself, ignored by them.

Finally, one came along who actually spoke good English. He was very helpful, and said he would arrange a car to take us to Herat. Not only were there no cars to be seen, but I didn't see any roads either. Then he asked if I wanted my passport stamped, or not stamped. I said I certainly wanted it stamped, not really understanding why he posed the question.

He just said, 'Well, some people who come here don't want their passport stamped.'

We set out for Herat in a broken-down Japanese car, with the wind-screen cracked. The first thing that came to my mind was water. I hadn't brought any. It was hot, and dusty, and horrible. The villages we went through were made of mud and straw. One of the projects that I had done back in Birmingham was the building of wells in this region where there had been a drought.

Eventually the driver stopped, and there was a dirty-looking river by the car. I was so thirsty I thought, 'I've got to drink something.' But then I thought, 'The children, they can't be drinking from that too.' In fact he'd just stopped to relieve himself, not for us to use the water. I kept telling him, 'We need water.' Finally he stopped by a pump well, and we went and pumped some water with great relief.

The roads were terrible, often not really a road at all. The dust was incredible. The children were vomiting. Throughout the journey I had some of the worst regrets ever of this trip to Afghanistan.

By the time we got to Herat it was afternoon. It was very, very hot and I didn't have any local currency. I managed to get the taxi driver to stop by a moneychanger sitting on a street corner. I had no idea of the rate, and I knew I had got ripped off pretty badly, but that was to be expected. Eventually we got to the hotel, and things just got a lot easier from that point. The next day I managed to get a flight, and it was fine, except that I had booked five tickets and paid for them, but they only gave us two seats, so we had to have all the children sitting on our laps.

When we arrived in Kabul I could see that we were in a city, a Third World city, but things looked reassuringly modern compared to where we had been.

We took a taxi to someone I knew who was working at Kabul University. Sheikh Abdul-Majeed, the scholar I used to refer to in Britain, had been expecting us. He was amazingly hospitable. He and his wife said we could stay with them as long as we wanted, until we got our own place sorted out. We stayed about three weeks, while I found a house and haggled over the prices of household goods.

One night there was a huge explosion. It sounded as if somebody had rammed his front door and broken it. Abdul-Majeed knocked on my door and asked me to come out. He had a gun in his hand. We went from room to room, checked upstairs and downstairs, and everything was fine. The next day when we were driving to the city centre, we saw that the Ariana Airlines office had been destroyed. It was a terrorist attack, probably by the Northern Alliance. That made me uneasy: what was going on?

Initially I phoned home about once a week, although it was sometimes hard to call because the public call offices were usually packed with people. I had to sit for an hour sometimes to get a phone call.

I soon found that Kabul unexpectedly had some Western aid workers with their families: Americans across the road, Germans next door to Abdul-Majeed. It was reassuring to feel that I was not the only crazy idealist who had turned up here.

One of the first things I did was to get Umamah into the school. It was very satisfying visiting it and seeing the reality I'd been thinking about in Birmingham. I got a great reception too. I started going over regularly, and getting involved in things like taking the kids to see the amazing Afghan game buzkashi, a kind of polo with men racing about on horses fighting over a dead goat.

About six or seven weeks later Shaker came, and moved into our huge house with his family. He took the top floor. It was brilliant, and our children all absolutely loved it. They felt free in the big space.

I soon got quite disillusioned with the Taliban after various personal experiences. One was a traffic accident I had with one of their commanders, who first refused to take responsibility for it, then lied about it, and then tried to buy me off with free fuel. Some of the foreigners who'd been there a while had other stories too, about things such as executions. So I kept away from the Taliban, and just went on with my own projects.

We had already built some wells in Kabul, and it was incredibly exciting and warming to see the tangible benefit. It felt quite different from sitting in Birmingham raising the money.

One day I was driving through the city centre with a friend and we noticed the main roundabout that leads towards the airport had its four entry points blocked off. I could see throngs of people all gathering around, and we decided to get out and see what was going on. As we got closer I saw four small cranes with something hanging off the end of each one on a piece of rope. I couldn't make out what it was, until I got closer. They were bodies, human bodies. Each of the four entry points had one. I'd seen dead bodies before but I'd never seen anything like this. I felt a kind of morbid fascination, but I found it really odd that women and children, families, were walking around and just looking. The most striking was that the mouths were open and the tongues were black. Even odder was the fact that people had stuffed money between their fingers, and notes were sticking out of their pockets. It was an Afghan tradition, someone told me later, meaning they had sold themselves to the opposition for a pittance, but I found the whole thing very shocking.

A week later the Taliban staged a military parade near the centre of Kabul. It was certainly more impressive than I'd expected, with tanks, armoured cars, mobile missile launchers, uniformed rank-and-file soldiers marching – out of tune and step – and even fighter-jet fly-bys.*

One of the things I loved about Kabul was that I kept meeting

---

* The US military later denied POW status to those few actually captured on the battlefield. This was on the pretext that they were not uniformed, without insignia, and militarily unstructured. This assertion was made despite the fact that the Northern Alliance were an even more shambolic military formation than the Taliban, and that US special forces themselves often dressed as locals to avoid detection.

people from so many parts of the world: Chinese, Arabs, Uzbeks, people from places like Malaysia, and others. Some of them had fought against the Soviets, and some of them had come as part of aid projects, especially a large number of Pakistanis.

As a result of talks breaking down between the United Nations and the Taliban, all the bakeries that the UN supported suddenly closed. Bread is a staple of the Afghan diet, and a Pakistani organization took over all the bakeries around Afghanistan, and funded them. I got to know some of these Pakistani aid workers quite well.

Once I visited the front line between the Taliban and the Northern Alliance, with the Pakistanis. I was told that the front line had been dormant for almost two years, there had been no fighting, and that was why things were prospering, people were coming back, and there was new investment. The front line was near a place called Bagram, about an hour's drive from Kabul.

There was spent and unexploded ordnance, and many abandoned villages, along the way. Rows and rows of grape vines were everywhere, growing all over the place, and white Afghan grapes are some of the most delicious I had ever tasted in my life.

We got to the rear line, where people were coming and going, getting their equipment ready, or eating, or just relaxing. It was all very, very simple. There were different sections for Pakistanis and Arabs who had come to fight with the Taliban. My Pakistani friends knew some of the Pakistani fighters, and they were the ones I visited. The Taliban were separate. The Pakistanis told me about some of the things that had happened there, and showed me where the front line was before, and then. To me it was just one huge, mountainous desert. They said that if I really wanted to go to the front line I'd have to be back before dark. We all drove over to have a look.

It felt weird and frightening to visit a front line. I kept expecting something to happen. But it was very, very quiet – until lunchtime. They had brought some food, a very modest plate of rice with some sultanas thrown in. As we sat down to eat, a shell landed. Overhead there was a huge bang, and then another and another. I felt really panicky inside and I just wanted to go home immediately. But of course I couldn't say that, it would have seemed so cowardly.

Everyone else just carried on eating, with the dust rolling up around them. I was looking around at the others, thinking, 'Are you not thinking what I'm thinking, then?' The fighters were used to it, but the ones who came with me from the aid organization did look a bit concerned.

When it stopped, I said, 'I thought the place was quiet?'

'This is quiet, really this is quiet. Nobody attacked and there was no push, this happens all the time. We do it to them twice as much.'

I was glad to get back to Kabul. It was a city I really liked. It was always busy, jam packed with people. And what I had heard about women not being allowed to go anywhere without a male member of their family was not what I saw in Kabul.

Zaynab and I constantly discussed the future and how long we should stay. I often asked her how she was really coping, was she happy? She had come from a very wealthy family and she had always had it very easy. She had sacrificed all that for me to be here. I so wanted her to be happy, and to give her everything she needed for the house, although I also didn't want us to be resented for obviously living at a totally different standard from most Afghans. But we were better off. All non-Afghans were better off.

The novelty of Afghanistan certainly hadn't worn off for me after a few weeks. There was so much more I wanted to discover. I wanted to go and visit all the places up in the north, which I was told were a lot greener, and there were a lot more historic sights that I wanted to visit.

Once I took the family to the zoo, but we saw bullet holes all over the place, and one solitary lion. He had also been a victim of an Afghan-style feud. He was called the One-Eyed Lion, because a man had jumped into his area and the lion had mauled him to death. The man's brother returned the next day with a hand grenade. That was how he lost his eye.

Kabul was full of such strange Afghan stories. And life was definitely enjoyable, mainly because of the people, the neighbours, all welcoming, very warm, and inviting us to dinner almost every day.

Apart from that, whatever time I had, I used on a project that I'd had in mind for some time. I'd bought some old classical Islamic texts, which I intended to translate into English from the Arabic. I thought they could make some interesting little booklets for our bookshop back in Birmingham.

On the night of 9 September 2001, I was woken by helicopters flying over our house, followed by the sounds of rockets and gunfire, but it stopped within an hour. The next day I heard that the night's excitement had been a retaliatory attack by the Northern Alliance, for the assassination of their commander, Ahmad Shah Masood – the Lion of Panjshir.

There was a varied mood in Kabul: the Pashtuns were generally pleased, the Farsis resentful, and the Hazara Shiites indifferent. But the overall feeling seemed to be that it was the end of the fighting. The Taliban had already captured 95 per cent of the country, and Masood's death, rumoured to have been an al-Qa'idah operation, would consolidate their gains. But two days later I was disturbed by another loud noise. It was Shaker banging on the steel front gate.

'Haven't you heard the news?' he said frantically. 'The whole world's turned upside down. America's been attacked. Thousands of people have been killed.'

There were no televisions for me to see the horrifying images of the victims of the attacks, and I simply failed to grasp the enormity of the event, until things began to change for me personally.

Nobody was sure what would happen next; most people I spoke to thought that the US would just attack bin Ladin's camps in Kandahar. We decided to stay, considering most people hadn't evacuated yet.

For several weeks nothing happened. Then on the night of 17 October I felt the earth shake. The explosion was louder than anything I've ever heard. The sounds of shattering glass filled the streets. I ran back home from the shop – where I was buying tomatoes – in sheer panic. The US cruise missile had landed far away, but the shock waves had broken our windows. Both Shaker and Abdul-Majeed had left their families with me for the day, so I had around twenty people in my house – mostly children – and I took them all down to the cellar and covered the windows with mattresses.

Outside, red tracer rounds fired from the Taliban anti-aircraft guns lit the sky. I realized it was time to go.

I arranged with Abdullah (the Kurd I met in 1998), his family, and another British family to leave together. We drove in our three cars for about an hour, to Logar, a desert town near the Pakistan border where we were all going to stay until the situation calmed down. For the children this was a fun camping trip, and they loved the freedom of the countryside, although it was just desert. The three families set up home together in a large compound, with five or six different rooms.

I used to drive back to Kabul every few days to check on our house, buy food and get news. US B52s were carrying out bombing sorties in daylight; the Taliban had no real air defences. The ground trembled with each of the carpet bombs that fell, leaving gigantic clouds of dust in their wake. During one of the bombings, near the city centre, I saw the shrapnel whizzing over my head. I was overwhelmed with fear each time this happened, but found that most Afghans just stopped in the street and looked up – seemingly more curious than scared. On one of these trips, when I went in a friend's car to meet my Pakistani friends north of Kabul, the news came that it had fallen. I had told Zaynab to expect me back home the same evening, or next day.

In fact Kabul hadn't fallen, but the Taliban had evacuated and there was no government, no law and order. It was now very dangerous, particularly for foreigners, as they would be robbed, kidnapped, or killed. No one dared to risk evacuation through Kabul, so, as my friends told me, they would take me via another route that led to Logar. But we got totally lost on the dark mountain roads. After nearly twelve hours we reached the main road, but there was a scramble of desperate refugees fleeing the city in all directions. I had absolutely nothing with me from the house and my vehicle was still in Kabul. I didn't know where I was going, everyone was panicking because no one had any idea what was happening or what direction we were heading. We just wanted to get away from the bombing.

On the Kabul road I asked my friends to take me to Logar, but they said they couldn't – they were going to evacuate to Pakistan through Jalalabad in the south. They wouldn't take me to Kabul either – it was just too risky for foreigners. No one was going back. I was distraught. How was I going to get to my family – and how would we evacuate without a car? One of the Pakistanis told me not to worry. He would help me to get to Logar if I came with him.

When we reached Surobi, en route to Logar, we saw a group of fighters come down a mountain road, aiming rocket launchers and AK47s at us. They were bandits. But just then four jeep-loads of retreating Taliban fighters came along. The bandits pointed their weapons down and left. The Taliban drove right past us – they hadn't even noticed the bandits.

But I heard the road to Logar was closed. There was no way to reach Zaynab and the kids. I'd lost my family.

I had never cried so much, or hated myself, as I did then, for my naivety, which had put my family in such danger. My only option now was to leave Afghanistan, and re-enter at a different point from Pakistan, where the road was open and closer.

We continued south, and eventually came to a point where the roads ended and the mountains really began. They were huge, snow-capped, empty, and incredibly beautiful. Our group, about ten of us, managed to hire a local guide who agreed to take us over the mountains into Pakistan.

Those two days on foot, fasting because it was Ramadan, were the most dramatic I had ever spent. I felt light-headed with the altitude and the fasting. When we stopped to pray, high over the world, it had a feeling of transcendence which calmed me even more than prayer normally does. We walked high up on tiny stony paths, with white peaks just above us. I was in sandals, picking my way through snow some of the time. We slept huddled together trying to feel a bit of warmth from each other. We had a few pieces of bread and bottles of water with us that we shared. We had bought them together, pooling our money, when we hired the guide.

High in the mountains we reached a small frozen river, and carefully crossed in single file. I was the fourth. When the man right after me walked across, the ice cracked, and he fell in. We joined hands together to help him clamber out, and as we continued our trek his clothes froze stiff on him. He, like all the others, was a real lesson in patience for me. None of them ever showed any impatience, never complained. I was the one who often felt, 'Why can't we stop, why can't we have a break, how much further?' I never said it, and I was embarrassed that I was even feeling it.

The guide was an extraordinary person who really knew his job. He had contacts who seemed to pop up out of nowhere and tell him things, including once about a group of armed bandits. When we saw them walk past our hiding place, behind rocks and trees, I immediately thought about being taken hostage, maybe killed. All of us put what money we had in our socks.

Then I heard automatic gunfire. Its sound bounced off the mountains so it was impossible to tell which direction it came from. No one moved. My heart beat so fast I could feel it pounding against my chest. And then the firing restarted, but this time I saw it: a lone man sitting on a precipice, firing in the air, at a drone aircraft – thousands of feet above. Apparently he was bored.

It was late at night when we finally crossed the border into Pakistan. We'd walked for two days and nights. We were hungry, exhausted, and looked like tramps. But my journey, I felt, had just begun. All the way along my friends told me that my family would probably have evacuated to the city of Khost, where I could reach them by entering Afghanistan from another route – one that I had crossed in 1993. But I still had no idea where my family were.

From Islamabad I spoke to family and friends and asked if there was any news. No one had heard a thing. I phoned my father in England to reassure him, but couldn't tell him that I'd lost Zaynab and the kids.

First, with the help of my evacuee friends, I contacted various organizations that were helping people leave Afghanistan. I went to meet some of the old contacts from Jamat-e-Islami, whose camp I had visited in 1993. The Taliban had closed down the al-Fajr camp in 1995, shortly after they took power, because the Jamat was backing the anti-Taliban alliance then. But now, like several other Islamic groups opposed to them, the Taliban found sympathy because the US had invaded Afghanistan, just like the Soviets had. Many of these groups had seasoned veterans and guides working for them, so I asked for their help.

While I waited at the guesthouse in the tribal border town of Bannu I came across many people who had evacuated from Khost, but there was never any news for me. When I told my story to anyone I thought could help me, I found even they were moved to tears. One of them suggested I forget the family, that if I hadn't heard from them by now they were probably dead, that it was 'God's will'. I didn't have any such knowledge, but I knew what I had to do.

I called family and friends in England to send me money for the guides I'd despatched to find my family. I tried to go with them, but they refused, saying it was too dangerous for foreigners. Each day I read some new horrifying story about foreigners in Afghanistan – murder, kidnap, rape, US bombings. One of the local papers reported that two Arab women committed suicide after local warlords defiled them. Others had been captured and used as hostages by greedy opportunists. And then there were the reports that came from the mainstream media like the BBC and CNN, which confirmed that the numbers of civilian dead was into the thousands. A busload of evacuees had been bombed in Kabul, an entire village massacred near Kandahar, a convoy of refugees destroyed near Khost – Khost, where my family was said to have gone.

The very atrocities that had so often prompted me out of my life of ease in Britain were now the stark reality that my own family might have met. I made a solemn promise to myself that I would never stop searching until I found them, or I died in the process.

I was distraught with anxiety and fear, as I waited each excruciating hour, still without news. 'Why did I not evacuate much earlier into Pakistan? Why did I leave to visit Kabul that day? Why didn't I take the risk to return through Kabul? Why did I come to Afghanistan?'

It had been three weeks since I last saw my family.

Finally, in desperation, I told my friends in Islamabad that if they didn't hear from me within a week, to contact my father and the British Embassy. I was going to Afghanistan, alone.

'Don't go anywhere!' Tariq yelled down the phone. 'I have some wonderful news for you. Your family's safe, right here in Islamabad, Moazzam. They're staying with a friend a block away from where you were.'

It was a tearful reunion. There were so many emotions. I had feared so much for their safety and cried till my eyes were sore. And here they were, at long last. After the initial tears of sadness and joy, Zaynab was beaming brightly. Typically, Umamah cried as I hugged her. Abdur-Rahman just laughed. And Nusaybah, not even three years old, said, 'Where my choc-lat baba?' The last time I saw her I promised to bring her some back from Kabul. I was three weeks late.

Zaynab told me about what happened that fateful night when I didn't return. The Kurdish family, my old friend Abdullah amongst them, had learned about the fall of Kabul and decided to evacuate to Pakistan. But I had not returned yet. They insisted that Zaynab and the kids go with them – that they were not going to leave without them.

Zaynab was distraught, even angry that I hadn't returned, but she had to make the right decision and leave. She left with the Kurds and another British family in a convoy headed for the border during the evening. In the panic she wasn't able to take more than one small bag of clothes between her and the kids. Besides, there was just about enough space for them all to squash into the vehicle like sardines.

They drove from village to village, avoiding aerial bombardment by keeping the lights off at all times, and finding that almost no place was safe to stop. It was bombs, bandits, and bribes all the way to the border. Over two weeks had passed by the time they all reached Islamabad safely, and all the while Zaynab had no idea that I was trekking the mountains of Jalalabad searching for her like a lunatic. They were all convinced by then that they'd never see me again. When Zaynab finally arrived in Islamabad, she and the British family went to Ali's house – someone we both knew.

Once our family was together again, and in the comforting familiarity of Islamabad, where I had aunts and uncles and cousins nearby, we were miraculously happy. We found we had a new baby coming, the other children were in school, everyone had new clothes, and I made another new home – the third in three months – with everything Zaynab could possibly want, so she would quickly get over the horror and fear she had been through. Family and friends from Birmingham sent us several thousand pounds to get us through this difficult period when we had lost everything we possessed in Kabul, and, again, I felt quite confident that I was doing something worthwhile in the region.

While waiting for Afghanistan to be safe again, so I could get back to supervising the schools*, I planned to start translating ancient Arabic texts into English – the part of the original Afghan project, linked to the bookshop in Birmingham, which I could just get on with here in Islamabad.

Several times, when I was speaking to my father on the phone, he urged me to come back to Birmingham, but I countered by asking him to come over and visit us. We had plenty of space in

---

* I have learned recently that one of the schools was destroyed by US bombs in late 2002, but there were no casualties.

our new house. We were going to stay in Pakistan for a while, and try to help some of the other evacuee families, including the ones that had helped mine.

It was then too that I finally saw the pictures of the September 11 attacks, and realized the scale of the damage done to thousands of innocent lives.

Little did I know that my own life in Pakistan would end so abruptly with my midnight abduction only two months later. Interrogations by the CIA, FBI, and MI5, and their decision to send me to back to Afghanistan would change my life for ever.

The first time I was separated from my family the ordeal lasted three weeks. The next time it lasted for three years.

6

'ENGLISH, 558'

We flew out of Pakistan to Kandahar very early in the morning. It was very uncomfortable sitting on the floor of the plane, with its vibrations running up my back and the noise of the engine filling my head. Flashing lights – obviously from soldiers' cameras taking trophy pictures – came and went in front of me, despite the hood's darkness.

From beside me a voice said in Arabic, 'Shall we pray, brother?'

A guard came and screamed in my ear, 'Shut up, motherfucker, if you speak again I'll kill you.'

Later, another guard told me that on the journey they had sat around us, with their knives unsheathed. The voice telling me to pray was the man who was shackled ahead of me in Islamabad before we boarded the plane. He had managed to tell me that he was a Libyan who was captured in Pakistan. It was so typical of a Muslim, whatever the circumstances, the act of prayer came automatically at the prescribed time.

Under the hood I felt I couldn't breathe properly, it pulled in and out against my mouth and nose with every breath. Not being able to see made me feel unbearably vulnerable; I thought I was going to be struck in the face, or worse, at any moment. When we landed and felt the air, it was bitterly cold, and my feet and hands were already numb. I had no shoes, only socks, as the Americans had taken away the old rubber slippers the Pakistanis had given me. Nor did I have a coat, just a shirt and trousers. I was marched off the plane bent double, with US soldiers pushing down on me, from either side, with what seemed like pointless force. I knew there were six of us, all handcuffed and hooded by the Pakistanis. Back in Islamabad, one of the Pakistani agents had briefly raised my hood when I asked him for a breath of air, and I had got a glimpse of the others, hooded, like me, and dressed in typical Pakistani shalwar kameez. I had no idea who they were.

During the handover to the US military, back at Islamabad airport, I had immediately felt a sharp contrast between Pakistani and American attitudes and treatment. The Pakistanis never shouted at me, or dragged me around, or shackled my legs during transportation. The Americans barked orders for silence, harshly shackled my feet, too close together, and dragged me into the plane, unnecessarily tightening the hood round my neck. I told myself this was going to be worse than anything I could have imagined, and I would need all my calm. Just after we had literally hit the ground and cleared the landing strip, hands forced me down into a prostrate position. I was very afraid by then. I could feel my heart pounding, and my head sweating under the hood in spite of the cold. The uncertainty about what was going to happen to me – would they kill me, would they torture me, would they humiliate me, and would I be able to keep my dignity – was hard enough to bear, but then I thought of my family, and how my father, with his weak heart, would be in agony if he had any idea of what was happening. I didn't want to think about my family at all, I didn't want the thought of them tainted with all this. I prayed that they would never have to see me like this. My lips moved over and over again reciting the comforting, familiar prayer, 'In the Name of Allah, with whose name nothing can cause harm, on earth or in the Heavens; He is the Hearer and Knower of all things.'

I was bracing myself for brutality, brutality that was, unbelievably, happening to *me*. I remembered how appalled I had been by the first images of Camp Rhino in Kandahar, and Camp X-Ray in Guantánamo, from the TV and papers I had seen and read while I was free in Islamabad. I remembered the last interview with the FBI agent, Mike, in the dining room of that comfortable suburban house in Islamabad, when he had said, 'Kandahar and Guantánamo will be very different, you know, they are under military jurisdiction, so you can expect harsh treatment.' At the time I hadn't let myself quite take it in, or imagine, what did he mean by harsh – hoods, beating, electric shocks like in the movies, false accusations, death threats?

I had not prepared myself for the naked aggression I saw from under my hood – brown suede US desert boots stamping on the backs of other prisoners.

'What are the gloves for?' I asked one of the soldiers, who I assumed was an officer from his way of speaking, which showed he was clearly in charge. 'You're not going to do full body searches, are you?'

'No,' he replied. 'Nothing like that at all.' His lie was transparent.

With the aircraft's engine still howling, I was dragged a short way through the waterlogged mud and thrown to the ground. The pain of the manhandling was bad enough, but my internal terror was even worse. I heard shouts and screams of prisoners and soldiers mingled so that almost nothing was intelligible. I did make out that some soldiers were yelling orders in English, then in Arabic, then in Urdu, in distinctly odd American accents. 'Shut up, *uskut, chup karo*; stay down, *qif fee makanik, neechay raho*; don't move, *laa tataharrak, hilna mutt.*'

One guard was almost lying on top of me, screaming obscenities in my ear. My hands were still shackled from behind; the hood was pulled around my neck so I could barely breathe. I gasped at the guard that I had asthma . . . that I could not breathe. He eventually raised the hood just above my mouth.

'Thank you,' I panted.

'Don't thank me, motherfucker!' he responded, tightening the hood again. 'And don't take my kindness for weakness.'

Two guards pulled me up, dragged me off again, with the shackles cutting into my ankles so painfully I wondered if they were bleeding. I couldn't keep up the pace because the chain was so short.

This was the beginning of 'processing', and I was past a state of shock, I couldn't believe all this was happening to *me*. The noise was deafening: barking dogs, relentless verbal abuse, plane engines, electricity generators, and screams of pain from the other prisoners. Maybe I screamed too. I was tripped onto the ground to the prone position again. This time I felt knees pushing hard against my ribs and legs, and crushing down on my skull simultaneously. I was pinned to the ground by this massive weight; I was not sure how many of them were on me – perhaps three. I couldn't move an inch. I felt the shackles being undone from the ankles, and then I felt a cold, sharp metal object against my legs: they were using a knife to slice off all my clothes, and I felt the cold even more, though the humiliation was worse. With the trousers off, the shackles were replaced against my bare skin. The process was repeated with the shirt – my arms were twisted behind my back, until reshackling was complete. I was pulled up to a standing position and the hood was removed. I thought that a pipe would be used next, to hose me down. Instead I was confronted with the sight of soldiers encircling me, screaming abuse and taking pictures again. I blinked at the camera flashes all around me. The body, or cavity search, that I had been told would not take place then followed. As it started, my imagination went wild with an even more terrifying and painful picture. I heard more screams of people behind me, suffering the same violence. Someone shouted out in Arabic, 'Be patient, my brothers,' quoting the Quranic verse, 'Verily, Allah is with those who are patient.'

I was then moved under a wooden shelter, and sat down so they could take portrait pictures for their detainee album: one with all my hair, and one after it was shaved off. The barber sadistically enjoyed his job, and as he shaved off my beard with a machine, he commented, 'This is the part I like best.' I wondered why he would say such a thing, but realized that he *knew* the beard was an important symbol of Muslim identity, particularly in this region. He'd obviously seen plenty of distressed reactions from others. As he pushed my head around to shave it, I tried to adjust my feet, so that I wouldn't slide off the stool. A guard shoved my feet further away from the stool and stamped his boots on them, really hard. 'Who gave you permission to move, motherfucker?'

The most humiliating thing was witnessing the abuse of others, and knowing how utterly dishonoured they felt. These were men who would never have appeared naked in front of anyone, except their wives; who had never removed their facial hair, except to clip their moustache or beard; who never used vulgarity, nor were likely to have had it used against them. I felt that everything I held sacred was being violated, and they must have felt the same.

I was shoved into the makeshift processing room, with my escorts, to face two FBI agents, looking completely out of place, identifiable by their 'FBI' baseball caps. One called himself Rob, and the other was Bill. They took my fingerprints, a mouth swab, and asked me, 'When was the last time you saw Usamah bin Ladin or Mullah Umar?'

They must have asked hundreds of men the same thing, and never got a useful answer. I had already heard another 'processed' prisoner ahead of me being asked the same question, and I got an idea of how utterly pointless their whole exercise against us was. When I said politely that I had never seen either of them, they were very surprised that I could speak English, and started a mundane conversation about English accents. One told me that he'd visited Stratford-upon-Avon – only twenty miles from where I lived – while I was standing there, with no clothes on, shivering. The guards mocked me for what they assumed was fear. 'When you've calmed down, we can start.' But I was shaking from the cold. They then pushed me down on the ground and repeated the earlier shackling procedure, but in reverse. I was then dressed in a thin pale-blue cotton jumpsuit and old shoes. They also gave me some underclothes, and a bakol: an Afghani cap, a symbol of Ahmad Shah Masood, the Northern Alliance leader assassinated on 9 September 2001. It was far too big.

The leg shackles and handcuffs were closed very tight around my ankles and wrists, so I could only move at a snail's pace. The guards thought it was deliberate, so they carried me in the strappado position: I was suspended in the air, with my hands cuffed behind my back, with both guards' arms hooked under mine, from behind my shoulder. Though it hurt intensely, I didn't scream in pain, but I did shout out that I had dislocated my left shoulder earlier. I was carried like this to an interrogation tent, finally dropped into a chair, and had my hood taken off.

This time I saw a young military interrogator, who asked me some personal details: name, age, address, was I married, did I have children? Then he explained the camp rules. These included, 'No talking to detainees', 'No concealment of food, or any other items', and 'Keep away from the razor wire'.

'No touching the wire at all,' he said.

'Is the wire electric?' I asked.

'Any failure to obey, or refusal to comply will result in punishment,' he said. Any attempt to escape would be met by force, with the use of firearms.

I was given the number '558', handed to me on an Enemy Prisoner of War (EPOW) card, and the number was also written on my back. I was told that I would be known as 'English' – because I spoke it, not because I was.

The Americans seemed smugly convinced that none of us had a clue about our whereabouts. 'I bet you don't know where you are,' one of them taunted. I knew it was Kandahar airport, as the interrogators in Islamabad had told me where I was going. (I had also seen pictures of Kandahar airport, which bore a crude resemblance to the Sydney Opera House.) I had also seen footage of the place on television, when the US Marines set up Camp Rhino, at Kandahar airport. It was a small satisfaction to be able to surprise them by saying I did know.

Processing ended when I was taken into a kind of disused barn made of corrugated sheet steel, rusty brown, with an earth floor, and divided into makeshift single cells by concertina wire. No windows. I was taken by two military police, or MPs, to the far end, to the cell in the corner. My cell contained two blankets, a shawl, a bucket, a plastic water bottle, and my asthma inhaler – nothing else. The Americans had taken my glasses away back at the airport in Pakistan, so I had to squint. I could see the person in the cell next to me, but I knew we were not allowed to communicate. He had covered himself with a blanket and looked as though he was actually able to sleep.

I could not sleep at all, although I was utterly exhausted. I was in shock; I couldn't believe that all this was actually happening to me. The noise of the generators powering the camp didn't help either.

There were some bullet holes in my corner of the barn, and I peered through them, trying desperately to get some idea of the conditions in General Population – one of the MPs had said that I would like it there. But it was dark, and anyway I didn't have my glasses. I heard sounds of talking and shouting: Arabic, Pashto, Urdu, Farsi, and English, all fusing together. I smelt something burning too – a slightly odd smell. I thought that perhaps there was a game of football, and a barbecue going on. Maybe the soldiers and the prisoners were playing each other. I remembered the old Second World War movies *The Great Escape* and *Von Ryan's Express*, where the prisoners were treated quite decently by the Nazis, and had a relative level of autonomy from their captors. After all we *had* been issued EPOW cards.

I looked around my cell, stunned by my surroundings. Then the bucket caught my eye. That was the toilet I was going to have to use. I remembered how the Pakistanis just put a towel over my head, an armed guard behind me, and then I walked along normally to the toilet. It was dirty and horrible, but at least I had my privacy. Here all I could do for my dignity was to wrap the blanket or shawl around me.

The American soldiers had to ensure that the buckets were emptied daily. It was not a task they relished, which became apparent when they started picking certain detainees to do it. Their legs were shackled, but not their hands. Although I never volunteered to do it, many others did. It gave them an opportunity to hear the news from newly arrived prisoners, and some MPs would allow the exchange of a few words. The first person who spoke to me like this I later found out was a Kuwaiti scholar. He simply said, '*Al-Faraj qareeb*,' deliverance is close. I knew it was a statement of hope, and I thanked him for it. But I couldn't help thinking, and hoping, 'Does he know something I don't?'

The barn was floodlit from both ends – day and night. A rusty steel sheet hid the cells in front of me. At either end of the barn there was a soldier with an M16 assault rifle, pump-action shot gun, or SAW light machine gun – terms I soon became familiar with, sitting in a mini-guard tower: 'Overwatch' as they called it. They sat there for hours, with a few breaks, and times when they would talk to other passing MPs.

I lost track of time during that long, miserable, night, but it must have been in the early hours of the next morning when the MPs came in yelling, 'Get up, get up,' kicking the concertina wire. Then something came flying over the wire. the MRE (Meal Ready to Eat), standard US military ration pack, designed for the field. We had fifteen minutes to eat, and everything had to be accounted for and returned, including the 'trash', as they called out when they came back. There were several different varieties of MRE, but initially no Halal ones. I had spent all my life eating only halal or kosher meat. But faced with either the MRE, or just eating the various crackers and peanuts, and starving, I ate, all except the ones containing pig. Like the others, I learned to rip them open with my teeth, though it was hard, and sometimes I saw people surreptitiously use the razor wire to do it. The MPs removed several things from the packages before we got them; spoons were potential 'shanks', water heaters could be used to make a 'smoke bomb', pepper could be 'thrown in someone's eyes', and chocolates were a luxury we 'did not deserve'. As we had no spoons we had to improvise, either using our hands, or folding up a bit of cardboard from the pack, or just sucking out the contents. So eating was another humiliation, and I dared not think of home food and all the care and love that went into it, or I would have lost my composure. I was determined they would never see me lose my composure.

One thing they didn't stop, at that time, was the call to prayer. I awoke to that familiar and welcoming sound, made dry ablution, and faced west for the dawn prayer. It had slipped my mind, but this day was Eid al-Adha – the Festival of Sacrifice, when Muslims commemorate the Prophet Abraham's order to sacrifice his son. It is a family day, the most important celebration of the year.

There was a most surreal moment when someone entered the barn saying, 'Eid Mubarak.' That was my first encounter with the International Committee of the Red Cross (ICRC). The man, an Arabic speaker, went from cell to cell distributing a cup, with the Red Cross symbol, containing some meat and a piece of bread. I assumed he meant well, but who could imagine saying 'Season's Greetings', to somebody shivering behind concertina wire, having gone through what we had? An MP who later earned the nickname Rambo, and who referred to me as Great Britain, came to ask me what Eid Mubarak meant. 'Eid greetings,' I told him. 'Culturally equivalent to "Merry Christmas".'

Besides a military escort, there was another man with the Red Cross official. He was Patrick Hamilton, from England, which seemed a little comforting (the reaction I had had for just a moment to MI5 in Islamabad). Patrick spoke fluent Pashto with the person in the next cell. When my turn came, he took down my personal details, gave me an ICRC registration card and asked me if I wanted to write a message. I really wanted to write to my wife, although I had no idea where she was. The first letter I wrote was to the Pakistan address, in the hope that she might still be there, even though the Pakistanis had told me that she had left. I wrote another one to her too, at my father's address, in the hope that she had returned to England, and one to my father, apologizing for having caused him stress. Patrick told me that the ICRC viewed our status as POWs, as far as rights were concerned, but that the Americans had labelled us 'illegal combatants', with no rights at all. I found it comforting then to think that this international organization would be calling for our rights, but I soon saw how powerless they were in front of the Americans.

I was kept in the barn for five weeks – isolated from the prisoners in General Population – and taken to interrogation at any moment, day or night. The process of removing a detainee from the cell demonstrated for me the larger picture of US military procedure, epitomizing the war on terror. Every time, the overkill amazed me, and that resentment of overkill used on me stays with me still.

When someone was going to be taken for interrogation I often knew beforehand, as I heard the request on the MPs' radios. 'Escort – MI. Request five-five-eight.' That meant military intelligence were asking the escort team (or escort agency as I called them), responsible for detainee movement, to bring in a particular detainee for interrogation – in this case, me. They gathered their team and the shackles, and approached the cell shouting the number, sometimes adding, 'You're going for a walk.'

There was no door, just an entrance made of coiled concertina wire. They had to wear protective gloves to pull the wire across each time they wanted to take anyone out of the cell. Apart from the two MPs on overwatch, with their automatic weapons trained on the prisoner, another stood outside the cell aiming a handgun. The prisoner had to 'assume the position', lying prone on the ground, legs crossed and bent at the knees, hands on the back of the head. Three other unarmed guards carried out the shackling or unshackling. It was a long process. It took five people to transport and shackle or unshackle one detainee.

When I left the cell I had to walk bent double, their hands pushing me down, and shackles rubbing into my ankles. Once unshackled inside the cell I was made to assume the position again, and they would run off to get out. These were the early days; things began to ease up a little as some familiarity set in.

In my second week the MPs brought me into the interrogation tent and told me that 'the pansies' were here to see me. That was my first meeting with MI5 in Afghanistan. It was just one day, for a few hours. Andrew, from MI5, who I'd met in Birmingham, walked in with another man called Matt, a tall, wiry redhead, wearing a rugby shirt. Again, seeing a British person, I had a feeling of hope, familiarity, 'I know this person, he's been in my house, I've even offered him a cup of tea.'

Andrew was an intelligent man, he spoke fluent Arabic in several dialects and was well read. But there he was, asking just the same questions as in the UK, about people I knew, places I'd been, the money my wife's family paid for our house. I asked him, begged him in fact, for news of my family. He said it was not his job to know that. Then he said, 'We're just guests of the Americans here, they're in charge, we are their close allies, and we've got some influence in how you get treated. Believe me, the better you behave with them, the better you're treated.'

It was nonsense. No one could have behaved better than I did. I had noticed Andrew was pretty uneasy when he saw me hooded and shackled, and he asked the MPs, 'Is that really necessary?' At the end he asked all the Americans to leave the tent, and he gave me a Mars bar, which I refused to take. He left, but Matt stayed for a moment, saying, 'Look, mate, I don't know what else to say to you, but it'll all be over one day.' That was the end of my expecting something from MI5.

I used to spend hours squinting to read the dietary and nutritional information on the MRE packs – how many calories I had just consumed – just to have something to read, to feel I was doing something vaguely constructive. I was used to being extremely busy, with so many pressures and demands on my time, especially in the schools in Afghanistan and with life at home. Here there was absolutely nothing to do. I walked round and round my cell, and from corner to corner, over and over again. I was at the end of the row of cells, so I could see one person. They had given him a Quran to read. We managed to exchange a few words when I borrowed his Quran. I was often asked to translate for other prisoners – to the Red Cross or the MPs – which gave me an opportunity to say a few words at the same time.

The first man next to me was soon replaced by a dubious but interesting character. He was a Russian* who had been held by the Taliban for spying, and handed over to the Americans by the Northern Alliance, after the fall of Kandahar. He spoke Arabic, Pashto, Farsi, Urdu, a little English, and obviously Russian. The Taliban had accused him of spying for the Russians and had imprisoned him for several years. The other person in there with him – two in the same cell – was a Syrian who was also accused of spying by the Taliban. I had read about him earlier, back in Birmingham on a website of Afghan news: he had apparently made some confessions. The Syrians had forced him to spy on the Taliban, and he had also been beaten and tortured by the authorities in Dubai. These two were kept separate from all other prisoners because they were thought to be under threat from the rest of us, but they were still prisoners, treated just as badly as anybody else.

I soon realized that the Americans were doing their utmost to scare us because they themselves were terrified of us. They had been told frightening things about us as part of their training: we were Muslims, Arabs, Middle Easterners, killers, terrorists. When MPs stopped outside my cell, often out of curiosity about 'the British guy', I made some attempts to talk to them. I tried to explain things about the region: the political and historical context, attitudes, sensitivities, ethnic and cultural diversity, religious doctrine, and linguistic nuances. I didn't understand all this myself, but I spoke several of the languages, I had travelled in the area, and had studied history and religion. I thought they would want to understand, that they would be interested. In fact,

---

* Airat Vahidov: released May 2005.

it was rather frustrating, as most were happy to remain ignorant, and were satisfied that the briefings they had had before being deployed had given them as much information as they needed. Anyway, how could I really hope to explain these things to a person who had never left, say, Georgia, or Tennessee?

I soon began to understand that most of them were part-time soldiers, National Guard or army reservists. 'Weekend warriors', as the active-duty units called them, had a total army commitment of an initial six months' basic training, then two whole weeks and six weekends a year. In a way I couldn't help feeling sorry for them, they had joined perhaps to get a visit to Hawaii or travel to Europe, or to help pay for college fees. They had never dreamed they would end up in one of the most volatile places on earth, guarding some of the most dangerous people in it – as they were told.

In these first five weeks I got to know several MPs, and an officer, called Captain Danner, a practising Christian African-American who I often talked to. He listened to our gripes, and appeared to be a man of his word. I could have reasonable discussions with him.

I once got involved in a conversation with him, translating via Arabic for the Russian, who had decided to go on hunger strike. The Russian wanted the MPs to know that the Taliban had held him for nearly three years. 'I am being treated here worse than when I was with the Taliban. At least the Taliban gave me a radio, cooked meals including fresh fruit and vegetables, respected my faith, and housed me away from a toilet. Here, under the Americans, I *live* in a toilet.'

Captain Danner, for all his goodness, did not like hearing that at all. He did start trying to make some changes, but really nothing changed. The US military operated under a ludicrously rigid and uncompromising system that annoyed a lot of people – MPs as well as prisoners.

Much of my time, particularly after dawn, was taken up memorizing the Quran. I had just learnt the chapter al-Kahf (the Cave), which Muslims are encouraged to recite, especially on Fridays. When I wasn't pacing around, I sat cross-legged on my blanket, or just lay down. We were not allowed to know the day, the date, or the time, though five times a day we could hear the call to prayer from General Population, which was then repeated by one of us in the barn. This was a small victory over the Americans: we knew dawn, noon, afternoon, sunset, and night. They would rather we didn't know. The call was a spiritual communication, reverberating around the camp.

I also spent time staring out of the bullet holes at life in General Population, wishing I were there too. But one of the MPs warned me to stop looking out or he would have the holes blocked. So I resorted to taking quick peeks when they weren't looking.

The view was of several wooden structures in symmetrical rows, with canvas roofs, like tents. The sides were open – just the top was covered. In each building there were between ten and twenty prisoners, all wearing the blue jumpsuits. Each structure was surrounded by two rows of concertina wire. There was some space to go outside and walk around, but I could see that only three people walked at any given time. I later learned that only three people could talk with one another at any given time too. They were not allowed to approach or move close to the wire. They were not allowed to shout across to the other people in the other structures, and anybody who flouted the rules was made to kneel, sitting up on their knees with hands behind the head, in the sun, from fifteen minutes to an hour.

Once I saw a scene that stuck painfully in my mind. An American soldier was pointing his shotgun towards the face of a prisoner who was crying, kneeling in that position with his hands behind his head. So often I heard that yell, 'on your knees, on your knees', and this man *was* on his knees. I could feel the American just terrorizing him to show off his power, and I couldn't bear the image of the prisoner's fear and loss of dignity.

I noticed too that a whole cell of ten, or more, prisoners shared one bucket as a toilet. I dreaded that. I had also discovered what the odd burning smell was: waste disposal. All those foolish thoughts of barbecues, football, and having a good time had gone by then.

After four weeks enclosed in the barn I felt desperately in need of air and sun, and I began agitating for exercise outside. When the ICRC came round we made regular complaints, usually about food. Often there was not enough food, as half the contents were taken out of the MREs, and we got a piece of mouldy Afghan bread as a supplement, or even as a complete meal. I protested to the ICRC that I had been in the barn for almost five weeks. I hadn't seen the sun or felt the air. I hadn't walked one step out of the place, except to the interrogation room.

Eventually, in response to the complaints, the Americans began a ridiculous system, which they called 'Operation Sun-Bob'. They referred to all detainees as 'Bob'. It was meant to be demeaning. None of us had had showers or baths, or had enough water to wash with, which meant, inevitably, bad smells. So they called us 'Bobs' (short for Bad Odor Boys, as I had overheard). Every little operation was given the suffix 'Bob'. 'Operation Wash-Bob' would be to take prisoners out to shower, which never happened to me. 'Operation Sun-Bob' was getting everybody in the barn out into the sun for a certain amount of time, because the complaint was that we didn't see the sun.

They went through the laborious system of taking each person from the cell in the same way they normally did for interrogations, which took an immense amount of time and effort. They brought us out of the cells, kept watching, and linked us up together using a string around the arm to attach one person to the next, so that we were all tied together as in a chain gang. We were all moved out in this tight chain, with MPs hovering around everywhere. It was a big operation, to bring us out into a place where we could stand in the sun for only two minutes. 'Next time you want to see the sun, look out of a hole,' one of them grumbled after all the trouble of Operation Sun-Bob. Our response was that if these were the conditions to get some natural light, we would rather stay inside.

By overhearing their radio communications I learned a lot about how the Americans operated, as well as gaining snippets of information. I knew the numbers of detainees getting punished, when an MP patrolling the camp radioed in, 'SOG [Sergeant of the Guard] – Rover. 217: failure to comply.' Similarly I heard the numbers called for interrogation and movements at the entrances and the various duties assigned to the MPs. Often they would refer among themselves to things I could easily relate to, and I would then be sure to mention them. It was a way of forcing some normal human relations. Many were very surprised to find I spoke English, and even more surprised when they learned where I was from. England triggered the interest of many of the MPs – even the ones who clearly believed anyone held by the US military was, by definition, a hardened terrorist – and they really wanted to talk to me.

Over the years, being a British Muslim held by the US forces would be something of a novelty with each new group of MPs. That had its disadvantages, as well as benefits. It meant that I had more interrogations. After all, they didn't need an interpreter each time, as they did with the vast majority.

One of the MPs I often spoke to was Cody, an Irish American who had been brought up on a Cherokee reservation in North Carolina. He told me how he had had to fight his way up to gain respect among the

Cherokee, and that he identified more with them than with white America. He said to me once, 'When I see you people here, it reminds me of *my* people. They were treated the same way. Their lands were invaded, they were slaughtered and imprisoned, their language and religion were not understood, and they were depicted, until recently, as savages and murderous heathens.' He even said that if any soldier dared to mistreat me, that I should tell him, and he would 'fix the problem'.

But over the months, between Kandahar and both our transfers to Bagram, I saw Cody become desensitized, and accept the demonizing process of regarding us as subhuman. He always treated *me* well, but then I was easy to get on with. We talked about Native American history and culture – which I was fascinated by – and about hunting, military life, his family in America, and his hopes for the future. But my final judgement of any MP came from how they treated others, people who were not as amiable or communicative as me. Cody later sank in my estimation because of his behaviour towards other prisoners, and his brutality to one in particular.

There were several other MPs I used to talk to who were from the 511th Military Police Company. One was Warnick. When I asked him about his origins, he replied, 'All I can tell you is I'm from the islands.' He looked like a huge Samoan rugby player.

Once, Warnick entered the barn and I heard him get into a conversation with an overwatch guard.

'Man, we've got our forces everywhere. We're kickin' ass all round the world: Afghanistan, Korea, Iraq, and now the President's talkin' about the Philippines. We're just like Hitler's armies rollin' on through,' the overwatch guard said, with evident satisfaction.

'Wait a minute. We're nothing like Hitler, we want to spread peace and democracy,' retorted Warnick.

And that was how I thought of him. He was a very decent sort of a person, with similar morals and values to mine. Many months later, in Bagram, we had several religious and political discussions. He was a law-enforcement officer, who had previously served in the US Marine Corps. His wife was German, and he spoke German fluently. He had a wonderful sense of humour, and he treated everyone with dignity, fairness, and respect. His appearance had a little of a Middle Eastern look to it, which, coupled with his behaviour, made him popular among most prisoners. Observing us at prayer times, he would often come around and mimic the raising of the hands in supplication, saying, in his strong Southern military accent, '*Al-Hamdu Lillah*' (Praise be to Allah). He even became a Muslim, though he probably didn't realize it. Teaching him some Arabic words once, I asked him to utter the phrase '*Laa ilaha ill-Allah, Muhammad ar-Rasul Ullah*' (There are no deities except Allah, Muhammad is the Messenger of Allah), the Islamic declaration of faith.

When he asked my opinion about the war, I told Warnick, 'I can understand the reaction of the US, to some degree, after the strikes against the Pentagon and the Twin Towers, that you need to prevent such attacks and arrest those responsible. But I can never accept that the occupation of a de facto sovereign state will resolve the problem.'

I added, 'Do you remember your own home-grown acts of terrorism, like the Oklahoma City bombing by Timothy McVeigh? The Michigan Militia trained him; he was responsible for the deaths of hundreds of people. Why didn't the US authorities raid, capture, interrogate, and torture all the people who were "linked" to him? Weren't they potential threats too? In fact the US constitution asserts its citizens'"right to bear arms". Here we're told that we are all potential threats to the safety of the US because we supported a struggle – over a decade ago often – against occupation in Afghanistan, Bosnia,

Kashmir, Chechnya, or Palestine, which al-Qa'idah was also aiding. So because we are united not only by faith, but also purpose, we must all be enemies of your country, posing a latent threat to the security of the free world. If that *is* the case, then you need to capture several million more people to remove that perceived threat. It's pure nonsense.'

After such a barrage of argument I often got just blank expressions. When I discussed this kind of thing with some of the more rational amongst them, the response was, 'Look, I'm here with my buddies, I don't understand the politics, it doesn't make sense to me.'

Some said, 'I don't understand why we're bringing all these people in. They can't *all* be responsible for the attacks on the US.'

But there were others who didn't want to hear these conversations at all. They believed that we were all dangerous terrorists who deserved to be here.'You know you are all here for a reason, we wouldn't have you here otherwise, would we?'

Cody told me that he had volunteered to join up after September 11. Despite his involvement with the Cherokee Indians he was really a Southern redneck. Because of my love of history and different cultures, I wanted to learn whatever I could about the South, and its attitudes to the North. Talking with one of the MPs, I asked him to define 'rednecks', 'good ol' boys', and 'hillbillies', and Cody more or less fitted the description of a redneck. He had felt the attack on the Twin Towers was an attack on the US as a nation, and told me how even some of his townsfolk in North Carolina had expected to come under attack themselves too. With several of his friends he had volunteered to come to Afghanistan, to pay back the Taliban. However, by the time we were talking, he had been there three weeks, and he deeply regretted his decision. He had imagined he would get involved in the nuts and bolts of a battle, but he had no idea of what modern warfare was like. Kandahar was desolate and bleak, and there was certainly none of the adrenalin and excitement he and his friends had hoped they would be part of.

Later I heard many MPs like him say, about Afghanistan and Guantánamo, 'We're just like you – only our prison is larger.'

My immediate response was indignation: 'Please, don't patronize me. You can see your family when you go on home leave, communicate with them by email and phone, and you'll return home as heroes, getting paid for it in the process. We are held here in limbo, without charge, incommunicado, our loved ones lost to us, our lives are shattered, *and* we are treated like animals.'

By the time many of them left, they were still bewildered by their experience. They had had no contact with the real Afghanistan because they lived just in their military base. Any other place was out of bounds. Perhaps there was some truth to their feeling of 'being in a larger prison'.

Shaker Aamer, my close friend who had lived with me for a time in Kabul, had also been in Kandahar, and several MPs spoke to me about how impressive he was. During one of the interrogations I was asked about him, and one of the MPs in the room overheard. He mentioned Shaker to me after the interrogator had left, while I was waiting for the escort team. 'He's an amazing guy, I can't believe I met someone like that here. Here he was, in shackles, with his hair shaved, and he spoke to me as though we were the best of friends. In fact, hearing the passionate way he talked about religion, I came within an inch of becoming a Muslim myself.'

'Why didn't you?' He replied by pointing to the US flag on his arm. I kept thinking about that. What had he really meant? Was this an admission that he thought his country had declared war against a faith? My faith.

The MPs also mentioned other British prisoners who had been

here earlier, but had been moved on to Guantánamo Bay. For instance, I heard that three lads from Tipton, outside Birmingham, had been held in the barn. The MPs told me they called them 'the Beatles'.

The MPs talked about one other British prisoner who had been there. I later discovered this was Feroz Abbassi from Croydon. I met him nearly two years later in Guantánamo. The stories they used to tell about this man they called 'the SAS guy' showed me how much the American mentality was geared to the creation of heroes and anti-heroes, so their enemies had to be the very worst characters possible, but highly trained, committed, and effective enemies. They were describing Feroz as a former SAS man who had joined al-Qa'idah, teaching them special urban- and guerrilla-warfare tactics. 'He was a real bad-ass dude, martial-arts and explosives expert – you could tell by his look, and the way he carried himself.' That was the rationale applied to reach some very far-fetched conclusions.

It didn't matter too much about the MPs gossiping like this. But it made all the difference when the interrogators were convinced that I was a highly trained assassin, veteran of the Afghan, Bosnian and Chechen jihads, with a black belt in jujitsu, fluent in eight European and Asian languages, and an Oxford graduate with a degree in artificial intelligence.

Interrogations went on, day by dreary day. It was any time, twice a day, three times a day, or sometimes not at all for days on end. It was five minutes. It was an hour, or ten hours. There was always the same show of force, armed guards at the door, or even in the room. Interrogation was generally with one person, and because they came from different agencies and had different agendas, it was not at all systematic. These were people trying to make a name for themselves, believing they could single-handedly crack a terrorist plot or network.

Nathan, a young Texan from military intelligence, interrogated me the most, sometimes with a colleague, a Japanese American called Lee. They were mostly in civilian clothes, in their early twenties and clearly not very senior. Nathan started with a given list of questions, which followed on from the line of questioning in Islamabad. Sometimes they asked only one question. Other times they asked me to go over every detail of my life, my primary school, my family, my friends, my neighbours, every journey I had ever made, everyone I had ever met. They wanted to go over and over the story of where I went in Bosnia, who I had met, what I did on my trip to Turkey, and on my trips to Afghanistan. I had told them everything, but still they went on and on asking.

There was never an accusation of being involved in anything, or having prior knowledge of anything. It was all about links between people. I got on quite well with Nathan, which may seem surprising, but I had always tried to like people, to see their positive side, and I wasn't going to change here.

Nathan explained to me, 'We are trying to judge people's intentions.'

'How on earth are you going to do that? As a law student I learned that two components are clearly required to constitute a crime: *mens reus* (the guilty mind) and *actus reus* (the guilty act). Are you trying to become some type of Orwellian Thought Police?'

I told him he must know by now from all I had told him about people I knew, places I had been to, that I had had plenty of opportunities to join al-Qa'idah. If I had wanted to find someone who could give me a reference to al-Qa'idah's training camps, through people I had met in Pakistan or Afghanistan, it could have been done.

He and I talked about other things too, away from the mass of irrelevant information he was supposed to accumulate. He really did want to understand the big picture of what was going on in the region, and in the Muslim world. But at the same time he was looking for promotion, he wanted to rise up the ladder, he wanted a Silver or Bronze Star, based, perhaps, on the numbers of interrogations he had carried out, or the numbers of people he had recommended for Guantánamo. I once overheard him talking about Combat Patches, for having served in a designated war zone, which struck me as ridiculous: I knew he hadn't seen combat in Afghanistan. But he was someone who treated me well, and with whom I had riveting discussions.

After five weeks I was really yearning to get into the General Population, just to be with other people. It became very important to me to get out of the barn, and I changed my tactics from being Mr Reasonable. I began pacing up and down the cell, kicking the wire, refusing to speak to the MPs. One of them, who I normally got on well with, came and asked me please to tell him what the matter was. I told him I could no longer bear being in the barn. I was hitting despair. Eventually I think it was that sergeant's speaking to Nathan that got me transferred to General Population.

As I walked into that open-sided place it was a wonderful moment – but I was still in a cage. Every single person in the cell came to shake hands, to embrace me, saying, 'As-salaamu alaikum,' and I felt such comfort from the warmth and affection of these men I didn't know, but that in a profound way I did. There were eighteen or nineteen of them: Egyptians, Turks, Chechens, Pakistanis, Afghans, Uzbeks, and Chinese. They were full of advice about patience, fortitude, and caution. But at that very moment of happiness an MP came along and radioed in some numbers for punishment. One of them was 558. I looked at him astonishment, as he barked at me, 'On your knees'.

'For what? I've just come into this place after five weeks in the barn.'

'You know the rules, no more than three people speaking at once.' I wanted to argue, but the others assumed the position and urged me to follow suit. I did.

That first night I lay down with the same two blankets I had had in the barn, with eight or nine people in my row, feeling very much stronger. The only thing worse than the barn was the toilet situation. Here in the cell we had one bucket, sometimes two, to share between us all. It was absolutely disgusting: hordes of flies and dung beetles crawling on the excrement. I trained myself to go only when everyone was asleep, usually very late, or even early in the morning before the dawn prayers. It was a way of keeping a little control and self-respect over that private area.

We used the old system of deciding when to pray, with the sun and the placement of the shadow. We prayed in congregation, during which the imam would make a long supplication. Depending on who led the prayer, the supplication would include appeals to God for the downfall and destruction of the US military, as well as for our own deliverance and for strength for our families. We all responded with, 'Ameen.' For exercise we used to speed-walk around the cell. I asked the ICRC to get permission for regular exercise, but they only allowed some minor stretching – no press-ups or sit-ups. Nothing that built up strength or stamina was allowed in Kandahar.

The days now were very different from in the barn, and in the two and half weeks I was there in the cell I learned so many people's life stories. I heard about so much suffering, so many people killed, so many people who had disappeared. I felt like in the early days in Afghanistan more than ten years before, when the Kashmiri fighters told me about their lives and I was so humbled by the thought of how easy I had had it, living in Birmingham. People talked about their families too, especially those who were married and had children. It was a very human thing – in the inhuman way we were living – to talk about something that was close to me.

Also, I learned the most mundane details of life in, for instance,

Bahrain, so that I was longing to go there, feeling I would recognize it. And people were fascinated by my stories of Birmingham, and of what it was like to be a Muslim in Britain. No one knew anything about that. I found myself telling them about England's green fields and villages with a nostalgia that surprised me – I hadn't ever lived in an English village. I told them too about Warwick Castle, and Blenheim and Buckingham Palaces, the Lake District, Loch Ness, Snowdonia, Stratford-upon-Avon, and Sparkhill. It was escapism, and I really enjoyed both the telling and the listening.

The ICRC brought us a chessboard. It caused some controversy and debate, as someone claimed that chess was prohibited in Islam, but another said that he heard from a senior Islamic scholar that it was permissible, and it was in fact backgammon that was prohibited, because of its use for gambling. I played a few times with Isa al-Bahraini.* It distracted me from the reality of life in a concentration camp for a little while, and the discipline of really thinking out the moves gave me some pleasure. We did not have much else to do apart from our long talks, and memorizing the Quran, which I couldn't do for more than an hour or so at a time. There were some booklets in Pashto, and Bibles in Arabic.

We used to have debates about the ICRC. Some people rejected them entirely, assuming they were missionaries in disguise – because of the cross – and linked to the Americans. I liked Patrick as a person, even if I found the ICRC sadly ineffectual. I saw the advantage of working with them, especially as the MPs despised them.

The ICRC had distributed some carom boards – a game with slid-ing discs, very popular in the subcontinent – which were about three

---

* Isa al-Murbati: one of six Bahrainis held in Guantánamo.

foot by three. We used to prop them against the wire when no one was playing, but the Americans soon took them away, saying they were an obstruction, blocking their view of us. They really did not like to see us happy.

The whole time there were American guards, weapons pointed, pacing up and down outside the cell. Sometimes they drilled in what they called 'full battle-rattle', as though preparing for an attack. There were eight guard towers and always MPs looking down at us from them through binoculars.

People's inventiveness and resilience in captivity were amazing. There was a lot of teasing between the Arabs and the Afghans, sometimes a bit harsh, but still funny. Isa had a running joke about one Afghan who never prayed with everyone else, even the other Afghans. Khayrullah prayed alone after everyone had finished. First, he whipped his shawl around the floor to clear the dust, and then he assumed a strange posture for prayer, his behind out, and his hands held well below his navel. Isa would mimic him, but exaggerating, whipping his towel all around, then standing to pray while his behind really stuck out, and his hands slipped right down to cover his groin, like a football player waiting for a free kick. People fell about laughing, enjoying that joke, daily – five times daily. Eventually some other Afghans convinced Khayrullah to pray with the congregation, and we lost that joke.

Another day three Afghans and an Uzbek made a little play of Americans shackling a prisoner. It was hilarious, but the paranoid Americans assumed that somehow the prisoners had captured a guard and were preparing to beat him up. There was incredible yelling and rushing about as they burst into the cell, pulled us all out, and dispersed us to other cells. Those were some of the moments when I realized how really pathetic they were, panicking at the slightest thing.

Our cells were raided very often, but randomly and without notice – though what they thought they might find after all we had been through was a mystery to me. The contraband that they *did* find, occasionally, included boiled sweets that were somehow left in the MRE packs, or extra bits of toilet paper. Screaming out the orders, 'Get to the back' of the cell and 'On your knees,' they rushed in, while we were all lined up at the back, with MPs across the wire aiming their weapons at us. Nothing in the cell was left uninspected. Everything was overturned. Then we were individually dragged to the middle of the cell, and systematically searched.

Early one morning, as all of us were performing our dawn prayer, the MPs burst into a cell on the opposite side. Finishing our prayers, we saw them drag the prisoners to the ground while they were still praying. Tarek Dergoul, one British detainee, was in that cell. I had heard that he was the other British national there, but I never did meet him.

Only once during all my time in Kandahar did I come out of the cell unshackled. That was the day of the sandstorm. It was around noon when it began, blocking out the sun with dust that painted the sky orange. Then the wind and rain came down so hard that several of our cells – makeshift wood structures – began to fall apart. By sunset the MPs had begun to panic, trying to figure out a way to move us. They didn't have enough time or manpower, so they decided to bring us out in twos and threes – unshackled. We were made to lie down encircled by MPs all pointing their weapons at us. After six of us were out, they moved us in an arc, a 'mobile killing zone'.

There was quite an atmosphere of apprehension building up in my last few days there, as rumours were flying around about people going to Guantánamo Bay. One group had already gone. Cody told me, 'There are orange suits around – and that means Guantánamo.' People really did not want to go there; even an Egyptian told me he would rather face his homeland's notorious prisons than go to Cuba.

When they came for me to leave the cell, I went around, said my salaam, and embraced everybody, even after the MPs had told me to get down on the floor. I thought, 'What are they going to do, rush me with a gun?'

Then, going to the plane, hooded of course, I had two particularly nasty MPs, who pushed me down so far that my chest was almost touching my knees. It was so painful. I tried to straighten up a little bit just as we were going up the ramp. As we got into the plane the first one punched me. I said, 'What's wrong with you? What are you doing this for? I can't walk. It's killing my back, breaking my back.' The second MP let up a little bit, but the first one snapped, 'No,' pushed me down, then threw me to the floor and kicked me in the ribs. Then he said, 'That'll teach you to resist.'

I thought to myself, 'How could I resist? What's wrong with you?' I seemed to be completely alone.

The plane took off, and I knew I was headed for Bagram, just as Nathan had told me. Optimist that I am, I thought that maybe there was a chance of being sent back to Pakistan from there. And at least it was not Guantánamo.

7

THE HARDEST TEST

Shackled and hooded, I arrived in Bagram from Kandahar, hoping I was prepared for the worst – whatever that might be. I knew what processing would mean, from Kandahar, and sure enough it included another humiliating strip-search in front of several guards and medics. But otherwise it felt quite humane, compared to the yelling and the mass-production-belt feel of Kandahar. I was given some thermal underwear, and another blue jumpsuit to wear. On the back they had written 180 – my new number.

The first thing I noticed was the near-perfect silence, except for the occasional sounds of army boots echoing around the building. I was taken, shackled but unhooded, to one of the interrogation rooms on the first floor. There was a flight of stairs on either side of a landing overlooking the main prison area. I could see about six rooms. As I soon discovered, some were used as administration rooms or as holding cells for high-value detainees, like the former Taliban Foreign Minister Wakil Ahmad Mutawakkil.* But most were bleak concrete rooms with the windows boarded up. The only things in them were a wooden table and cheap plastic chairs.

---

* Released May 2005, invited by President Hamid Karzai to stand for elections.

I was put into a room and made to sit down facing the door. Above it there was a bright security light glaring in my face. This first interrogation was short. I was faced with two civilian interrogators. They only asked me some basic personal details, confirming the papers they had from Kandahar. But they told me to expect much longer and more intense interrogations in future – by other people.

Coming out of the interrogation room, I got my first overview of the prison. It was a huge disused factory, a relic of the former Soviet Union's ambitions, from a time when it was the enemy of both Islam *and* the West. There were pieces of abandoned machinery, and warning notices on the walls, with inscriptions in Russian.

As I came slowly down the steps, the chains clanking, thoughts rushed through my head about this extraordinary place. I recalled how the USSR met its own Vietnam right here, and now the Americans had come 'to help the country', just as the Soviets had claimed. Two global superpowers, in little more than a decade, had occupied this land – one of the world's poorest. The historical parallels were uncanny. I thought back further to when this desolate landlocked country had been coveted by Tsarist Russia and the British Empire in the Great Game. I thought back to Kandahar, where an Afghan had told me what he remembered of the Soviet occupation: that initially opposition was undisciplined, weak, and slow, but within months the resistance movement, armed with .303 Lee Enfield rifles, had grown strong enough to unite several factions against the common enemy and inflict damage on the invaders. The Russians had been invited into Afghanistan, but by a pro-Soviet regime.

On the way back from interrogation, passing the cells, I noticed something else: each cell had its own name, written in bold white marker: *Somalia, Lebanon, USS Cole, Nairobi, Twin Towers,* and *Pentagon.* I wondered what all these names and places had in common. Was the

USA unleashing pent-up rage, seeking vengeance for every military engagement it had lost or terrorist act that it had suffered? Well, almost. The common denominator was Islam. Although it was alleged that al-Qa'idah was responsible for some of these attacks, what could they possibly have had to do with Lebanon (presumably the bombing of the US Marine barracks in Beirut in 1983), or with Somalia (the botched US *'Black Hawk Down'* encounter a decade later)? Anyhow, what the hell did I have to do with any of them?

From my first impressions, I felt that things might be a little better here: there were certainly far fewer detainees, and that meant fewer guards and interrogators. I was taken into cell four, and then I understood the unnatural silence.

'No talking with detainees allowed,' said the guard as he opened the padlock on the door, and asked me to step into the airlock that led into the cell itself. Standing, walking, praying in congregation, or sitting in a group, were not allowed either, he told me. I soon learned that the rules in Bagram often changed without notice, but for the present these were in force.

'Aren't you going to remove the shackles?' I asked.

'They stay on for a week, or until the SOG [Sergeant of the Guard] says. Just holler if you need the bathroom, one of the MPs will undo the shackles, and return to lock them when you're done.'

I found an empty corner to set down the two old blankets I'd been given, rolling one into a pillow and covering myself with the other. Like Kandahar, the whole place was illuminated with mobile floodlights that were only off during a power failure. I had to cover my head to try and sleep. I found it very difficult to move around with the handcuffs, but then, remembering Islamabad, and thinking myself lucky to be small; I twisted my wrists, and found that the shackles slid off my hands with little effort. I slept every night with the handcuffs tucked under my blanket – empty – until they were finally removed.

The prison area I was in had six cells separated by coils of concertina wire, so that I had a good view of the adjoining cells, the main floor in front of the cells, and even the first-floor landing area where the interrogation rooms were. The entrance to each cell had a rough door made from strips of metal, then a corridor of about four feet, and that led to another identical door, which opened into the main cell area. This second door was controlled by a piece of thin rope that the MPs pulled and released in order to isolate the prisoner from the rest of the cell during shackling and opening of the front door. The soldiers called it the airlock, or the sally port. The floors were wooden, covered with cheap Iranian carpets, originally red, grey and beige. At the back of the cell, a rusty oil barrel cut in half was the toilet. The guards emptied it only every few days. That first day the stench hit me hard, and gave me a constant headache. The smell got steadily worse as the numbers of prisoners increased.

During the first few weeks there seemed to be no more than twenty or so detainees in the entire building. But every few days I saw new ones trickle in. The cell I was in first – number four – contained only four other people: a Tajik doctor, an Iranian student, and two Afghani taxi drivers. In cell five, to my left, I could see six people. I soon found out that they included an aged Afghan, an old Palestinian, a Saudi, an Egyptian, and someone I assumed was African, but soon knew was a fellow Briton, Richard Belmar. Although talking was strictly forbidden, I did manage to exchange a few words with him, and have brief conversations with the Tajik and the Iranian – in Urdu. They told me they had both been there about a week. They seemed as bewildered and anxious as I was. I could see that cell six held another four prisoners.

The other prisoners soon discovered that I could communicate easily with the Americans, without an interpreter, and they constantly asked me to translate their requests to guards and medics. I was very happy with the role of translating, as it gave me the opportunity to speak to other prisoners about all kinds of unrelated things, and to exchange news right in front of the guards, who didn't understand a thing.

To my right, cells three and one were empty, but I could see that cell two held a solitary man. I still had not got my glasses back since the handover to the Americans in Pakistan, but I could make out that this prisoner, dressed in grey shalwar kameez, had long black dishevelled hair, and often appeared to be talking, though not to me, or anyone else that I could see.

'Aaa-nimal!' an MP passing cell two shouted, comically twisting his head. He was talking to the inhabitant of cell two, who I assumed was very dangerous, considering his isolation and his name. 'How you doin' today? Shake your head for me, like on *The Muppet Show*. Go on, do it and I'll give you a piece of fruit.' 'Animal' responded with a series of grunts and curses in Pashto. As he walked passed my cell I asked this soldier, whom I had spoken to once before, why they called him Animal.

'I don't know why this guy's here. I think he's crazy. He refuses to brush his teeth or to take a bath, and talks to himself a lot. But he looks like Animal from *The Muppet Show*, and he looks a lot like Charles Manson as well.'

At the end of almost two weeks the cell populations were reshuffled. I was shackled and moved to cell six. I came in, carrying my thin blankets, and saw four prisoners staring intently at me. I whispered, '*As-salaamu alaikum,*' and sat down in a space near the front, to the left of the door. I got a muted reply in unison, '*Wa alaikum as-salaam.*'

The first person to speak to me was Sa'ad, a Pakistani man who had studied and grown up in Saudi Arabia and Indonesia – where he had been captured. Sa'ad was plump, and in his mid-twenties, but he looked a lot older. He told me that his late father was a former Pakistani ambassador to Saudi Arabia, where Sa'ad had studied and memorized the entire Quran in his youth. After his mother's death, his father married an Indonesian woman, and they moved to Jakarta.

In a whisper, when no MPs were near the cell, he began to tell me a very strange story, which left me with more questions than answers. He said that he and his stepmother had both been kidnapped by the Indonesian security services, and he had been sent to Egypt, where he was held in a tiny room and interrogated brutally for three months, before being handed over to the Americans. He told me that in Egypt he could hear the screams of another man from a room nearby. He was haunted by those screams, and he told me how he had heard them again, very loud, despite the noise of the aeroplane engines, on the flight to Bagram, and was terrified for himself. From my first cell I had watched a man, who was often made to stand, but kept fainting and dropping to the floor. Sa'ad told me that was the man.*

We talked often, usually at night when the guards were a little more inattentive. By this time also we had begun to master the art of ventriloquism. I had been made to stand a few times as punishment for talking, when the guards had been too close.

I talked too to Ahmad, from Saudi Arabia. He was arrested by the Pakistanis in Lahore – where he had been living for many years – and was sold by them to the Americans, he told me. Ahmad was often taken for interrogation. He told me that he was questioned by an Arab American, originally from Egypt, whom I soon found held a lot of power in Bagram. Ahmad had been stripped naked after he refused to

---

* I was later convinced this man had been an Australian, Mamduh Habib: released January 2005.

cooperate, and he had threatened to kill the interrogators if they touched him again. As time went on though, this Arab interrogator softened his approach.

'Wouldn't you like a woman, Ahmad? How many years do you think you'll survive without one? If you cooperate with us I can make things very easy for you.'

Ahmad enjoyed telling me his riposte. 'And why would I need a woman? Can't you see,' he said, pointing to his groin, 'my trousers are filled with the aftermath of many a wet dream?' That was the last exchange both the interrogator and I had with Ahmad before he was sent to Guantánamo Bay.

Food was a real problem. They gave us kosher/halal ration packs twice or sometimes three times a day. There were ten different varieties, but it was still utterly monotonous. Nothing was cooked and nothing was fresh. To make things worse, they opened these ration packs up, and split off various items, so we only got certain things that they had decided to give to us, perhaps because they were the least tasty. I'm not a big eater so it really didn't affect me so much, but some of the larger ones really suffered. The pack came with a very flimsy spoon, but to the guards even that was a potential weapon. They made a very emphatic point about counting all the spoons from every cell.

There were no washing facilities in the cell, and we were only taken out for a bath once a week. For once the shackles were taken off – in a caged washing area – and each of us in turn was given one bucket of cold water, though I was always desperate for the chance to wash, no matter how cold it was. Not having water to wash with after using the latrine was disgusting, and the guards insisted that water bottles were for drinking only. They said that anyone found using them to wash with would be punished. We had 50ml water bottles – often from Muslim countries like Kuwait, UAE, Turkey, and Oman. They were rationed and recorded. At the height of the rationing we were allowed only two a day. At one mealtime there was no drinking water at all, and one of the guards said, 'There's not enough. You guys are drinking too much. You're consuming more water than the military.' That was obviously impossible, as there were no more than twenty of us, and hundreds, probably thousands of soldiers. Besides, I'd heard some of them actually complain about the steak and lobster dinners they were getting, or the brands of soda that weren't to their liking; there was no way on earth they would settle for two small bottles of water per day.

'If you're not going to give us any water, then don't give us any food either,' I said, giving him back the hated plastic pouch of the MRE.

'So you're refusing your meal?'

'Yes. And so are they,' I responded, pointing toward Sa'ad and Ahmad, who also came to the airlock and returned the packets, asking me to translate their grievances too. 'The rules change here all the time. How can you expect us to manage with no water at mealtimes? Anyway, you give us only one or two items from the MRE and throw the rest away, so what have we to lose?'

That led to my first punishment. The new soldier seemed surprised by this salvo of complaint in perfect English, and sped off to consult his superiors. He returned shortly with the SOG and three other guards, and asked me to step into the airlock.

'Go get your shit, you're moving,' one of them said.

I was shackled and taken to cell three, the largest of all the cells, which was empty. I was made to stand for what seemed like several hours. But as a direct result of our refusal to accept the meal packets, I soon learned from one of the guards, the water ration increased to four 50ml bottles a day. Not enough, I thought, but it would do. Most importantly, it had taught me a lesson: assertive, focused protest eventually produced results.

The monotony of the days, which passed so slowly, made me desperate at the thought of how each precious one was irreplaceable. That time was lost, time which could – which *should* – have been spent with my family. Each night, as I covered my head with the old grey blanket to shield my eyes from the glaring floodlights, I played back in my mind scenes from my old life, several times over. I thought mostly about school and childhood, though I didn't think about my dad – that was too painful. And I tried never to think about Zaynab and the children and the last years together. Sometimes I let my mind run through what I might do once I was released. I still really believed deep down that this whole nightmare was transient, and I would be home soon.

These particular soldiers in Bagram had a communication method that aroused my curiosity about their personalities. They did not attempt to conceal one another's names, using, Private P, Specialist A, or Sergeant S (as the MPs did in Kandahar), because they were using nicknames like Superstar, Skeletor, and Superman. It was Superman who had spoken to me about Animal, my new neighbour in the adjacent cell.

As the rules did not allow talking of any sort within the cells, some MPs found it perfectly appropriate to punish Animal for just that. 'No talking, Animal, even if it is to yourself.' He was ordered to stand up for an hour, during which he continued chatting, singing, and laughing to himself. After a few minutes he looked up towards the ceiling as if someone was telling him something. 'Kenuh?' he asked himself. Then, contentedly nodding his head as affirmation, he sat down. I almost choked with laughter as the infuriated guards entered the cell and forced him to his feet again. Animal had just told himself to take a seat – in Pashto.

The rumour was that Animal, a harmless Afghan tramp, clearly in need of psychiatric care, had been handed over by the Northern Alliance for a paltry sum. He was never once taken for interrogation in all the time I saw him there. Eventually, he was moved to cell four, this time not alone. His companions included a Chechen; Superman assumed he was Russian, and he made derisive comments about the USSR, Lenin, and Stalin. More typical Yankee ignorance, I thought. Didn't he even know that Stalin's treatment of the Chechens – despite their valiant resistance against the Nazis – was the worst in their entire history? And here was the all-American Superman thinking that he'd surprised this Vladimir with his knowledge of past Soviet leaders.

When he first heard me speak, Superman expressed his surprise, asking, 'So where are you from, dude?'

'Have a guess, see if you can recognize the accent.'

'I know, Scotland.'

Also in cell four was a very young pale-looking Arab boy, who seemed angry rather than bewildered or sad. He went on hunger strike from the first day. Though we were in separate cells – I was still alone – I tried to speak to him through the wire, but he would not respond. However once he shouted, in Arabic, towards someone new in cell six, 'My Lord has informed me what you've done. You said that I pledged my allegiance to Usamah bin Ladin, didn't you?'

For this outburst, and for refusing his meals, he was taken to cell one, alone, and made to stand shackled and hooded. I saw him shake his head so violently that the hood came off and fell to the ground. The guards entered his cell, replaced the hood, attaching it with pieces of tape to hold it in place. He shook his head again, scraping it against the floor and the wire to dislodge it. Eventually he stopped moving, and the Egyptian interrogator entered with the guards. He removed the tape and raised the hood a little, saying a few words to the boy. The guards soon left, taking the hood with them.

One day, I saw three guards struggling with a heavy object, moving slowly toward cell two. They had to lift it up into the airlock over the metal doorframe, which exhausted them all, including the powerful Superman. Eventually, they dragged it near the back of the cell, a few yards away from the toilet. It was some kind of giant circular steel bracket, perhaps used for oil or water pipes in the Russian era. One of the guards then dragged in a long, thick steel chain, looping one end through the bracket and carrying the other end out through the airlock. Sometime later, I saw a new prisoner brought into cell two, shackled and bent over double, and deposited between the bracket and the toilet. The chain was then attached to his waist, so that he could not even reach the toilet unless they slackened the chain from the airlock. His movement was restricted to a 180-degree arc around the bracket. As he was unable to reach the toilet, he used the area where he slept to relieve himself. The smell was terrible, but worse was having to witness the man's humiliation. I complained to the guards, and I heard others do so too, about the inhuman and degrading state this man was forced into. Finally they did slacken the chain. But they hadn't finished with him.

I had negotiated with the guards to allow us some exercise time daily. In fact my first PT sessions were done with arm and leg shackles still on. But still, we all enjoyed exercising, even though many prisoners had very little experience of physical education. Watching some of them perform hip-thrusting press-ups and uncoordinated star jumps was hilarious, sometimes eliciting comments from MPs. 'Retard PT!' a passing soldier screamed out, with an uncontrollable burst of laughter. But physical exercise was used as a punishment too. The chained prisoner, who I believe was Uighur (from Turkistan in western China), was screamed at for hours with orders to do push-ups, sit-ups, squats, star jumps, and butterfly kicks. By the time they had finished with him, he was lying on the floor in agony. They carried him out on a stretcher, and I never saw him again

During this time in cell three, separated from all other prisoners as a result of my disruptive behaviour, I was taken upstairs to interrogation several times. Almost a week after the water incident I was informed by a man called Gary that I was separated from the others because I'd incited them to hunger strike. I told him that the incident had happened almost seven days ago, and he replied that people were 'slow to respond, but eventually have'.

Shortly after that, Agent Ryan of the FBI, an Irish American from New York, questioned me along similar lines to his colleagues in Kandahar.

'All of you know that I haven't committed any crime, nor have I been involved in one. I have done nothing to harm any American at all, and you've shattered the lives of my family and me for nothing,' I said passionately.

I still believed in protesting my innocence, although no one had ever told me what crime I was supposed to have committed.

'What crime are you proposing to charge me with?' I asked.

'Support and facilitation of terrorism.'

'But how can my sending a few hundred pounds, during the early nineties, to Kashmiri freedom fighters, or visiting their training camp, be regarded as hostile intent towards the US? Tens of thousands of people have trained over the years in camps dotted around Afghanistan. Admittedly al-Qa'idah ran a few, but many others were entirely independent. In fact, the one I visited in 1993 became part of the anti-Taliban alliance. The Taliban shut it down when they took power, years before there were any hostilities with the US. If you were to add up the number of people who had donated money to these camps, and/or attended them, the figure would run into millions. Forget Guantánamo, the entire island of Cuba would not be large enough to accommodate us all.

'There is no reasonable court in the US, or the UK for that matter, that would attempt a prosecution on this basis. I was questioned in the UK about these very same things, and released because there was no crime. There was only perception and supposition.'

'After 9/11, Moazzam,' Agent Ryan came back, 'the rules changed. We have new laws, and according to them, you're already convicted. The US has done with fighting wars with its hands tied behind its back. Look at us now: we came right in their backyard. I'm not supposed to tell you this, but I like talking to you: a few days ago there was a firefight with some of your Taliban buddies. We sent 'em all to Allah, except the ones we caught, who you'll be seeing shortly.'

As I was returned to my cell I saw the guards gathering up many pairs of shackles. In my hitherto empty cell they had already laid down several sets of blankets. Soon enough the new prisoners were brought in, one by one. I walked over to a few of them, as a sort of welcoming gesture, along with my 'salaam'. At least their beards had been left alone, although their heads were shaved. By then it was evident, even to the Americans, that beard shaving was offensive to most detainees, particularly elderly Afghans, who were the majority in this new batch. In Pashto they are called the *spin girre*, the white hairs.

The next time I saw Agent Ryan I said, 'Congratulations. Seems like the remnants of the Afghans you despatched to Allah are part of the elite Taliban octogenarian and geriatric units.' Agent Ryan went red, but didn't respond. However, he said that someone new wanted to talk to me.

The man called himself Mark. He was in civilian clothes, short hair, clean shaven, probably not very much older than me. He was left alone with me in the interrogation room. I knew that was unusual, and I wondered what was coming. He said he was with the CIA, and had previously been stationed in Syria. Now he was here to ask me if I was willing to work for them. In Kandahar, the FBI agents, Koh and Bill, had also asked me to work for them: 'turn state's evidence', enter 'a plea bargain' and a 'witness-protection programme'. It sounded like a Hollywood movie.

'We'll even have your family sent over to the US; your kids put in a Muslim school,' one had said.

'And you'll buy me a Lamborghini too, right?'

'No,' came the answer, 'a Yugo.'

But, prestigious-car requests aside, they were deadly serious.

And now, here again was a man from the world's best-known intelligence agency asking me to sell my life and soul in order to see my family again.

'You're an intelligent, well-educated man, fluent in several languages, physically fit, well travelled and connected with the types of people we're interested in. If we had someone like you working for us we could have infiltrated al-Qa'idah and pre-empted any attacks,' he said.

'I thought you already *did* have plenty of people working for you. It must have somehow been in your interest not to hinder a strike against your own country. I find it hard to believe that the great CIA was incapable of penetrating al-Qa'idah, with the resources of the world's largest economy at your fingertips, with your operatives everywhere – and even a former head who had once been the most powerful man on earth.'

'I've heard these conspiracy theories, and I'm not here to discuss them with you. Here's my offer: you work for us and we can move mountains for you. I might be the agent assigned to you, or that might change over the years. We would meet sporadically and you'd report on all those people and events that we'd assign to you. Your family and you would be taken care of for life. We look after our people, Moazzam, because if word got round that we fucked our own contacts, nobody'd get on board. We could arrange for your escape and have it printed in the papers. For sure al-Qa'idah would try and contact you just to use the escape as propaganda, and ask about their men held by us. But let me tell you this as plain as I can: if you run, there isn't a corner of the earth where we couldn't find you. We know where your family are and I would make it my mission in life to track you down, with the gloves off. Now, you've got something to think about, until I see you next.'

The thoughts darted around in my head, 'Is this my chance to get out? Should I take this opportunity, and then run? But where could I run to? Britain, Pakistan, Iran, North Korea, Cuba . . . ? If I make it to England, surely they won't turn me over to the Americans? Britain values its own status and laws too much to do that, surely? But there are new laws now, and who knows what they entail. They were already investigating me before I left, and all this has just added fuel to the fire. Maybe I could hide with family in Pakistan? No, I can't get them involved. The two-faced, hypocrite "Paki" government would just as easily sell their own mothers, as my family – as they did me. But I don't know anybody or anywhere else . . . What if I actually agreed? What if I really worked for the CIA? They would definitely take me on. He *had* said, "You're intelligent, well educated, fluent in several languages, fit, perceptive, observant . . ." Can I sell my life in the hereafter? The same life that prompted me to begin this journey in the first place? How would I ever look my family, and society, in the face? What about those tenets that I live by, perseverance, self-control, and the indomitable spirit? I've done nothing wrong, hurt no one, killed or attempted to kill no one, planned to kill no one, so I have to believe that justice will prevail. This can't go on for ever! But what about Zaynab, and the kids? Perhaps I'd be a stranger to them, if ever I'm released by these inhuman . . .'

I told myself, 'This is it, your own personal trial, your test of faith. Pass it and you're free. Fail and you lose everything: family, honour, dignity, self-respect and your afterlife.'

'Wherever you are, death shall meet you . . .' says the Quran, which I read every day. Its message is that life is temporal and what you do in this world prepares you for the next. The verses from the Quran that resonated most came from the chapter al-Mumtahinah (the Test), and I felt they were directed right at me.

'O you who believe, do not take My enemy and your enemy for friends: would you offer them friendship while they deny what has come to you of the truth . . . And I know what you conceal and what you manifest . . .

'If they find you, they will be your enemies . . . and they ardently desire that you may disbelieve. Your relationships would not profit you, nor your children on the day of resurrection . . .' My head was reeling and throbbing with my thoughts.

I was taken back to my cell with this internal argument raging inside. I had not replied to the CIA offer. I never saw Mark again, nor heard any more of his proposition. I thought it over, and wondered if it was just a ploy to see if I'd jump at the chance or if I'd refuse. I guessed he probably wasn't expecting me to reply. The next time I spoke to someone from the Agency the options had changed.

*

One of the confusing things in Bagram was trying to distinguish all the people in civilian clothes, and work out who ultimately ran the show. It was obviously a military facility, with all these MPs in uniform guarding us. But it seemed they were working for the interrogators, who came from various agencies. Most of them were in civilian clothes. The military interrogators (MI) also had the option of wearing civvies, but they were easily distinguished from the others, usually a lot younger and often wearing their military-issue desert combat trousers or boots, with a Gerber multi-purpose knife attached to their belts.

I could see that a prisoner was treated by all of them as well or as badly as his interrogators regarded him.

In May, I met interrogators from the FBI and CIA, who didn't like me at all. Two FBI agents began the questioning, convinced I was involved in some complex nefarious web of plots: from planning to assassinate the Pope to masterminding al-Qa'idah's finance operation in Europe, or being an instructor in one of its Afghan training camps. They had their perceptions about me, and were searching for ways to confirm them – preferably from my own mouth.

By now I'd been raised to the status of some rogue James Bond-type figure. They thought I was a graduate from some prestigious British university, that I was fluent in a dozen languages, that I was an expert in computers, and several martial arts.

'Had it not been for this ludicrous situation I'm in, I would have been flattered by your assumptions,' I once said to them. 'I should ask you to write my résumé – I'd find a job anywhere.'

It would have been funny if it hadn't been so terrifying, being in the power of these people who actually believed their own fantasies. Part of it came out of their examination of my laptop, which they had taken away from the house in Islamabad. They produced various pictures from files they had undeleted and printed.

'What do these pictures mean? Why have you got these pictures on your computer?'

At the time I was utterly confused and just couldn't think. 'Where *did* they come from? Why would I have these images on my hard drive?'

But when I was calm enough to think it over, I realized that no one has any idea of every single image stored on their computer. If any of the interrogators had had any basic knowledge of computers, they would have realized that the folder 'Temporary Internet Files' stores all images clicked on or that have appeared on any website visited, so that it doesn't take as long to load up next time. 'Disk cleanup' automatically deletes unnecessary files from the Temporary Internet Folder.

They presented me with some pictures. They included a camel spider, BBC correspondent Kate Clark, and the Pope. 'These deleted pictures were recovered from your hard drive, but we undeleted them. Now tell us what you were up to, why did you have pictures of the Pope?'

One of them, Major Idiot, as I called him to myself, said, 'If anything happens to the Pope, and I find out that you were involved, I swear I'll break every finger in your hands. I'm a Catholic too.'

It was just too ridiculous to take seriously, so I said, 'Well, bully for you, mate.' They really didn't like me taking it as a joke and they were getting ready to take it out on me.

Then they started asking me about my finances. 'Fifty thousand pounds sent from an account in Jersey to your wife's account in Britain. What was that for?'

'A house. My in-laws gave us money for a house when we first got married. Just go and check it out.'

'Are you sure this money wasn't sent to Afghanistan?'

I just didn't know how to answer such absurd questions. Everything about our house transaction was on the record. And didn't they know that Afghanistan didn't have a banking system? There were no banks you could transfer £50,000 to.

Then they asked if I had been an instructor in one of the Afghan camps. They claimed some detainee had said, 'My instructor in the al-Faruk training camp was a Pakistani called Abu Umamah' (Abu means father in Arabic, and Umamah is my older daughter's name). They insisted that in a sworn statement from a ranking member of al-Qa'idah, I had been identified as an instructor in al-Faruk.

It was a whole year later, in Guantánamo, that I discovered the truth behind this accusation. It was frightening, knowing they were playing with my life, basing their evidence on such poor intelligence. I hadn't read Kafka, but I knew the expression Kafkaesque. It was happening to me.

The CIA agent, introduced to me as Martin, simply sat there, staring at me. He had deep burning blue eyes, which seemed to want to pierce my mind. It was a classical interrogation scenario that could have been a movie. But it was me. There was a floodlight pointing down right into my face. The two FBI agents were sitting either side of Martin, who held an M16 against the table. Two others, Major Idiot and someone called Alex, sat behind me.

'Tell us what you were planning, Moazzam,' said Niel, one of the FBI men.

'To translate classical Arabic texts into English . . .'

'No, not that,' shouted Marti, the other FBI agent. 'You know what we're talking about, just admit it. Were you planning a suicide operation? Were you planning gas attacks? Were you planning to assassinate . . . ?'

'What the hell are you talking about? I think you've seen too many movies . . .'

A voice from behind, Alex, said, 'Were you fighting on the front lines against American and British forces?'

I turned around and said, 'Wait, just a minute. Just because I told you I visited—'

'I'm getting tired of this shit,' yelled Niel, which made me turn back around.

'Do you want to see your children again?' Marti said, producing a printout from his folder. It was a picture of Umamah when she was two years old, with another child. 'Because it doesn't seem like you care very much about your family. You're being very selfish. Think of what would happen to them without you – your children, your wife . . .'

'Stop it! Just stop it! Leave my family out of it. I've done nothing to hurt anyone; no American has been harmed from anything that I have ever done. And I haven't planned anything either.'

My heart was breaking thinking about my daughter, and I was full of sorrow and anger, afraid of the future. I wanted to die. I wanted them to die. What right had they to desecrate the memory of my wife and children? These bastards had destroyed those innocent lives.

Suddenly one of them pulled the chair away from me so I had to stand. 'Get up off your ass. You've lost the dignity of deserving to sit on a chair when you're talking to us,' said the Major.

Then others all walked out, leaving me with Martin, the CIA agent. He was still staring at me. It must have been several minutes before he spoke.

'Moazzam Begg,' he said, raising his hand in a fist, putting out his thumb, and then turning it upside down – the 'let him die' gesture of a caesar. I felt seriously worried and scared to the core, just from the atmosphere.

Then he said, 'I've decided to send you to Cairo, where you *will* talk.' He told me that Ibn as-Shaykh al-Libee,* who was supposedly the highest-ranking member of al-Qa'idah in US custody, had been sitting just where I was, a few weeks before. 'He played the same games with us as you did, and we sent him to Cairo. He talked there within two hours. You'll do the same.'

I'd seen on the news, what seemed like years ago, in another life, that the Americans had caught Ibn as-Shaykh, who they announced as their biggest catch in the 'War on Terror'. I did not know him, but I had met detainees in Kandahar, who had been in the camps, who said that he was not a member of al-Qa'idah.

After that first heavy interrogation they took me into another room and left me there. Guards tied my hands behind my back, hog-tied me so that my hands were shackled to my legs, which were also shackled. Then they put a hood over my head. It was stuffy and hard to breathe, and I was on the verge of asthmatic panic. The perpetual darkness was frightening. A barrage of kicks to my head and back followed. Lying on the ground, with my back arched, and my wrists and ankles chafing against the metal chains, was excruciating. I could never wriggle into a more comfortable position, even for a moment. There was a thin carpet on the concrete floor, and a little shawl for warmth – both completely inadequate. I lost track of day or night, because not only was I usually in the hood, but even when they took it off for me to eat the window was boarded up and although there were little gaps, I couldn't tell if it was natural light. Eventually, some-

---

*The CIA extracted a statement from Libee that Saddam Hussain had trained al-Qa'idah in the use of WMD. This information was used in the justification for the US invasion of Iraq. In 2004 Libee retracted his statement, which was made under torture. *Brigadier General David R. Irvine. Alternet, November 2005.*

one came in and removed the hood and readjusted the shackles to be in front of me.

I was there in isolation for about a month or so. Once they kept me from sleeping for about two days and nights. A guard kept coming in, and if I nodded off, he woke me. By the end of that I was completely drained and disorientated. I never knew what was going to happen. Sometimes they did take me to an outside toilet – used by the military, as there wasn't one upstairs. But even then I was hooded, and the hood only came off when I was in the latrine area. There on the wall, in big black letters, were the words, 'Fuck Islam'.

For days on end I was alone in the room, and then they came for me and went over and over exactly the same ground: the camps, my role in training, my role in al-Qa'idah, my role in financing 9/11. Sometimes it was the CIA, sometimes the FBI; sometimes I didn't even know who they were. All of them wanted a story that didn't exist.

There are no words to describe what I felt like. I don't even want to remember it.

I was surprised to see Nathan, the interrogator from military intelligence, when he came in.

'You're all tied up, what happened?' he asked.

'They are threatening to send me to Egypt to be tortured.'

'You know, that shit really does happen, Moazzam.'

Oddly enough we two had enough of a rapport so that I did trust him a little. Nathan was quite young, and we'd had a lot of conversations about many things, back in Kandahar. We'd talked about films, history, in particular the Spartans, and Julius Caesar's campaigns, and the Arab–Israeli conflict. He talked about his experiences as a mixed-race child growing up in an all-white Texas neighbourhood. Things that he'd told me about before had always happened. That day he told me about something that absolutely chilled me, and that I would never forget.

'There was a case of a person who was picked up in America, and sent to Syria where he was tortured.* Of course, we [Americans] don't take part in anything that takes place there, we're simply observers.'

I believed it.

I thought Nathan was trying to be truthful, but he was a low-ranking soldier who wanted to impress the big shots from the CIA, so there was some point in trying to scare me further, in the hope that I would reveal something.

CIA Martin, was, apart from MI5 Andrew, the only interrogator I ever met who struck me as intelligent and knowledgeable. He was very well informed, he spoke Arabic fluently, he knew about Islamic history, he knew about the region, he knew about the differences between various communities in Arabic countries. But, unlike Andrew, he was also quite menacing. His threats were often unspoken. Martin was the real deal, and all the other interrogators, FBI agents, and so on, were a joke in comparison.

Martin came and sat down in my cell. He gave me his piercing stare and said, 'I have decided not to send you to Egypt. We checked your story about the computer and it made sense.' To be fair to him, it seemed to be his decision, as the FBI were not satisfied at all. They really had no idea about computers. Once they brought in a computer-generated picture of someone for me to look at, which was quite blurred. When I said, 'This picture is not clear, it's pixelated,' Major Idiot said, 'I wouldn't have known that term. You're obviously very well informed about these things.'

'It's not that I'm knowledgeable, Major, it's that – if you'll forgive me – you're not. My seven-year-old daughter knows what pixels are,

---

* Abdullah al-Malki: see Epilogue.

like most primary-school children where I come from.' I really wanted to ram home the point that their computer ignorance had nearly sent me to Egypt to be tortured.

'Do you know this man?' Alex asked shoving a computer-generated printout in front of me.

'Is that Ibn al-Khattab?' I asked astonished. It was a picture of what appeared to be his corpse, and some words in Russian. Were the Americans in Chechnya now?

'Yes it is. Your buddies are dropping like flies.'

'From Allah we came, and to Him we return,' I whispered – the Quranic response to death. 'I've never met him – but he was a hero in the Muslim world. What have you got against him? Has he done something against the Americans?'

'Didn't get a chance. I admit I don't know much about him – but I know he was a terrorist.'

'Well, *I know* that the Russians call him that, but he was a mujahideen leader who only ever attacked military targets. The people of Chechnya love him . . . Do you speak Russian?'

Alex took back the paper.

I later learned that Khattab had died of poisoning, and that it had nothing to do with the Americans.

For a while, my interrogations seemed less crude and cruel. They were offering me deals again, including a witness-protection programme to testify against anybody and everybody that they wanted. In return I would be free in some sort of environment for my family to visit me, perhaps in America, or somewhere else, at a hidden location, but under house arrest. Surely, I told them, there had to be a crime that I had witnessed or took part in, something tangible that they were accusing me of. 'You can't just tell me that "We want you to be a witness against everybody."'

'You will eventually be sent to Guantánamo, and you will be held there indefinitely, and you will never see your family again,' they threatened. In the same breath, waving a phone in front of me, Marti said, 'You are only a phone call away. This is a satellite phone, and it can call anywhere in the world. You just have to agree with us if you want them to speak to them and see them again.' But the offer was a mirage. Things got worse.

I began to hear the chilling screams of a woman next door. My mind battled with asking questions I was too afraid to learn the answer to. 'What if it was . . . my wife?' They clearly registered the look on my face. I was sure that in all their reports they had written, 'Get to this guy through his family . . .'

I was always asking about my family. I was looking for somebody among them who would have a little bit of human compassion. I prayed that someone would say, 'OK, we can do anything to this guy, but let's at least give him the solace of knowing that his family is OK.' But none of them did.

For two days and nights I heard the sound of the screaming. I felt my mind collapsing, and contradictory thoughts ran through it.

Once I thought, when the screams started up, 'I am just going to slip my wrists out of the shackles, hit the guard, grab the weapon off him, and go next door to stop what is happening.' But my other thought was, 'Just give them whatever they want.'

I began to think that the only thing I could do to end this misery and terror was to pretend to admit being involved in some terrorist plot. But it would have to sound reasonable. Of course I could probably have told them anything. I toyed with the idea of telling them that I planned to get a donkey laden with explosives and send it to a market frequented by Americans. A 'suicide-donkey' mission. But before I invented a story, they changed their minds.

Eventually I did agree to say whatever they wanted me to say, to do whatever they wanted me to do. I had to finish it. Stories about bomb-laden donkeys wouldn't do. I agreed to be their witness to whatever.

At the end of it all, I asked them, 'Why have you got a woman next door?' They told me there was no woman next door. But I was unconvinced.

Those screams echoed through my worst nightmares for a long time. And I later learned, in Guantánamo, from other prisoners, that they had heard the screams too and believed it was my wife. They had been praying for her deliverance.

My thoughts at that time were not just about my wife, but about the family too. What had happened to my children? Where were they? Knowing these men as I did now, I couldn't put it past them to torture women, or even children, to get the answers they wanted from men. In their own minds they were completely justified in doing things like that for the bigger picture – 'saving innocent American lives', as they so often put it, as if no other lives were innocent in this world, or worth saving.

The memory of those screams was even worse than the physical humiliation. It was worse than being kept naked, even worse than the beatings. I tried to forget all those assaults, as my body healed. I imagined that the interrogators were patting themselves on their backs for their psychological techniques. 'We didn't really beat him up that bad; we didn't really hurt him.'

8

DEVIL'S AGENTS

When I was brought down to the cells again I was with a new group of people, mostly Arabs. They had been captured in various places, and came from Mauritania, Libya, Egypt, Algeria, Yemen, Sudan; there was even one from Russia. The one I got closest to was a large, polite Sudanese called Ameer. I was right next to him in the cell. When we spoke, wary of the guards, he told me that he was captured in Pakistan, where he had come to assist the Afghans after the US invasion. He felt they needed all the help they could get. I briefly met another British man,* who came in with Ameer but was only in my cell for two nights, so I never got to speak to him very much.

I got to know Ameer as he told me about his interrogations. Nathan had been questioning him. Often Ameer asked me, 'What should I do? Should I tell them why I came?'

'You know, in any normal situation I would say the truth is always the best option. It always is. But in this situation you don't know what is going to happen, what their reaction will be. So I don't know what to tell you. Here, they'll use the truth against you, though not in a court. We'll probably never be given the chance to argue our case.'

---

* Jamal Kiyemba: at the time of writing, he is still held in Guantánamo, and is expected to return to Uganda.

Ameer told them the truth anyway. He was sent to Guantánamo. I was still in Bagram.

Another man I spoke to frequently was a Libyan who had lost his leg in a minefield during Gaddafi's war with Chad. He had a particularly difficult time, because, initially, the Americans took his artificial leg away so he had to walk around on his knees. And when it was time to change our empty water bottles, the MPs would not let one person take water for the whole cell. Each man had to come up to the airlock to exchange his own water bottle. One of us would always stand up and try to get the Libyan's water bottle for him, but they told him to come over himself. He was an amazingly resilient man. Eventually he got his prosthetic leg back. Then he was sent to Guantánamo.

I couldn't believe my eyes one day, when I saw my local shopkeeper step into the cell. The last time I saw Deen Muhammad I was buying groceries from him in Kabul, just before the evacuation.

Deen told me he'd been captured and sold over in Pakistan as an al-Qa'idah sympathizer, because many of his customers were foreigners. Many people I met in custody believed they had been sold in the same way. Several interrogators later confirmed to me that this was common practice. Deen was very upset and often in tears when he told me about his young family. How would they manage without him? They were all refugees from the war.

When I first arrived in Bagram I was given a copy of the Quran – just like everyone else. When the group of prisoners that Deen arrived with asked for theirs, some of the guards began playing games.

'Extra, extra! Come get your Quran – your holiest of holy books. Learn how to kill Americans . . .' Instead of handing it to Deen, the MP threw the Quran down in the airlock. There was uproar – people were screaming at the guards. I felt so powerless. These soldiers had no idea of what it was they were insulting. Muslims believe the Quran is the revealed speech of God. I couldn't understand where this hatred had come from. I could certainly never imagine any of us doing the same with the Bible.

When I analysed it, though, it became clearer: to the soldier, the Quran was just a book – paper and ink. If in his mind he could justify our abuse as human beings, then what was a book?

I had a discussion with a guard once, a born-again Southern Baptist, who at times found the war at odds with his Christian beliefs. 'I convince myself each day that you guys are all subhuman – agents of the Devil, so that I can do my job. Otherwise I'd have to treat you like humans, and we don't do this to people where I come from.'

I had already negotiated with the guards to allow us at least an hour of exercise every day before lunch. I led the exercise in my cell and the adjacent one, where people could see me. The other cells were led by anyone with some experience. Richard Belmar was one. I started off with stretching and warming up, and then on to press-ups and sit-ups. It was a very rigorous workout to build up strength and speed. But I also included running and circuits. Exercise was the only thing I ever looked forward to – at that point.

The ICRC visits, just as in Kandahar, although sporadic, were a welcome break and an opportunity to write home. I wrote to Zaynab – not knowing if or when she'd got any of the letters I wrote from Kandahar – that I was getting fitter than I had been for quite a while, which must have surprised her. It gave me quite a sense of satisfaction that this was something I initiated, and which lasted until I left a year later. Exercise was a good distraction to set my mind on something else, and fight depression, even though it only lasted for an hour a day.

I needed every pastime I could invent for myself. People were being released regularly, although they were all Afghans. Even in that I managed to find some comedy.

A detainee would usually be told about his release a day or two or even just a few hours before. One of the Afghans in my cell was told he was going home – after almost two months in prison. These emotional times always left me with a tantalizing thought of release. The Afghan gathered his belongings and went to each detainee embracing us all and saying goodbye. Then he walked over to the airlock, where the guards shackled him and took him to the next cell and left him there. He wasn't going home after all, it seemed – they'd only moved him. The poor man looked dazed and confused. Almost everyone – detainees and guards – burst out laughing. It had all been a joke. He was going home, but I'd asked some of the friendlier guards if they'd tease him just a little before he left.

All non-Afghans were sent to Guantánamo. This was particularly difficult for me, since the friends I made were gone usually within two or three months, while I was left behind. Months had passed since the interrogations had ended, but I still didn't know what was planned for me.

When I thought about it, I wondered if the FBI had arranged for me to be sent to the US because I had agreed in principle to do whatever they wanted me to. I knew I would never in my life witness against someone about something that I had no idea of, but I did think that if I got to a court, then I could really speak the truth. A court would be a platform to expose the truth.

As time had passed, I had begun to build a rapport with some of the guards. Partly because, after a few months, I had already been there a relatively long time compared to the normal turnover, but also because I was useful, helping with translation, and taking care of the daily exercise.

Then, in July, Andrew from MI5 reappeared. Much of our talk was quite mundane and I wasn't even sure what he came for this time.

When he produced a list of names of the imams of mosques in Britain, I began to realize the magnitude of how Islam itself was being targeted. But I couldn't see the connection between me, in shackles here in Bagram, and some obscure mosque in West Yorkshire that I'd never heard of.

Andrew also wanted to go over and over my trips to Bosnia and the Afghan camps in the 1990s – round and round, always the same questions. He wasn't particularly interested in why I went to Afghanistan in 2001, although I kept telling him about the school, the well-drilling, the poverty . . .

I told him what had been done to me during the interrogations in May, emphasizing that the Americans had really intended to send me to Egypt to be tortured. I asked how he, and the British government, felt about what their top allies had done and were threatening to do. What would they do if it really happened? He said that MI5 would never deign to be involved in things like that. I said that surely any information gathered by the Americans via abuse and torture had been shared with the British. He didn't answer that. He just reiterated that Britain would never take part in rendition and torture.

'But it happened. It happened to me, Andrew. Most of their lines of questioning couldn't have been taken without your full knowledge and cooperation. That is undisputable. It was only because of that intelligence officer finally applying a little *intelligence* to their non-existent evidence of those computer photos that I didn't go to Egypt. It would have been easy for them to do it, very easy. I have no access to any legal representation; I have no consular access, even though there is a functioning British Embassy in Kabul.'

'How did you know about . . . ?'

'I heard it from one of the new detainees, just like I heard about Operation Anaconda and the Royal Marines' Ptarmigan Operation.'

'But I thought you weren't allowed to talk to . . .'

'We're not.'

I asked him if some agreement was reached between the British and the Americans, for Richard and me. 'Sometimes they say I'm going to a Pakistani prison. Then I'm told it's going to be Guantánamo or America. Nathan told me that Britain has officially requested the return of all British nationals.'

'Did he? I'm not aware of any formal requests like that. All I can tell you is that it's all in the hands of the Americans – they're calling the shots.'

'If President Bush decides that I never go back home again, that's completely acceptable to you?'

'If that's his decision we can nothing do about it. He's in charge.'

Andrew reiterated that my only option was to cooperate with the Americans. 'That's the only way you will ever see an end to this.'

Strangely enough, I rather liked Andrew, as a person. He was quite a contrast to most of the Americans I'd met. I liked the fact that he was cultured, and aware of regional customs and sensitivities. I once mentioned the film *Black Hawk Down* to him. He said, 'I'd never watch a biased propaganda film like that.' That quite amazed me.

'If we were sitting in a cafe,' he said, 'discussing political viewpoints, you'd be quite surprised at some of mine.' I tried to picture myself at some chic London coffee bar – with or without him.

Even his accent, compared to the Americans', was refreshingly familiar. The fact that he was British helped me maintain the illusion that MI5 was on my side. I kept reminding myself that he had said, 'I can be your mouthpiece to the British government.'

But I knew this was MI5, and its world was a very murky one. They could say and do whatever they wanted. They materialized and disappeared without notice, like ghosts – or spooks. Before he left Andrew said, 'I'm sure I'll see you again, Mr Begg. After all, I have been haunting you for the past four years.'

I began feeling more optimistic when I finally received the first letter from home. It was from my stepmother, and in it she said they were in contact with Zaynab, and soon she and the children would be back in Birmingham. Zaynab would have our baby there. That gave me some peace of mind, after all the horrible things I had imagined.

I told the others in my cell about what had happened with Andrew, and they were all optimistic, saying that perhaps it was a sign the British might be taking me back. Everyone noticed who was taken out for interrogation, and we were interested in analysing every detail – which direction they were heading, or how long they were out for. I saw the MPs take Richard too; I believed that we would probably share the same fate and really hoped there was something good happening for us Brits. But there wasn't. All this analysis and anticipation drove me mad. I was trying to decipher the psyche of something completely irrational: the US military in Afghanistan.

I used to watch carefully a whiteboard they had up opposite cell three. All the numbers of the detainees were written on it, in sequence. Different colours for the numbers denoted varying detainee status. Red meant ordinary conditions, green meant ill – usually tuberculosis – yellow meant special conditions, like sleep deprivation. Blue meant destined for Guantánamo.

In August I received a one-sentence message, which someone from ICRC read to me: 'Male child born on 28th June, mother and baby well.' He was, I later learned, named Ayub (Job in the Bible). Back in my cell, I told the others about the good news and made a prayer for my child and Zaynab. Then I covered myself with a blanket, feigning sleep, and wept.

Things had changed a lot since I first arrived, when there had only been about twenty prisoners. Now they had built isolation rooms, and the regime had changed so that every single person who was brought in was put on sleep deprivation. Later on they built other cells for sleep deprivation, constantly playing ear-splitting heavy metal tracks by Marilyn Manson to break down new detainees. Once they even played the Bee Gees' *Saturday Night Fever* soundtrack all night long. Hardly, I thought, enough to break anyone I knew.

I often found humour in the most unlikely places. It was one of my tools to counter the grim reality of life. Many of the soldiers, being from the South, liked listening to Country and Western music, which most detainees regarded the same as all other 'English' music. But I had the misfortune of knowing better.

'We'll talk, we'll all talk,' I said in half-jest when they played it, 'just turn that crap off, please.' At first, some MPs didn't know how to react to unexpected remarks like that, as I saw from the grim looks on their faces. But most were pleased to find someone on the other side who could humour them, as well as himself.

Sometimes though, the sheer ignorance was amazing. There was a big commotion once, as guards and interrogators gathered in front of the new detainee in the airlock of cell three. 'You Nazi scumbag,' one of them shouted at him. This Afghan villager had a swastika symbol tattooed on his forearm.

I called over one of the interrogators and said, 'Slow down for just a minute. Where do you think the Nazis got their symbol from?'

'Uh . . . I'm not sure. Hitler?'

'The symbol is over three thousand years old, and its origins are right here. The Aryans came from Central Asia.'

'Not the ones we have . . .'

I continued, 'The national Afghan airline is called Ariana; the word

Iran has the same root. Hindus and Buddhists use the swastika to this day as a symbol. I'm sure this man knows as much about Nazis as he does about Bonnie Prince Charlie . . .'

'Who?'

'Never mind. I really hope you don't think that there's a new conspiracy between the Taliban and the Aryan Brotherhood.'

He went up to the shouting guards, whispered something, and they all walked away from the 'Nazi'.

Some things got better over time. Our clothes were exchanged occasionally for one thing, and we had a proper shower – usually freezing cold – instead of just a bucket. But these communal showers were a problem for us all. It is humiliating for a Muslim to be naked in front of other people, and some of these men simply refused to enter the shower. They were shouted at, screamed at, and dragged in.

One evening a polite and cheerful Afghan, Abdur-Raheem, went into the shower with us, but the cold was too much for him and he dropped down and had to be taken to the hospital.

There was cheap soap and shampoo in there, and bundles of communal towels outside. We didn't need a comb most of the time, as our hair was usually shaved off every month. At least we had our own numbered toothbrushes. But to clean our teeth we had to enter the airlock from the cell one by one, and be handed a plastic tub with the brush and a toothpaste tube.

One afternoon in July I heard one of the guards yelling, 'What the hell do you think you're doing?' I heard a scuffle, and then some dull thuds, behind cell three. Then I saw Cody, the Irish American I knew from Kandahar, and another MP from North Carolina, dragging a limp body past our cell to the medical room. I could see bruises on the detainee's face, covered in dust, as they pulled him past my cell. They must have radioed for help, as all sorts of medics, doctors and officers, including the new female commander, Major Stuart, rushed into the medical room. Eventually the door opened, and guards carried out a stretcher, with only a man's feet visible.

The story was that this young Afghan had tried to escape. He had inched away the barbed wire beside the toilet at the back of the cell. Whenever we used the toilet we took a blanket and hung it up at either end of the surrounding concertina wire for privacy. This detainee had prepared the barbed wire so that he could push the barrel away and crawl through when the time was right and the guards on the wooden catwalk behind the cells were not around. Usually there were one or even two guards patrolling there, so he must have picked his time.

Later that evening, Cody came over with his arm in plaster, and started talking to me. I was already used to a lot of the guards feeling they could confide in me. But I could not believe it when he began telling me in detail about what he had done to that detainee. *He* had shouted, 'What the hell do you think you are doing?' Then, he told me, he jumped on the escaper straightaway. The other guard on overwatch saw it too, and jumped down from the opposite end. Cody told me he started hitting the detainee so hard that he felt he had fractured something. The other guard had used Thai-style elbow- and knee-strike techniques. I didn't know whether they knew they had killed him.

But I soon had the death confirmed from Warnick. After he let on to me that the man who tried to escape was dead, he realized he had made a mistake and confirmed everyone's fears. Later he tried to dismiss it, saying, 'Oh no, he didn't really die, the reason they covered his face was just to scare people. You know, "This is what happens if you try to escape."' But I didn't believe him. When the ICRC (Red Cross) came next, I was not the only detainee to report the death.* Another soldier, Damien, confirmed the death to me a few weeks later. 'That man was due to go home the following week – only no one told him.'

After the Arabs were sent Guantánamo I was left in the cell with just a few Afghans and I couldn't communicate with them too well. I was sad and quiet and spent my time making all kinds of lists on some small pieces of paper the guards gave me. I listed new PC games and speed-up Web connections. And I studied the French vocabulary lists, numbers, verb conjugations, and phrases, which a Mauritanian detainee had taught me. I also wrote a great many letters.

Red Cross visits sometimes meant a letter from home and a chance to send off the numerous letters I had previously written, on different days, but all with the same date. It was sometimes hard to write because nothing changed for me, and time dragged so slowly. I got more depressed when I heard from Zaynab that she was very upset, and I often deliberately did not tell her how low I felt. I once told her too, 'I don't know anyone else who has stayed here so long.'

Sometimes I wrote just brief reassuring messages home, and other times I wrote, trying to share the children's lives in whatever way I could. I wrote to Zaynab asking her to start our lawyer working on getting back the money the Americans had taken from our house in Islamabad.

I couldn't really understand the relations between the ICRC and the Americans. I thought at first that they were closely involved, but then I discovered that the Americans didn't like them and thought they were interfering. I stopped handing my ICRC letters to the Americans

---

* It was accepted by the Americans that several deaths occurred in Bagram. Both in Guantánamo and after my release I was interviewed by the FBI and other US agencies about this killing, as well as the one I witnessed a few months later. Seven US servicemen have been charged in relation to the two deaths in 2002.

as I thought they did not pass them on. I got extremely frustrated by not knowing what would arrive and when – in both directions. I wrote numerous letters from Bagram, but only ever received a handful.

I soon made two very good new friends. One was Sharif, a young Afghan who had lost an eye a long while back in a factory accident, and who spoke fluent Arabic, very good Urdu, and some Uzbek and English. The second was a Russian, Saeed. I liked them both particularly because they awaited the daily physical exercise routine as eagerly as I did, and they were rather practised. Sharif had done martial arts in Pakistan's refugee camps, where he grew up. Saeed had been a lieutenant in the Russian army.

Sharif knew a great deal about Afghanistan and its politics, and I was not the only one who liked to ask him about that. The interrogators were very keen on talking to him, and often called him out. He told me that his father had been executed by the Russians, buried alive with other political prisoners near the centre of Kabul in the Pul-e-Charkhi prison.* He told me about his arranged marriage, and that he'd never seen his wife until the wedding night. He was adamant that his mother's choice was fine for him. He was very traditional in how to lead his life, but quite modern too. He really disliked the Americans being in Afghanistan, and saw them as the same as the occupiers who had killed his father. But on a personal level he was warm to them and talked to them very reasonably, trying to explain to them that what they were doing to his country was totally wrong. During the Taliban time he had run an unlicensed school (like ours) for women, teaching them English, and accepting the risk that went with that. I liked Sharif's complexity. No stereotype fitted him. He had a sense of humour, finding comedy in things that most of his countrymen did not.

---

* The *Financial Times* has reported that the US is planning to build a high security prison here.

My grandfather, Abdus-Sattar Begg, in the 1920s (right) and his brothers, Mahmud Begg (centre) who was killed fighting Pashtun tribesman during the British Raj, and Ghaus Begg (left).

My brother, Azam, and me with my father and stepmother, shortly after they were married.

Flying kick: I'm practising one of the many aerial kicking techniques taught in Tae Kwon Do.

The Lynx: standing (left to right) are Budda (died 1998), Corruption, Bones, Marky, Arif, Chico, Boot, Mo, Wayney and Olly. The second row is (left to right): me, Khan, Enzyme, Sigi (died 1990) and Sam (died 2005).

I'm on one of the mountains surrounding the Al-Fajr camp close to the Pakistan border (1993).

Outside the Convoy of Mercy Aid Distribution Centre in the Bosnian village of Ostražac, near Jablanica (1994).

My children, Abdur-Rahman, Umamah and baby Nusaybah, shortly before my trip to Turkey.

على نفقة ال
عبدالرحمن ابو ثا بت

Hand-pump well installed near the city of Herat during the drought in 2000.
This one was in the name of my son, Abdur-Rahman.

US Air Force B-52s conduct carpet-bombing on frontline Taliban positions northwest of the Afghan capital, Kabul, 31 October 2001.

Hooded and shackled detainees are transported by US forces.

Guantánamo
prison.

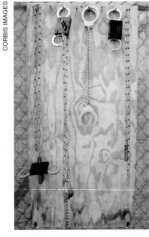

Leg irons and
handcuffs used to
restrain detainees at
Camp Delta.

A US soldier stands
outside a maximum
security isolation cell in
Camp Echo, where I was
kept for twenty months.

Entrance and check point leading to main cellblock in Camp Delta.

My father and Terry Waite campaign for my release in front of the US Supreme Court, Washington (2004). Corin Redgrave is standing behind my father.

Former detainees and their relatives at the Amnesty/Reprieve Conference, November 2005. Standing (left to right) are: Tahir Abou Khalide, cousin of Mohamed C. (Chad); Mohammed Sagheer (Pakistan); Rustam Akhmiarov (Russia); Martin Mubanga (UK); Jamal al-Harith (UK); me; Abdullah, brother of Adel Hajee (Bahrain); Airat Vakhitov (Russia). Seated (left to right) are: Rabiye Kurnaz, mother of Murat Kurnaz (Turkey/Germany); Nadja Dizdarevic, wife of El Hadj Boudella (Bosnia); Fatimah Tekaeva, mother of Rasul Kudayev (Russia).

The Begg family are reunited: Zaynab, Umamah, Abdur-Rahman, Nusaybah, Ayub and me (2006).

A new batch of senior citizens was brought in around then. One of them was so old he said that he'd lost count of his years, but the MPs said he was in his nineties. This man's back was grotesquely stooped and he could only walk by shuffling a few steps at a time. When I asked the guards for his hearing aid, they refused to give it, saying it was a potential security hazard. We were all sickened to the core – including some MPs. 'I didn't come here for this shit,' Cody, of all people, said. He told me he had even refused to process the old man.

Apart from the three of us – Sharif, Saeed and me – everyone else in our cell, then, was old enough to draw his pension.

But one day, a young Afghan boy, Shams, was brought in to our cell. He was only fifteen. The guards just deposited him and his stretcher down in a corner. Shams had been shot in his upper thigh, and the bone was shattered so he couldn't walk. He couldn't make it to the toilet, he couldn't get his own medications, or his water, or his food. And he couldn't wash, so he started smelling quite badly. Sharif and I were given the task of helping him, but after a while Sharif was moved out of my cell. I ended up not only helping Shams, but also teaching him how to walk again. I taught him all the different types of leg-strengthening exercises I could think of. Sometimes I got annoyed and shouted at him because I thought he was being too soft. I wanted to shock him into making the effort to walk. Eventually he did, but it took several months. He used to put his arm around my shoulder, and we would walk slowly around, in the cell. It gave me a very good opportunity to walk around myself.

Shams told me the story of his wounds: US helicopters had descended one night and attacked his house during a sweep of the area. He fired his uncle's weapon at them. They fired back. He was hit, and captured – with his uncle.

Every now and then the Americans brought someone into our cells who aroused suspicions amongst the detainees. There had been at least two who had previously been in my cell, going around unhindered, asking the oddest questions, and offering help after release. Sharif was good at spotting the Afghan ones. One of these men may or may not have been a plant by the Americans, but I had a bad feeling about him. He claimed he was the victim of tribal feuding, and ironically part of a pro-Karzai militia*, sold over to the Americans for a fee. Sharif told me this man liked sleeping with young boys, and I was appalled.

There was a strange incident involving this man and a young woman soldier. I knew that particular soldier was a lesbian, as she had joined in a conversation I had had with Nathan once, about difficulties years back with girlfriends. 'Ain't that the truth,' she said, 'I get the same shit with my woman.' She had really short hair and looked like a handsome boy. One day she came to exchange this Afghan's water bottle, and he grabbed her hands attempting to stroke and kiss them. She in turn grabbed his hands, pulled at him through the cage, screaming and shouting, until all the other guards converged, opened the cell, dragged him out, took him away, beat the crap out of him, and then brought him back.

Sharif saw all this, and he insisted that the Afghan did not believe that she was a girl, and that if he had known he wouldn't have approached her.

Warnick told me about an al-Qa'idah operative they had captured. He told me this was a really dangerous, vindictive, highly trained terrorist, who had attacked a convoy of American soldiers that happened to be driving along minding their own business and helping people. This terrorist had taken a grenade and thrown it at the convoy and

---

* Hamid Karzai became president of Afghanistan following the downfall of the Taliban.

killed a soldier. Warnick said that he had been given the task of guarding him on a rota of shifts. The detainee had been really badly wounded, he said, his chest was pitted with buckshot and he had lost an eye.

The boy's name was Omar. He was a fifteen-year-old Canadian, and I spent a few weeks in cell two with him. The medics came to see him every day to give him eye drops and check on his wounds. He had been stitched up and I could see the extent of the huge wound across his chest. Of all the detainees I met, my heart bled for him more than any other, because he was not only so young, but also he was one of the softest characters I have ever met. I just could not see him being the type of malicious kid running around with grenades to throw at unsuspecting American soldiers that Warnick claimed he was.

Omar told me an entirely different story. He said he had lived with his family in Afghanistan for many years. When evacuations began he was left behind, with some others, and ended up in the house of an old man, Baba, also in custody. Americans raided the house with helicopters and killed everybody in it, apart from Omar, and Baba, who was shot in the leg. A Special Forces unit came in for a clean-up operation, shooting at the bodies on the ground. Omar was on the ground too, but terribly wounded. One US soldier died, and his comrades blasted Omar with a shotgun. Then Omar was brought to the army hospital in Bagram, where the MPs, with typical US military tackiness, gave him the epithet, 'Buckshot Bob'.

Omar was treated terribly badly in revenge for the death of that soldier. The guards often screamed at him and pushed him around. When the 511th left, the new guards, as always, came in pretty gung-ho, convinced that we all deserved to be there. They often took Omar out of his cell and made him work like a horse. They made him carry barrels of water, fill the water bottles up, carry boxes of food. They called him a murderer.

Omar had many difficulties to bear.* One of them was that his brother had been captured in Kabul by the Northern Alliance earlier, and had actually agreed to work for the CIA after the Americans sent him to Guantánamo. The Americans took him to work in various places like Bosnia and the Middle East, before he eventually gave up, and told his whole story to a newspaper.

Later on in Bagram there were at least some Americans who recognized what Omar was really like, and that he was a minor who should have had better treatment. I told one of the interrogators that the new group of guards was treating him really badly, and he eventually spoke to the sergeant of the guard.

There was a lot of rumour-mongering, and scare tactics by guards and interrogators then, telling people they were going to Guantánamo. I soon saw there were no fixed criteria. Everything was up to the interrogator. He or she made a recommendation, and the chance of that recommendation being accepted was almost 100 per cent.

In my case I knew they had run out of questions at the end of May, but they still kept me in that limbo for months. This was a whole period, a block of time, which was very, very long. Reflecting on it is quite upsetting for me.

By the time the 511th left I was usually coming out of my cell most evenings to help with meals. Doing this gave me a little bit of autonomy. I made many suggestions to the new MP unit of how we should reorganize the procedure. Tons of food were being thrown away every week – and yet we went to sleep hungry every night. I even asked the lieutenant to donate the food to the local children, rather than throw

---

* Two years later word came across the blocks in Guantánamo that Omar's father had been killed in a shoot-out in northern Pakistan. Omar was designated for trial by military commission in December 2005.

it away. Eventually, some officer saw reason and the food was finally given to us – minus all potentially lethal contents, like black pepper or water-activated phosphorus heaters. This was another major achievement for me: I'd successfully negotiated extra sunflower seeds and peanuts.

Sharif, Saeed, and I were the three usually taken out for this job. Occasionally Omar was with us too. We sat down on chairs outside the cells, in long hand- and leg-shackles that allowed us more movement. The guards sat in front of us, and we all talked together, as though we were friends. Most allowed us to eat whatever we wanted from the packs, and even to use the heaters to warm them up. At the end we took the food packets and placed them outside the cells, ready for the next day.

Sharif was soon released, and then it was usually just me and Saeed sorting the packs. But one day in October, I noticed something on the whiteboard. Saeed, Shams, Omar, Richard Belmar, Jamal Kiyemba, and others had their number colours changed – to blue.

After this group was sent to Guantánamo, I was often reluctant to prepare meals. But that changed when I met the soldier who left the most lasting impression on me in Bagram. Stephanie was a labour-relations student from Ohio in her early twenties, and one of the more cultured soldiers who I met. She was almost the only soldier who took part in meal preparation with us, as opposed to the ones who just sat and watched. During that time I discovered that she loved English literature and poetry. We discussed Thoreau's *Walden*, which I had recently read, and *Mere Christianity* by C. S. Lewis, which had been sent to her by her sister. I talked to her about Islam, and even wrote a few sheets comparing the history and beliefs of the two religions.

When I finally received a photograph of my children, I showed it to her. Her instant response was, 'I've got something I think you'll like.'

She brought over some writing paper, with a pretty floral design, for me to write to the children on. I even asked her to check some sentences I'd written to my wife in French, when I discovered that Stephanie was fluent.

During meal-preparation times, we often talked about life in America, Britain, and Afghanistan. Stephanie was someone I believed genuinely wanted to help the people of Afghanistan – not imprison and kill them. 'I'm not like these people at all,' she said once, referring to her colleagues. And she wasn't.

There was a rumour that detainee 'one-eight-zero', the small British guy, was a trained assassin, paid tens of thousands of dollars a kill.

'Do you mind if I ask you a question?' Stephanie once asked me.

'Not at all.'

'Is it true you're an assassin?'

'And what if I was?'

'Oh, nothing. It's pretty cool, actually. I've never met an assassin before.'

I didn't know whether to be flattered or to take offence, but I decided, in the end, it was a bizarre compliment. 'Neither have I.'

Stephanie was a young, impressionable, almost naive Army Reservist. We enjoyed talking to one another. But some guards noticed that she was talking a little too much to the detainees for their liking. That bothered her a little, but she told me, 'I just can't be like these guys. I have a different outlook on life from most of them, even though I love the guys in my unit.'

I wrote to my family about all kinds of things, including the insects, which infested the place during the summer, especially camel spiders, which I had actually researched on the Internet even before we went to Kabul. One of the images I was interrogated about on my laptop, back in May, was of a camel spider. Still a bit of a schoolteacher, despite the circumstances, I wrote carefully, '. . . the camel spider is the only ten legged spider in the world, and, I believe, not an arachnid (technically not a spider). But it grows to bigger than the human hand-size, moves like a race car and has a bite that causes flesh to decay . . .' I spent many sleepless nights because of those spiders, especially after I had seen a couple of detainees who were bitten by them. Their flesh decayed and started going black. Sometimes, when the guards felt like sadistic fun, they caught camel spiders, put them in a bucket with a scorpion, and watched them fight. Once I saw a guard who had one in a box throw it at the old man, Baba, in the airlock.

I wrote letters sometimes just to poke fun at the Americans, not really expecting them to be cleared. One of them, to my dad, said, '. . . I had a discussion recently with someone about the US's major contribution to civilization (after talking about Ancient Greece, Egypt, Mesopotamia, India, China etc.). I pondered for many hours and then came up with the answer – peanut butter (both smooth and crunchy). My co-debater was not amused . . .'

Evans, a young, black art-history student from Indianapolis, was interested in English literature, as well as black literature, which aroused my curiosity. I always talked to guards about the books they read, and Evans certainly had plenty. We discussed the works and varying philosophies of Booker T. Washington and W. E. B. Dubois, and Martin Luther King and Malcolm X. In my teens I had a particular liking for R&B, reggae, and hip-hop – which surprised Evans.

'You're the hippest, most conscious black man I've ever met outside America,' he said once.

The Afghans and the Arabs already had books that were brought in by the ICRC, but there weren't any in English. Evans kept me supplied quite regularly with books from his own collection.

I most enjoyed reading *Warriors of God*, a comparison between the lives of Saladin and Richard the Lionheart, and Mario Puzo's *The Family*, about Pope Alexander VI in Renaissance Italy. I also read a Tom Clancy novel for the first time. *Executive Orders* begins with a bitter pilot flying a passenger plane into a building on Capitol Hill, killing the entire US cabinet. Islamic terror cells then launch biological-weapons attacks around the US. This provokes a former CIA head, now President, to launch a war, devastating Iraq and Iran. The parallels are uncanny, but the book was written in 1996.

I read many books in Bagram – all from individual guards. They included books about brain science, anthropology, Winston Churchill, the War of Independence, the American Civil War, the Second World War, Vietnam, and even Afghanistan. I used to list them all carefully, and note quotations and facts that might be useful – someday.

The atmosphere in Bagram was very dependant upon the sergeant of the guard in charge of the soldiers, and I learned soon enough that they could take all of our small privileges away in a flash.

There was one particularly nasty character I didn't like at all, and his attitude and behaviour towards the other detainees were a catalyst for how those under him behaved with us. I once saw him and several guards do a cell search in a brutal way that expressed his character perfectly. Everybody was told to get to the back of the cell, down on their knees, hands behind their heads. The guards entered and searched, lifting all the blankets up, and throwing everything around. He didn't care about walking on everybody's blankets and over the places where they prayed. In fact there was one person still praying at the time, and the sergeant grabbed him, dragged him by his hair to the other end of the cell, and threw him where the others were kneeling, and shouted, 'You should be praying to me, asshole. I'm the only god you have here.' In our cell we were told to turn away and not to look while the search was taking place, but we had already seen enough.

It was around this time, late 2002, that another Afghan was brought into the cell where I was held. The routine then was that new detainees got the very-loud-music treatment, the isolation cells, and the sleep deprivation, as preliminaries for entering the main cells. But before they were even brought into the cells they were held for some time in the airlock. At any given time several people could be held in the airlocks for each of the cells. This Afghan was in our airlock. I could see from how he was standing, sort of lolling, that he'd been put on sleep deprivation. I only ever got to see his face once because he was always made to face the guards, and he was always standing.

People often had to sleep in the airlock, even though there was very little space, but he didn't get that luxury. He was told to stand. He'd been taken to the interrogation cell once or twice and brought back to stand again. I remember his number was 421, and the reason why I remember that is because eventually, when he had disappeared, his toothbrush was still there on the shelf outside the cell with ours, but he was not with us.

One evening in the airlock, after standing for so long, he just slid down. The MPs came and made him stand up by shackling his hands to the top of the airlock gate, above his head, completely above his head. He started saying some things, making noises, probably trying to appeal to somebody, but it was all unintelligible to me, I didn't understand what he was saying. But it was evident that he was very, very uncomfortable and he was asking for help. Eventually he slumped, and they came into the airlock. But instead of untying him and letting him go, to see how he was, they started punching him, and one of the sergeants, who was under the particularly brutal one, started punching him in the ribs really hard. Then they undid his shackles, reshackled him after they took him off the gate, and they dragged him off to the interrogation rooms. We never ever saw him again.

Later that night another soldier, a Puerto Rican who was very decent in his dealings with me, was running up and down, shouting, 'We're going to get in the shit for this.' So I knew that something really bad had happened. And then the rumours started that 421 had been killed. Some of the other Afghan detainees who had been held in the isolation cells came down and started talking about it, and word spread.

As far as Bagram was concerned, the disappearance of one detainee wasn't really such a major incident. So many people used to come and go, and I could never be sure where anybody had gone. Sometimes though I could see the euphoria when someone was told they were going home. The person was so happy, he walked around and embraced everybody in the cell and shook hands. The guards would say, 'No, you can't do that.' But he didn't care anyway because he was going home. The Americans let them have their blankets to take with them.

It was around this time that Bisher al-Rawi and Jamil el-Banna, from London, appeared, and I started talking to them when I could. I had met Jamil once before; he came to the shop and bought some things. I had never met Bisher before and I didn't even know whether he spoke English at all, let alone public-school English. But when I saw him speaking with the guards I realized he certainly did. I was extremely shocked when I first saw the two of them there, because I imagined that Britain must have actually been handing over its people directly from Britain to the Americans. It felt like a huge blow to me. I thought, 'There's absolutely no way out of this now, this has become so huge.' I was envisaging truckloads of Britons coming over to Bagram and Guantánamo.

Once I managed to ask one of the guards if they could bring the other British man (Bisher) out when I was sorting the meal packets, and they agreed as long as we spoke English. Bisher and I spoke cautiously, at first, but within minutes we were discussing our stories. I was particularly desperate to learn more about the UK and what he'd heard about my case. But he didn't know very much.

Back in his cell, Bisher was so assured, so English, so concerned about trying to help everyone. I even saw him once trying to teach an Afghan how to brush his teeth – by moving the brush, not his head. I managed to lend him some of Evans' books too, by throwing them over the wire into his cell.

I also spoke to Jamil once when he was in the next cell. But one of the interrogators must have noticed from up above, as they took him into interrogation. They must have said something to him that frightened him, as he didn't speak to me any more after that. Jamil had the odd nickname Kenny Rogers, though he'd probably never heard the name before. He did actually resemble the country singer. Once they asked him to sing half a verse that they taught him from 'Coward of the County', which he did: out of tune and very loudly. Jamil didn't appear too upset at that point and I had the impression that he thought he was going to be there for a short time, that perhaps the Americans had realized their mistake.

I could never have imagined then that nearly three years later I would be at home writing a book while he would still be in Guantánamo.

After all of these months of not seeing the sun, or any natural light, the Americans finally decided to build us a so-called recreation yard. They shackled us up, put jackets on us, and gave us silly hats, because it was so cold, and took us out one by one. Then we were all linked by one chain running through all our shackles so that we were in one line. We went outside into a place that was walled off, no view at all, just walls all around. There was a large, thick wooden bench, to which they attached the chain, and where we could sit. If one of us stood up, all had to stand up. If one sat down, all sat down. If one wanted to walk, all had to walk – and only in an arc around the bench. This was supposed to last no more than ten minutes, but after about five minutes we all agreed it was a waste of time and we would rather go back in. That was the sum of my recreation time outside my cell.

Otherwise I sat, in the exact place I was assigned to sleep, for the whole time except the hour-long exercise period before lunch. In fact, I sat down for a whole year.

The person I was mostly left with after that was a Saudi who had been picked up in Azerbaijan and handed over to the Americans. He was treated very badly. Mohammad Ahmed was the brother-in-law of one of the 9/11 hijackers.

The guards said he was 'a real hard-ass al-Qa'idah dude . . . and a Saudi ex-marine'. They made him work like a dog, carrying water around, up and down, pretty much what they did with Omar. They really tried to humiliate him. I asked the guards to stop, but they just didn't care.

We two got along fairly well, but if ever I came to a point when I was really close to having a fight in the cell, it was with him. Mohammad was typical of one kind of Saudi arrogance in his attitude and behaviour.

Once I asked Mohammad to roll up his blanket for exercise time, but he'd decided that day he was not in the mood and stayed lying down, obstructing everyone else. I started rolling his blanket myself, but he rolled it back out. There was some eyeballing between us, but I didn't want to get into a fight. Realizing that all the detainees would run over his blanket, Mohammad eventually folded it away and just sulked in a corner. We didn't speak after that at all for several weeks, until the day that I left. I looked at him, and he looked at me, and he shook my hand and embraced me and said, 'I'm really sorry about what happened. I apologize.'

'Sometimes these things happen.'

I witnessed two fights, both in my cell. One was between a huge Afghan, about seven foot tall and massively built, probably over twenty stone, and Mohammad. It was over something ridiculous, like who brushed their teeth first, or something equally stupid. Mohammad went over to him and kicked him in the face, and the huge Afghan got a plastic bottle of water and tried to hit him with that. In the end I ran in between them and pushed them apart. The other fight I witnessed was between two Afghans who were pro- and anti-Taliban. They fought in a catlike way, scratching, biting, and slapping, but no kicks and punches. Again I jumped right in between them and pushed them apart.

Ramadan came round again – my second away from the family. This time I wasn't still in shock, like in Kandahar, and I felt incredibly sad and alone. It was horrible. We weren't allowed to talk, we weren't allowed to pray in congregation, we weren't allowed to do anything at all. The worst thing was missing the special Ramadan prayer, Taraweeh, in congregation. The guards wouldn't allow it. They did not even give us anything to break the fast. In fact, for the first two weeks in Ramadan they didn't give us any food at all until ten o'clock every evening – five hours after sunset. That was clearly vindictive, and they knew it. They even had dates, which were brought in by the ICRC, but they wouldn't give them to us until the night. On the actual day of Eid, which is supposed to be a feast day, the ICRC brought in some little doughnuts for us. The guards didn't give them to us until the next day, which was too late. It was like celebrating Christmas on Boxing Day.

They had actually made us fast on Eid day. That night when I came out of the cell for meal preparation, I told Stephanie about it. She felt really bad, and she went back to where the guards were, and returned with her own ration of soup, cookies, and chocolates called Kisses, for me and Abdur-Raheem, the Afghan who'd fallen in the shower. 'Just to let you know we're not all alike, we're not all the same.'

Abdur-Raheem was impressed, it was quite beyond his experience of Americans. 'This girl's really good.'

'I know,' I laughed. 'She just gave us some kisses.'

There were not many such nice human moments, and after Ramadan, the sense of time passing became unbearably painful. I wrote to my father:

Dear Dad,

As-salaamu alaikum . . . It is nearing a complete year since I have been in custody, and I believe there has been a gross violation of my human rights, particularly to that right of freedom and innocence until proven guilty. I still don't know what crime I am supposed to have committed for which not only I, but my wife and children should con- tinually suffer as a result. I am in a state of desperation and am beginning to lose the fight against depression and hopelessness . . . Conditions are such that I have not seen the sun, sky, moon etc. for nearly a year . . . I have more than served enough time for whatever has been 'perceived' about me, yet I still see no end in sight. I hate so much to place this burden upon you, and do as a last resort to alleviate this injustice. Please remember me in your prayers, Your Son, Moazzam

Sharif had told me that the Americans were releasing him because he passed a polygraph test. Before he left he told me to request one. At the end of the year, in desperation, I wrote a four-page letter to the Americans, which detailed the murders that I had witnessed, the general appalling treatment, and my constant request for a polygraph test. I put down the questions that I believed were most important to answer: 'Have I been involved in an act of terrorism? Have I been involved in hostilities against United States? Have I had any prior knowledge of any acts of terrorism? Have I funded any acts of terrorism? Was I a member of al-Qa'idah, or any other similar group?' But I never had any response, ever.

What was so special about me?

Finally, in January 2003, one of the better interrogators I had met, Jay, called me in and said, 'You're going to Guantánamo. Things will probably be better for you there and from there you'll get a solution. Anyway, you're going, you have no choice.'

Could it possibly be worse, in those small cages, than Bagram? I wondered.

Like everyone else, I'd always dreaded the very idea of Guantánamo, and every time a group left – about four while I was in Kandahar and Bagram – I'd had a sense of relief that I was not with them. But by the time my turn did come, I had come to the point where I felt anything would be better than Bagram. I was sick and tired of the place, of the rules and regulations, of the food, the attitude, the smell, the lights, and, above all, the limbo. I'd had enough. Even the thought of the tiny cages at Guantánamo, which I knew about and thought of as dog kennels, was bearable because it seemed like a progression towards a court, a proper hearing, maybe on the American mainland. One step backwards, but two steps forwards, I told myself, optimistic as always.

But I was not prepared for solitary confinement in a room deprived of any natural light. I could not have imagined I would be held alone in those conditions for twenty months. Nor could I have anticipated that the Americans were preparing to force me to sign a confession written by them.

When we came to leave Bagram we were kitted out for the journey with a jacket and an orange hat as well as the orange clothes we already had. We had already had our hair shaved, again, and I'd heard from the guards that it was in case we might hide a pin or a minute weapon of some sort in our hair. It was ridiculous overkill, as usual – where would we get such a weapon? We were all shackled, with a chain around the waist that was attached to the handcuffs. And our legs were shackled in the usual way. We sat there in two rooms, waiting, with some people sporadically being escorted to the toilet, knowing the flight might be thirty-six hours or more. I decided that however long it was, I was not going to be humiliated, and I would hold on. I did, for two days.

Most prisoners had been told stories to make them fear life in Guantánamo. I'd seen two Afghan men in adjacent cells particularly distraught by the prospect. When they were told that they were going, they broke down in tears. One literally could not get up, because he was so physically and mentally overcome by the very idea of going to Guantánamo – the end of the world as far as he was concerned. He felt that his life was over, that he was never going to see his family again. One of the interrogators, a young Hispanic woman, had actually told him as much. 'You might as well write a letter to your wife saying that you're never going to see her again.' The only reason why he was being sent to Guantánamo was because he refused to confess to being a member of the Taliban. They tried unsuccessfully to bribe him, saying that if he agreed to what they were accusing him of, he wouldn't go.

There were others too protesting their innocence, like a young Pakistani, a seventeen-year-old, who they'd got on the border somehow. He maintained that he was working in Afghanistan as a bricklayer. He was captured by the Northern Alliance. As he had darker skin, and was obviously not from the region, it was enough for the US to think he was probably up to something nefarious.

We sat there shackled, waiting to get on the plane. I was thinking about how I was actually looking forward to it. Compared to Bagram, it was progress.

In the waiting room Stephanie sat down between the former Taliban minister, Mullah Mutawakkil, and me. He had been kept separately from all of us. I knew that Stephanie was sad to see me leave, and she just sat for a few minutes without saying a word. Then she stood up, reached out, held my shackled hand, and shook it. It was a brave thing for her to do, considering there were other soldiers close by, and all the other detainees were looking at her in astonishment. It was embarrassing, but I was touched. She was just a girl doing a job. That was the last I saw of her, and of Bagram, because then my senses were blocked with goggles, earmuffs, and facemask.

Then I felt something on my back. 'Hey, one-eight-zero,' said one of the MPs, 'you're gonna be five-five-eight again in Gitmo, so I'm gonna write it on your shirt.'

I could sense that people were moving out one at a time, until I heard the screams. The same humiliation that had greeted me when I arrived in Kandahar bade me farewell when I left Afghanistan. It was the harsh reminder that no matter how well I got on with the guards, I, and everyone else in orange, was still the enemy.

My last memories inside Bagram Air Base detention facility are of my own tears, and screams.

9

A SOLITARY ECHO

They took us on some sort of truck across to the plane. I could feel the open air for the first time in months, but I was also stifling in the mask. They manhandled us up the ramp, and as the goggles were not completely tight against my eyes, if I leaned my head back a little and forced my eyes down I could just make out rows of seats, along the length of the aeroplane. The prisoners sat in the middle, back to back, and the guards were seated in front of us. And what I noticed straightaway, as we were handed over, was that the guards were wearing khaki jungle combats, whereas the guards in Bagram wore desert combat uniform. I told myself, 'I'm now entering a completely different phase of custody; I have to keep positive that it is progress.' But soon I could not think about anything except how miserably uncomfortable I was. The earmuffs pressed really hard against my ears, I found it very difficult to breathe through the facemask, and of course I couldn't see. With the din of the engines, the pressure of the shackles around the waist, and the handcuffs, I felt I could not last long.

Then they gave us a peanut-butter sandwich; 'Typically American again,' I thought when I tasted it. But I couldn't raise it to my mouth because of the hand-shackles attached to my waist chains. I tried to hunch my head down to the sandwich, but it was impossible. The guards finally realized, and they went around lifting up the sandwiches, and sometimes some water. But I was getting desperate to be drugged so I would be out of all the misery, so I kept doing something to get the guards' attention. Despite the pain of the chains rubbing on my skin, I pushed my wrists or my arms against the goggles or the facemask or the earmuffs to get them off. Each time I did it, a guard got up and put them back again. I did it several times, and they came back and readjusted them. I could see that there was a row of guards sitting in front of us, maybe fifty or more, and I supposed the same behind us.

I had heard from a guard that several detainees had been forcibly drugged on previous flights to Cuba. I couldn't bear the thought of sitting in this position for nearly two consecutive days. I shouted over the roar of the engines to whoever could hear me, 'Can I have a sedative, or something, to drug me, please? This is unbearable.' The guard went away, and someone who I assumed was a medical officer came, and gave me some drugs to swallow.

The next time I remember anything was in a daze in Guantánamo. The first sensations I felt were intense heat and humidity. I realized I was out of the plane, and the shackles I had on were different. There was a chain going from the waist to the ankles, which restricted my movement even more than before. That was my introduction to the 'three-piece suit', which I soon knew only too well. I was still half dazed and vaguely felt there were a lot of MPs around. In and out of a vehicle, in and out of a shower, into more orange clothes, I was barely conscious. The guards on both sides held me up for a few steps, and I noticed the ground under my feet was very different from anything I'd seen in Afghanistan. There were small light-brown sun-baked rocks, it seemed a lot drier, hotter . . . and I could smell the sea. It was distinctly different to the smell of the sea in Britain. But I could definitely smell the sea.

I was in Camp Echo – or Eskimo, as they called it at that time – although I didn't know it just then. I was taken into a room where they took off my hood, goggles, earmuffs, and facemask. The guards took me to a cell in the corner of the room, asked me to step up and in, and locked the door. Then they asked me to stand with my back to the door so they could take the shackles off, through the bean-hole, an opening in the cell door covered with a metal flap controlled from the outside. They undid the legs first, and then the padlock at the back of the waist, then I had to turn round and hand them over the rest of the chain that had gone from the wrist to the ankles. Then they undid the wrists, and I was free in my little cell. My cell, my new home, measured about eight foot by six foot. It had a toilet in there, an Arab-style toilet, all metal, on the ground.

I didn't know what I was expecting, but it was not this. I looked around in utter bewilderment, almost unbelief. Nothing had changed, in fact things were worse. From Kandahar to Bagram, from Bagram to Guantánamo: each time I thought things were going to get better, but they actually got worse.

What could be more bleak, or grimmer, than being in a cage like this? I thought. I could not even see out of it clearly as it was covered with a pale green steel mesh, doubled, with one part of the mesh set vertically, and the other horizontally, so they crisscrossed one another. I could barely see through it, it was a strain on the eyes. I felt I was really back to square one.

It is considered a sin in Islam to despair, but in Bagram, during the worst days of May 2002, I had been unable to hold despair at bay. Here in Guantánamo, in this steel cage with its mesh sides, steel roof and floor, steel bed, steel toilet, all inside a white, new-looking brightly lit room, I felt despair returning as I took in my surroundings for the first time.

All I had in the cell was a sheet and a roll of toilet paper, not even my glasses. I asked for something that I could use as a prayer mat, and they brought a thin camping mat, which became my mattress for the next two years.

I wanted to pray immediately. I asked the MPs which direction was east, but they weren't sure. That told me there were no other prisoners here, otherwise the guards would have known, since all the detainees would have asked the same question. Or was it that they feared my knowledge of directions could allow me to calculate my position on the island – a potential breach of security? I performed my prayer, and then I sat for a while, thinking. Looking at the paintwork and clean linoleum floor outside, I thought it was obvious that this place was recently constructed, and probably had never been used before.

Then I lay down. I was still feeling quite hazy from the drugs on the plane. They gave me something which they said was a blanket, but which was made of a plastic-type material. There was no cotton or wool or anything like that in it, and it couldn't keep me warm with the air-conditioning on – which was how the guards kept the room most of the time.

Later on I was told it was a suicide blanket – meaning it could not be torn up to make a noose. I didn't understand why they gave me that. I didn't think they understood either. I think they didn't understand a lot of their rules and procedures; they just followed them because, as many would say, 'It says so in the SOP' (Standard Operating Procedure manual).

I lay there, wondering why I was in this place, separated from everyone else. I realized I was completely alone, but I never imagined it would last for almost two years – never allowed to see another prisoner. I thought that they still saw me as a prize catch. They had studied me in all that time in Bagram: I wasn't a troublemaker, I didn't go on hunger strikes, I didn't swear, shout, or hurl things at the guards, but they saw me as very influential amongst the prisoners. They did not understand that because I spoke English, Arabic, and Urdu, and had some education, it was natural that the collection of people they had in Bagram – villagers, young boys, people who had never had contact with Westerners – would look to me to help them negotiate all kinds of things. This time, however, they weren't keeping me with others.

I slept heavily, the drugs from the plane still in my system. The next morning a guard brought me the first cooked food I'd seen in a year: breakfast. I'd been told to expect cooked meals in Guantánamo. It was a big disappointment. There was tea and awful powdered milk in polystyrene cups. Both were cold. The cooked breakfast was revolting. Rice, green mushy peas, and a boiled egg, all mixed together. I couldn't eat it. I told the guard, 'I'd rather just have the cup of tea and that's all.'

On the evening of the second day the person who had told me that I was going to Guantánamo, Jay, turned up, with another man called George. Jay was an interrogator in Bagram, the one I'd given that long letter to, for the authorities. He had told me, 'Your letter managed to get further up the ladder than you realize.' I was pleased to see him, a familiar face, and without the malice I'd encountered from others. When two others came in, however, my heart sank. It was Marti and Niel, the two FBI agents from Bagram.

The guards locked them all into the outer part of the room, then came to my cell, shackled me with the three-piece suit, and brought me out.

I sat down at a table the guards had brought in, facing Jay and George; Marti and Niel. The latter two were both huge, obese, with the style of New York street cops, perhaps Irish American.

Rob, a colleague of theirs, had told me in Bagram how they boasted a combined mass of over 500lb – not something to advertise, I thought. They may have known precisely how to operate on the streets of New York, but they were out of their league here. Also, they knew they weren't subject to any checks and balances; they didn't have to worry too much about scrutiny from superiors, or Internal Affairs, as they would have back in the US. They had autonomy to do whatever they wanted; they could extract information from people in any way they liked. That was the way with all of the law-enforcement and intelligence agencies I'd experienced in Kandahar and Bagram. The CIA's unscrupulous methods rubbed off onto the others. Much later, the FBI tried to paint themselves as the squeaky clean ones, who saw all of this torture going on, and started speaking about it as though they were not involved. From my experience, they were an integral part of the process.

This time I knew these two would not threaten me with Egyptian-torture techniques, because Jay was there. In Bagram, when a new batch of MPs had arrived and heard about the Canadian boy, Omar, accused of killing an elite US soldier, it had been Jay's intervention that prevented them from continuing the abuse they had already meted out to him. In fact, Jay gave me a little hope once, saying, 'Guantánamo is going to be the beginning of the end for you.' But even my optimism knew better.

'You're never going to see your family again.' Marti's words in Bagram came back when I saw his face. 'You could be facing execution by firing squad, lethal injection, or gas chamber.'

In fact they did threaten me again. 'We want you to read and sign these documents,' they said, placing six typed pages in front of me on the table. They had written my confessions.

There were three copies – one for me, and on their side of the table, one for Jay and George, and one for Niel and Marti. They told me that if I didn't sign, several different things could happen, none of them good. They included sitting in Guantánamo for many years before anybody even looked at my case, then a summary trial – a formality before conviction. 'It's going to be one very short trial, they're going to look at the evidence we present, and they're going to take that on face value. That means you'll be imprisoned for life, or you could face execution, or both – execution after a very long time.'

I read through the pages in utter disbelief. My first reaction was, 'This is terrible. The English used here is terrible. Nobody could ever believe that I would write such a document.' Then I thought, 'This could actually be good – anybody who knows my style of writing would know that I am not the author, I don't write like this.' It sounded uninformed and adventurous, more like the ramblings of a hysterical sixteen-year-old college dropout than what one would expect from the Federal Bureau of Investigation. I recalled that during one of the interrogations Marti had said to me, 'Stop, already! Stop using big words.' Besides the pathetic English, I read the 'facts' with complete amazement. It was full of exaggerations, lies, and presumptions. There were names in there that I hadn't even heard of, which they knew only too well. The document claimed, amongst other things, that I was a longstanding member of al-Qa'idah; I had trained and taught in their camps; I had financed them, including giving funds that had gone to the 9/11 attackers. When I asked how they had reached this conclusion, they told me that I had already admitted attending and sending financial support to 'the camps'.

It was maddening to hear them refer to 'the camps', as if every training camp in the recent history of the Muslim world had been under al-Qa'idah's umbrella. Logic and reason, again, seemed to have got lost under an avalanche of assumptions. I actually laughed as I read through the terribly written papers that were so potentially damning.

They were obsessed with the word 'al-Qa'idah'. Their document suggested that almost everybody I'd ever met in my life was a member of al-Qa'idah. It said that I'd attended and sponsored 'al-Qa'idah's Jamat-e-Islami camp . . .' Were they really ignorant enough to assume that Jamat-e-Islami, the third largest political party in Pakistan, was a subsidiary of al-Qa'idah? Had they, maybe, mistaken it for al-Gam'ah al-Islamiyyah of Egypt? Both were part of the Islamic revivalist movements in their respective countries. Both had supported mujahideen forces in the eighties, against the Soviets. But that could be said of hundreds of groups and parties, including the CIA. Or was it a deliberate exploitation of the ignorance of most Americans, a few of whom would be looking at statements like this, but couldn't tell the difference?

The statement also claimed that I had financed a man I'd never even heard of – involved in a plot to bomb a US airport, in 2000 – but omitted to mention how, where and when I'd met him. It said that I had provided 'housing for terrorist suspects and their families, whilst belligerent acts were committed against the US', but again failed to mention who these people were, or exactly what they were accused of. I, of course, knew they were referring to an answer I'd given previously to one of their questions, when I told them that some women and children, whose men were presumed missing, had stayed with my family for a few days in Pakistan. They included some of the Kurdish people who had helped evacuate my own family. The statement gave no explanation how these women and children were members of al-Qa'idah, or had been hostile to the US.

Also, it was alleged that my bookshop in England was a recruiting centre for al-Qa'idah, who was our sponsor; though I had thought it was supposed to be the other way round. Hadn't they just said that I was funding al-Qa'idah? It was ridiculous. Reading it, I thought, this is cloud-cuckoo-land. And then they asked me to sign it.

I looked at Jay, picked it up and said, 'Have you read this nonsense?'

'If you'd seen the draft before, Moazzam, you'd have thought we were nuts.'

'There is no way I'm going to agree to sign this rubbish,' I protested. 'First of all, it's full of lies, and secondly I don't write like this. These are not my words. So if you want my signature on this, then let me make corrections, add some explanations, remove all the incorrect statements and absolute misrepresentations.' They allowed me to make some selected alterations, but kept in the most blatant untruths, like being a front-line fighter with al-Qa'idah, and, money I had sent to Kashmiris in 1994 being used in the September 11th attacks.

I felt surprisingly calm. I was imagining the damage this statement could do them in court; it would expose much of their tactics too. However, I didn't know what the parameters of the law were anymore: everyone had said that after 9/11, new laws had taken immediate effect in the US, and that was frightening. How could American laws apply, in retrospect, to a British citizen, who had never travelled west of Dublin, for crimes that never existed in the first place? Were they going to judge me on what Nathan had said in Kandahar: 'We're determining cases based on what we think were your intentions, and on our intelligence reports.'

My mind was whirling, but I still believed there was no way that any competent court in the world was going to look past the first sentence of the confession.

It was comforting that Jay knew exactly how bad it was . . . and he was prepared to say this in front of the FBI. I really despised those two for the demeaning job they were prepared to do, and this was just more of the same from them. I'd noticed the insidious way that they'd come in: late at night, asking the guards to leave the room, so there would be no witnesses. It was all supposed to be very fast, 'Here's the paper and here's the pen, quickly read through it and sign.'

They took it away after I'd made the corrections. They must have had a computer and a printer in the vehicle, because there was no other building around Camp Echo, as far as I understood. They all went out and told the guards to come. They locked me in the cell again. Then the four were back within ten minutes. They put a new document in front of me, and I went through it again. I made corrections, but this time they wouldn't allow any. They were getting agitated. 'Stop playing games with us, we know what you . . .' I could see the same anger rising that these men had had when they ordered my punishment back in Bagram. I couldn't forget for a moment that these were the same men.

'You could be shot by firing squad, Moazzam, do you understand?' Marti said, seeming like he was controlling himself.

'They've built an execution chamber here, I've seen it,' Niel followed.

'Have you forgotten about your kids, your . . .'

'OK, OK, just give me a minute.'

I'd thought about this before, many times, since the last time I saw them. Finally I resigned myself to whatever would come. Despite the insinuation, there still wasn't a crime in the statement, certainly not one that I could see. 'You know what, it doesn't make any difference, I'll sign whatever you want, but I have to do something first.'

I told them I wanted to go into the cell. I prayed that this would be my way out. I asked Allah for this document to be a means to expose their lies. The prayer is called al-Istikharah in Arabic: the prayer of asking guidance for the right choice. Afterwards I signed. I asked them for a copy but they wouldn't give me one. That was it. I never saw any of them ever again.

It must have been really late by the time they left; the lights weren't as bright, but still on, as always. I felt I'd taken a huge step, which would affect everything in the future for me, for the family. I felt that I'd literally signed my life away. I began to make endless notes to present as arguments for the defence attorney and the court that I now expected would materialize within days, as they'd told me. They were expecting me to plead guilty to whatever charge was alleged. But I had other plans.

I only had a blunt two-inch pencil to write with, and it soon wore down as the mass of argument accumulated into twenty pages of rebuttals.

I started to write home too, beginning every letter with, 'In the Name of Allah, Most Compassionate, Most Merciful', and 'My beloved wife'. I told Zaynab that I thought of her and the children every single hour. I felt ambivalent thinking of home: I didn't want its memory of warmth and gentleness tainted by this sordid scene around me, but I did need that softness and familiarity to retain hope.

I wrote Zaynab a nine-page letter – small writing on lined A4 paper – after about six weeks. I gave her advice on all the minutiae of family life, which she had had to organize without me. I tried to help with the choice of schools, and the struggle against her own and Umamah's asthma, I encouraged her to make a routine for herself including exercise, joining a fitness club, swimming, or doing stretches at home, and some study project for herself. I tried hard to encourage her to feel proud of herself: 'You said that you have achieved little in your life. That is not true. What sacrifices you have made, and difficulties endured (and continue to do so) have made you an extraordinarily rare person. Your intentions have been pure (to please Allah and to keep me happy). Whatever mistakes, miscalculations etc. – they have been mine – for which I am paying the price. In my sight, and the sight of the Lord, I believe, your station has been raised immensely, and think you have helped secure your own place in the Hereafter – the Garden. I know you want things to change when I am released. But they already have – Big time. I want it all to be different, spending all my spare time with my family – pursuing our welfare in light of the time lost and uncertain future.'

I wrote again after about another six weeks: 'I love you so much and miss you terribly. I look forward so much to your letters, yet, shortly afterwards I feel gloomy and miserable . . . I have to be honest and admit that I try my best not to think of you and the children, as it is so painful thinking about how you are all living your lives without me now, and all of our times together in the past. There is so much more I want to share with you in life, as well as the children, and I want more than anything to have the opportunity to make amends for the mistakes that I have made – particularly in relation to you – my family. I have it all planned in my head; I don't know what will become of them (the plans), but they include some major readjustments to my/our former life-style.'

Once, I wrote to my father using terms I doubted the Americans understood, like saying I was 'sent to Coventry', implying isolation; or that I was 'living like Sheba', after the name of the German shepherd dog I had when I was a child. But he never got the letter anyway. I felt I never wanted Dad to see the petty humiliations of how I was living, like the silly little toothbrush, measuring no more than an inch, that I attached to my index fingertip to clean my teeth, and the tiny translucent tube of toothpaste about two inches long; or the food, like the ground meat made into a leathery steak, which was so repulsive that I vomited when I tried to eat it; or the water bottles from which they removed the tops in case I'd use them to squirt water, or worse, at the MPs.

I made a calendar in those early days of 2003, sketching it out on a piece of paper. One of the ICRC workers in Kandahar had told me not to think in terms of days passed, particularly, I think, since he'd thought those days would turn into weeks, months, and years. But marking off days on a calendar also gave me days to look forward to, hoping for relief.

I soon began to see that here nothing was consistent – except inconsistency. Nothing that was true in Bagram would necessarily be true in Guantánamo. Rules, procedures, were different. Anything that I'd gained over there, I would not automatically get here. I couldn't understand that, and it became symbolic for me, of American military attitudes and behaviour. Empathetic guards had told me how they too were confounded by strict military rigidity and meaningless protocol. 'There's the right way, the wrong way, and the army way,' they used to say. They had taken my glasses again – like the early days of Kandahar. They took away my letters – the few I'd had in Bagram, pictures of my children, and notes that I'd managed to make. I never saw them again until the day I was released.

The soldier sitting guarding me meticulously recorded in the logbook every move I made. When the soldiers came on duty, they picked up the book and began noting every detail: each time I ate, slept, used the latrine, went for recreation and showered, read the Quran, had a medical visit, had an interrogatory visit or made any requests, or complaints – which I seldom did.

The level of paranoia was astounding, at the start. For instance the new green enamel paint in my cell began to chip off a little, close to where I was lying. Out of boredom, I started pulling at it with my nail, and it chipped away a little more. There was a space measuring, perhaps, one inch by three inches, of paint scraped off. During one of the cell searches they did when I was in the recreation yard, they noticed the chipped paint. They did not say anything to me directly, but they whispered in front of me, as if I couldn't understand, or wasn't there, 'He's chipped away at paint in his cell; we need to get the doctor here, and call BMW.'

'BMW?' I thought. 'Who, or what, could that be?' The medics and doctor gave me a full examination to see if I was eating the paint to make myself sick. Was this a new way to attempt suicide? Luckily, the US Navy doctor put them out of their misery, saying, 'He would have to consume a hell of a lot more paint than that,' pointing to the patch in the cell, 'to harm himself. There are definitely much easier ways.' (BMW, I learnt, from speaking to the guards, was in fact BNW, the acronym they'd given to First Sergeant Walker, the non-commissioned officer-in-charge (NCOIC). It stood for 'Bad News Walker'.)

I spent a lot of my time concentrating on routines, like exercising, and pushing myself to continue memorizing the Quran, which was much more difficult to do alone. At the beginning, I had twice-weekly periods of exercise outside the cell, outdoors in the sweltering heat. I was shackled up in the three-piece suit to be taken out of the cell, and the room – which was elevated on stilts. So as I went out I managed a glimpse of the sea from above the green plastic fence which surrounded the whole of Camp Echo. They put me in the recreation ground, and I had first to stand by the bean-hole, where they reached in to remove, or replace my shackles. After that I was left free to go round the yard for fifteen minutes – then I would get a shower. This process was referred to as 'shower and rec'. I often teased the MPs about this. 'If it's "shower and rec", aren't I supposed to shower first and then exercise?' This 'rec', for recreation, was an insult to the concept. What *recreation* was I getting?

I could hear a strange buzz from the electricity pylons, and the odd cry of the mynah bird, which sounded to me like a squeaky wheelbarrow, as I wrote to Zaynab. Seeing blue sky and cotton clouds was a pleasure, after all that time of total deprivation of natural light in Bagram. But comparing internal mental notes of the differences between here and Bagram I concluded that the situation was just as bad, or worse. 'Out of the frying pan, into the frying pan,' I said, when the guards asked which I preferred.

Outside the yard, armed infantry patrolled. Some on foot, some in a Humvee with a fixed machine-gun on top, as though somehow I could have escaped. It was very hard to motivate myself after exercising with a group in Bagram, and I couldn't do much because of the sheer heat. But if I had rec in the evenings I ran hundreds of laps, which in flip-flops was hard work. There was nothing to see, except some electric wires, and the three guards, sitting looking bored watching me. A special dog handler with his MWD, military working dog, was always on hand, just like the infantry patrol outside, whenever I was taken to rec. In fact, I couldn't go for rec until both infantry and MWD had arrived. US military overkill, again. The dogs and handlers alternated, but there was one especially volatile dog that was always barking, even at the soldiers. Once, his handler, a young, heavyset, blond soldier said to it, 'Hey, do you want to chase some orange meat?' He must have assumed I didn't speak English, as he added, 'It's just like watching a mouse run around in a cage.'

I stopped, looked him in the face, and said, 'Yes, but this mouse has two legs and speaks English better than you do.'

I went on running. I could see his jaw had dropped, he couldn't say a word, until he finally managed a lame, 'Yup.' The soldiers behind him rolled about with laughter. That story circulated for more than a year, from soldier to soldier. It made me reflect about how very fortunate I was to speak English, and how, in solitary confinement, I was so much more vulnerable to how the guards behaved with me, as they could get away with anything. In General Population there were always other prisoners to support me.

I had promised myself right from the start not to lose my self-respect and dignity, at all costs. I wanted to keep up a high level of spiritual, mental, and physical activity. I didn't just go for set routines, because I thought flexibility would help me adapt to the constantly changing rules. I set myself certain goals that I wanted to achieve. With the physical aspect it was mostly press-ups, abdominal exercises and stretching. I had started including one-armed press-ups too, but when I saw the guards getting excited about logging it, as though it was some remarkable phenomenon, I went back to ordinary press-ups. My record was a hundred in two minutes and I used to compare that, and stomach crunches, with some of the friendlier guards' records from their physical-training tests that they had to take every few months. They were quite embarrassed to tell me how comparatively easy their tests were.

In the first six months the person I saw most was Kim, as she introduced herself, an officer of the newly formed Criminal Investigation Task Force (CITF). She was responsible for interrogating me, though I never considered her an interrogator. She was a tall, smart-looking woman, in her mid-thirties, with long mousy-blonde hair and a pleasant manner. Kim helped to ease my situation in many ways. She was able to get my glasses back, change my flip-flops to rubber shoes, get more reading material and the occasional snack.

Initially she came with other interrogators, then later by herself. She was one of those who felt comfortable for me to be unshackled in front of her. She often came, I felt, just to talk; she seemed to realize that isolation was taking its toll on me, and she wanted to understand more than to interrogate. Sometimes she took notes, but other times we just sat and chatted. It was difficult to know for sure whether her concern was genuine, or just an attempt to gather more intelligence: I concluded that it was both. What I did know was that no previous interrogator, in Kandahar or Bagram, had spent more time, showed more compassion, or appeared more impartial, than her.

Kim talked about herself too, perhaps more than was allowed. She was quite responsive and non-dogmatic when I said something damning about the American war on terror. She seemed to be a fairly simple person who was trying to understand how to solve the problem of terrorism, as opposed to how to fight it.

'Kim, I'm not sure how to respond to you sometimes,' I said once. 'After all, I'm considered your enemy, and here you are treating me nicely. Many of your predecessors wouldn't have behaved like this, so I don't know what to make of you.'

'You're not my enemy, Moazzam, I really wish the best for you. I mean that.'

'You may not see me as the enemy, Kim, but the government you work for clearly does.'

She didn't reply.

Another visitor arrived one day with Kim – someone very different. The first British consular delegate for detainees in Guantánamo had arrived. Martin was a tall, balding man, in his fifties, with a formal quality about him. He became my only contact with the British government during my years in Guantánamo, but it was a relationship full of disappointments. That day he was wearing a horrible pink shirt and white slacks. I looked at Kim, thinking she was dressed well, and I thought, 'How embarrassing! The American's done a pretty good job, but this man looks . . .'

Martin had two other people with him, though not from the

Foreign Office. Lucy and Ian both identified themselves as MI5 agents. Lucy was quite unlike any previous MI5 official I had met. She was very talkative, with a passion for soap operas and film, which, to my amazement, she talked about endlessly. Ian was different. He seemed to want me to feel reassured. But that was all part of the deception. They were doing nothing for me, and presented me with yet another set of questions to answer.

Martin utterly confused me. He was from the Foreign Office, but was questioning me with MI5. It was impossible for me to distinguish between the two, despite the introductions. I thought they were all the same. He annoyed me even more with one of the first questions he asked me, 'I need to confirm that you are British. Can you tell me the name of your secondary-school headmaster?'

'Yes, Mr Goodfellow. Are you seriously telling me you are trying to confirm whether or not I am British? You have MI5 here with you, they already know who I am, and they've even been to my house.' Then I asked him, 'Why has it taken the British government so long to react?'

I couldn't understand him answering with a question, 'Why do *you* think it's taken so long?'

I had many things I wanted to say – none of them polite. But because this was the first person I saw whom I thought might help resolve my problem, I kept quiet. I didn't want to get into an argument or create a hostile atmosphere. Perhaps he had meant, 'We couldn't get here because the Americans are in control.'

I tried to probe a few things here and there, getting into a conversation with Ian, who seemed the most approachable of the three. Finally, we touched on the subject of Northern Ireland, and I asked how things were there at present.

'Sorry, can't tell you that.'

'Why not?'

'Well, I'm under strict orders not to discuss current affairs.'

It was quite depressing to hear that he felt such an unrelated issue would constitute a breach of US national security in Cuba. The British stayed for a couple of hours, and they came back the next day too. It was, apparently, a welfare and intelligence visit, all in one package. They asked me lots of questions about people in Britain, about who I thought was a potential terrorist ready to strike against British interests around the world, or in Britain.

'Anybody, everybody, and nobody. How do you figure that out? I don't understand how you expect me to respond to that, when I've never been involved in acts of terror, or know anybody who has.'

But I thought they were just following a line of questioning, which had begun a long time ago.

I told them about the statement – the false confession – that the FBI took from me, explaining carefully the way it was done, and that I had been refused copies. I said on purpose in front of Kim, 'I do not believe I will receive a fair trial from the Americans.' And I looked at Kim when I said that, because although I'd got on quite well with her, I wanted her to know what I thought of her government, and to know that I'd registered the concern with mine.

They asked me about Abu Hamza, the Islamic cleric from Finsbury Park Mosque, and even the whereabouts of the controversial Muslim scholar and refugee in London, Abu Qatada. I was incredulous. 'Do you know how long I've been in custody for?'

It had been well over a year, but they were adamant they were asking a completely reasonable question.

They also brought me hundreds of photographs of people, most of whom I didn't know. Sometimes they even brought pictures of the back of somebody's head, or an arm or a leg, and asked me, 'Do you recognize this?'

I tried my best to distinguish between the Americans and British, but it became increasingly clear that they had cooperated to keep me imprisoned, and intended to use my incarceration for the maximum benefit of the intelligence services. But what could that benefit have possibly been?

Before I was captured I had found little use for the word 'oxymoron', but I soon discovered its multiple applications were quite appropriate in reference to military intelligence, as many MPs themselves would joke: 'You can't be in the military *and* intelligent at the same time.'

Their information too was all so confused. After my signing the statement, the Americans began adopting a less adversarial approach towards me. They began behaving in a much more friendly way.

Mike, the last FBI agent I'd spoken to in Islamabad, and Rob, the agent I'd met in Kandahar and Bagram, both came to my cell on a visit to Guantánamo. Mike asked me out of the blue, 'Do you mind just lifting up your shirt? I just want to see if you've got any marks.'

'You have photographs of me completely naked when I was brought in.' But I lifted the shirt anyway.

I realized that the Americans had a poor system of information exchange, and little cooperation between the myriad agencies, which were actually vying against one another. 'The right hand does not know what the left is doing,' one of them had said in Bagram. It made me think of the Prophetic saying, 'When you give charity, let the right hand be unaware of the left hand's charity', which is clearly a guard against trumpeting one's own generosity. But here, information was regurgitated, and then cut and pasted into a file that one group had compiled, whilst another duplicated, adding to it their own two pence – or two cents' – worth.

I only unravelled the mystery behind Mike's strange request, and why, in Bagram, CIA Marti had insisted that I had been an instructor for al-Qa'idah, more than one and a half years later, when I was finally moved out of Echo. A detainee told me he had trained in al-Faruk – al-Qa'idah's camp, near Kandahar – and said he was questioned about somebody who had the same name as me, a Pakistani, who had been an instructor there. But, as he said he'd told the Americans, the man was six foot two, unmarried, spoke no English, and had a bullet wound in his chest. I'm five foot three and my chest is unscathed.

But assumptions and questioning didn't stop there.

'Have you ever seen this man before?' asked Rob, producing a photo of an African-looking man.'At one of the camps, maybe?'

'No. Who is he?'

'John Muhammad, ring any bells?'

'No. But the most common Christian *and* Muslim name, all in one? Must be American.'

I didn't know it then, but Rob was talking about a former US soldier responsible for the murders of twelve people in the US. And why had Rob asked me? The man had a Muslim name and knew how to shoot.

'How about the name Abu Musab al-Zarqawi – does that sound familiar? He might have been in Afghanistan when you were there.'

'Never heard of him. Who is . . . ?

'It doesn't matter.'

Little did I know how much I'd hear that name again back in England.

'What I don't understand about you, Moazzam,' said Rob, 'is why you ever left the UK and came to Afghanistan – of all places? If you're not part of al-Qa'idah or the Taliban, what did you leave Britain for – *with* your wife and kids?' The Americans – and Brits – were always baffled by my motives and intentions for travel.

'Why do I need to be part of any group to travel anywhere? The answer is quite simple, Rob, but you'll probably never understand. You're white.'

'Ah, come on. I have plenty of black friends – and lots of Muslims too.'

'Really. How many of them do you visit regularly? How often do your kids play together – outside of school, if they go to the same schools? Do you even live in the same areas?'

Rob didn't answer.

'And that's America, where at least black people have been for around four hundred years. I was born and brought up in England – but I never saw myself as English. And neither do the English. I know English history, English language, and English literature better than a lot of English people. But I'm not white, and I'm not Christian. And my ancestry is from another world. Don't misunderstand me. Britain has the best multicultural society in Europe, but still in most parts of the country I feel out of place. I'd like to go to an English country village, with my dark skin, my beard, and my wife in her hijab and not be stared at or singled out. In fact I'd like to do that in the areas that neighbour the one where I live. I'd like the people to see that we generally want the same things in life, that they should not feel threatened by me. I want the English to like me, because they are accepting – not just to tolerate me, *if* I'm trying to assimilate. I don't know how much of this you understand as an American, but in many ways you are more acceptable to British society than I ever could be. After all, you're white, and I take it, Christian.'

'I understand that: you wanted to go somewhere you fitted in – didn't stand out too much. But why Afghanistan?'

'Just think for a second, hypothetically. If I was white *and* not a Muslim, would this question arise? There isn't a place on earth where you won't find a British ex-pat. In Afghanistan I saw white

Europeans – and Americans – living and working, with their families. They didn't wear shalwar kameez, most of them didn't speak a local language, they weren't dark-skinned, they didn't pray in the mosques . . . and yet no one questions their intentions. Some of my ancestors are buried in Afghanistan. I dressed like the Afghans, I prayed in their mosques, I speak a language most of them understand, and I felt sympathy for them that went beyond a simple humanitarian one. These people have suffered immensely – not just from wars that your country has supported, but also from natural disaster. I wanted to live in an Islamic state – one that was free from the corruption and despotism of the rest of the Muslim world.'

'So you chose the Taliban?'

'I chose Afghanistan. I admit I have made mistakes – but had it not been for 9/11, I think I would still be living happily in Afghanistan.'

'Probably as a member of al-Qa'idah, or the Taliban.'

'I knew you wouldn't understand. The Taliban were better than anything that Afghanistan has had in the past twenty-five years. You weren't in Afghanistan – not before nor during the Taliban. Child sex, rape, looting, robbery, murder, and opium production only ended when they took control.'

'And in came amputations, floggings, and executions . . .'

'Oh, and has the US abolished the death penalty? I don't agree with many things the Taliban did, but some of these things were happening before the Taliban – worse in fact. Afghanistan is a tribal society. Even in your own country there are specific laws for the Indian tribes that most other Americans would find abhorrent. I know the Taliban isolated themselves with their strict application and interpretation of *sharia*. But I am sure it's regressed to how it *used* to be, now that the warlords are back.'

Back in Bagram I remembered Sharif telling the Americans that poppy production for opium had tripled since the fall of the Taliban, and that the warlords, many of whom were allied with the Americans, had restarted the child-sex rings.

'Anyway, Moazzam, had it not been for 9/11, we would never have wasted our time in Afghanistan.'

'I used to believe that. But it simply isn't true. I think Afghanistan was in your sights for a while. The fact is you will never tolerate the existence of a purist Islamic state – anywhere.'

For around six months, I remained in my cell inside this stand-alone room, where the lights were always on, though dimmed a little at night. I could barely tell if it was light outside or dark, except during recreation, when the door opened or when the MPs changed shift. I had to ask them for prayer times, as I could not hear the prayer call from the main camp. All I could hear, most audibly in the rec yard, was the US national anthem at 0800 hours and sunset. The soldiers stopped in their tracks and saluted the flag – wherever that was. I got heartily sick of that sound.

During this time they were building the rest of what would become Camp Echo, which included another twelve cells. I could hear the noise of machinery and banging. There was another tapping noise I often heard too. It was usual for people to knock before entering the room, and when the guards went to answer, expecting medical staff, or interrogators, they looked around searching for the visitor. But if they found nobody was actually outside, they soon discovered, it was the redheaded woodpecker. Just like Woody from the cartoon, its mission in life was to annoy some and amuse others. It was certainly considered a distraction by a visiting colonel, who issued the MPs 'woodpecker-patrol' duties, stalking the area, armed with pebbles, firing volleys at the unsuspecting bird. Did this colonel really have nothing more meaningful to do?

Later, after I was moved to another cell, these two rooms would be called 'the Secret Squirrel'. It was a code phrase, which meant nobody knew who the two people held here were. They were held by a different unit of the military, were interrogated by special interrogators. My status now was lowered to that of semi-top-secret. The MPs in Echo had no idea who I was, or what I was there for. All they were told was that this was a very high-level person held in the war on terrorism. I was the first person in Camp Echo, this new isolation unit, so I must be somebody big.

Once, Colonel Nit-Pick, as I'd named him by then, a tall, elderly African American, came in and reprimanded one of the soldiers for not sitting in front of my cell watching me twenty-four hours a day. The MP was in the corner of the room as this colonel walked in on him. 'Soldier! You are on the front line now. And this is like abandoning your duty on the front line. If you were to do that on the front line, several other soldiers would be killed because of your action.'

I thought to myself, 'Which John Wayne movie has he walked out of? And why is he reprimanding a soldier in front of me?' This tactless colonel had reached the common assumption that the guy in the cage, in orange, like the rest of them, didn't speak or understand much English.

He said, to the soldier, Foster, 'This here is a very important person, you have to keep a watch on him all the time.' 'Now I'm a VIP,' I thought to myself. 'Colonel Nit-Pick knows nothing about me at all; he's not involved with my interrogation, he doesn't even know what languages I speak, so how would he know that I'm an important person? He's come to that conclusion because I'm here in isolation.'

Foster was quite a strange young man, but in many ways typical of lower enlisted part-time teenage soldiers in Guantánamo. He liked talking about cars, or 'trucks', as he would say. In the UK people don't publicize the fact that they own a truck and expect others to think it's hip, but a truck, it seemed, in the US was not a huge articulated lorry, but a four-wheel-drive jeep. Foster liked talking to me when he was on guard; I supposed it was to alleviate the boredom. He used to tell me all kinds of fantastic stories about himself as a hero, about fighting against several people at once, about driving his truck on a vertical incline up a mountain where no man had gone before, or visiting an island in the Pacific, where his father had been stationed, close to nuclear-waste deposits that attracted a feeding frenzy of crabs and mutated them into the largest ever recorded in secret history. I asked some of the other guards about him and they said, 'He's just a story-teller, don't believe everything he says.'

Foster once gave me one of the real prizes of this period. There was supposed to be one library officer, who went round the cells visiting people and at least gave them one book once a week. But that never happened to me, though some soldiers went down a few times to the library and picked up a book or two for me. Foster picked up three recent *Time* magazines, brought them over, and left them on the table outside my cell. I was sure they weren't meant for me; I was not allowed any current affairs material, and anything that they gave me in my cell had to be logged. But seeing the magazines were still there after shift change, I said to one of the MPs, confidently, 'Can you give me my magazines from the table, please?'

'Sure,' he said, 'no problem,' handing me my first batch of contra-band.

When I first looked at them, it was the colour pictures that seemed so vivid. And so I read about the *Discovery* shuttle disaster, the Bali bombings, the attempted attack on the El Al plane in Mombasa, the Chechen hostage-taking in the Moscow theatre, the escalation of hos-tilities in the Indian subcontinent, and the capture – yet again – of

Usamah bin Ladin's right-hand man. The underlying theme seemed to be the war on terror, and that things were getting worse.

When Kim came by, and said to the MPs that I was not supposed to have *Time* magazine, I'd already finished reading. 'You can take them, I've read them all, thank you.'

Otherwise I was lucky if I got anything other than brain numbing suspense novels, courtroom dramas, *Reader's Digest* Condensed Books from the 1950s, *National Geographic* magazines from the 1970s – with many pages ripped out. But there was also literature I loved, nineteenth-century classics like Dickens' *Bleak House*, *A Tale of Two Cities*, and *David Copperfield*; Emily Brontë's *Wuthering Heights* and Dostoyevsky's *The Brothers Karamazov*. But some books that I would never have read ordinarily, I quite enjoyed, like *Lord of the Rings* and even a Harry Potter. The strange thing was that I enjoyed every single book I read. I even read a romance novel once – out of sheer desperation. I looked back at it afterwards and I thought, 'What was I doing reading that crap?' It was escapism, like watching a film, submerged in that world. Some of those books I devoured in hours, and straight afterwards yearned to read something new.

Boredom had really set in; I certainly couldn't exercise all day long, and memorizing the Quran had its limits. I was longing for more informative books to read, or even, I thought, to enrol in a university study programme. I knew that prisoners around the world had obtained their masters and doctorates from inside a cage. But that was far too ambitious.

To fight the dreary monotony of daily existence I began making lists again, much of them from memory: lists of books I'd read and wanted to read; lists of words, particularly useful adjectives. I also made lists of Latin and French words and phrases; a list of interesting notes and quotes from the books I'd read; a list of words with their etymological origins – from Hebrew, Urdu, Arabic, and Latin; a list comparing the symbols of Arabic, Hebrew, and Greek languages; lists of nations of the world and their capital cities; a list of the periodic table of the elements, with corresponding atomic numbers and symbols; lists of every prayer I could remember, in Arabic; every companion of the Prophet Muhammad; a list of the most notable and influential people in history; a list of all the subjects I'd like to study; and a log of every letter I sent and received.

Writing home very carefully was also a defence against boredom. I spent a lot of time and effort thinking about what I was writing; I was not just writing a letter for the sake of it, I was thinking hard about the impact, mainly on my wife, of every sentence, every word of advice I was giving her. If it got censored, or stopped, or just put aside because someone had decided that they did not want it to go through, I felt it was a right violated. I always kept very controlled, but this was one area that made me really frustrated. I had the right to communicate with my family and vice versa.

I regularly complained about censorship, and about letters not arriving. They always gave the same answer, 'We don't know, it's gone through . . .'

They just wouldn't give an explanation. They never said to me directly, 'Look, we have decided to block your letters and we're going to let through or block whatever we want to.' That would have been a lot more honest and truthful than them playing this game of, 'Oh, well look, you're allowed to write, you're allowed to receive letters.' I think they played that game just to show the Red Cross that we were actually given the right.

Still, I rarely felt angry at most of the individual MPs. One of them, a young woman from Maine, was very friendly and curious, and when she came into my room she sat right by my cell and started talking.

She was very interested in learning about Islamic culture and the Arabic language. She even ordered books on these subjects after talking to some of us. She was married, and she had a child. Once she told one of the dog handlers that her husband was upset with her ordering books about Islam. I found out later, from Foster the big talker, that the person that she was talking to was a black Muslim, although that was not obvious from the way he talked or behaved. I overheard him saying to her, 'Your husband should to be a little more open-minded, and a little less ignorant before he makes statements about a religion that he doesn't know.'

I know of two US soldiers who converted to Islam in Guantánamo. The first I only heard about from guards, but he was said to be a Puerto Rican who even prayed on the blocks with the detainees. I heard his conduct was deemed 'fraternization with the enemy' and he was removed from the island. The second was a young black woman from the South. I spoke with her a few times in Echo and found that she came to her decision after much contemplation, study, and discussion with prisoners. She was not sure about publicizing her decision as she knew there would be open hostility from many soldiers, similar to what she'd already witnessed, against Muslim civilian and military personnel stationed on the island. She was certainly one of the more thoughtful ones and I could understand why she was looking for something different.

I used to overhear the soldiers talking to each other often. And many of them also told me about their day-to-day lives; about the uncertainties of military life – in the shadow of Afghanistan and Iraq; about the pressures of PT tests; about promotion, or demotion (I saw Foster and another actually fight in my cell room over it); about finances, about family, about girlfriends and wives. In fact, one soldier committed suicide by shooting himself when he found out that his wife had left him. Others, I heard, had even committed murder after long tours of duty, when they returned home to find their sweethearts had moved on. One young soldier was removed from Echo after he broke down in front of me because his wife had left him, after learning he committed adultery – a punishable crime in the US Army – with a girl in Guantánamo. On top of all this, many soldiers were terrified of a prospect that the average person does not have: being sent into battle.

As I started learning about their ambitions in life and what they hoped to achieve, it cemented an assumption I had already made, that they were exceedingly materialistic. I know what it means to feel fulfilled by an act of charity, at home, or in a foreign land. But there was little sense of anything like that from how most of these soldiers spoke. They seemed to have few convictions, even about joining the army. From what they said, relatively few had joined the army as career soldiers. They had not even signed up for the active army, as most were National Guard or Army Reservists, never imagining they'd have to serve as full-time soldiers for a significant, often crucial, part of their lives, until they were activated and deployed.

As time went on they felt more confident with me and included me in their conversations. The only difference was that I was in the cage. Sometimes they would say they hated being in the military and felt they were in a cage too. Not just physically but because they were unable to get out of the army. To some of the more whingeing types I said, 'Well, good, because when you joined the army you knew what America was like, you knew what the American military had been doing for the past ten to fifteen years.' They said they didn't know, and that was probably true. They really did not know much about the world beyond their personal preoccupations.

Over time I learned a lot about some of those personal preoccupations, and became close to some surprising people. One was a very young soldier called Carlson, who went through an amazing meta-morphosis in Guantánamo. He'd been told by one of the officers, about me, 'Do not talk to this guy. He's very manipulative and he's very dangerous. He may sound nice but he's highly trained in martial arts and he's a . . . one of the worst people that we have here.'

Carlson looked like a typical American redneck, who never seemed to be too happy to be giving me anything I asked for, such as tooth-paste. Later I understood that he was like that because he'd just split up with his girlfriend who he wanted to marry, and he was devas-tated.

One day I read a poem out loud to Kim and he overheard it. It was my first-ever poem to Zaynab, and it was a very intense and romantic poem about her, but also stressed how she was my friend above all. There was even a little phrase of French, 'je t'aime', to end it.

When Kim left, Carlson came round and said, 'I heard your poetry, it's really good. I've written a poem too; do you want to hear it?' He read it, and it was about his relationship with the girl who he was ter-ribly in love with, but who'd dumped him while he was in Guantánamo. He told me his whole story bit by bit, and I became his confidant. In the months that followed, I heard every twist and turn of their story: 'She wants to come back to me,' or sometimes, 'She's with somebody else.' He was confused, and she was confused. As I fol-lowed their story, they both seemed to me so young and so typically American.

We talked about so many other things, and about what was going on. I knew he really felt for me, he was upset that I was in there, and by the time he left there was a real friendship. It was quite odd, because apart from talking about literature, travel, photography, and just human things, we did not really have much in common. He was nineteen, and I was thirty-five. He loved drinking, he'd tell me about getting drunk and vomiting all over the place, and I really didn't want to hear about that, and told him so.

Once Carlson took a four-day leave to Puerto Rico, and took hundreds of photographs. He brought them to show them to me in the cell. Nobody had ever done anything like that before. He was very good to me. I tried to help him with advice, about what he should do, how he should manage the immense debts which were why he was in the army in the first place.

Carlson told me that he didn't realize quite what a mess he was in until they put him into Camp Echo and he started talking to me. He told me about things he'd done in other parts of the camp, without telling me which detainee was involved. 'Some of the things I did with him, I can't believe that I did that.' He didn't go into detail about exactly what he did, but he mentioned that he slapped him around a few times, and that they did things to this person that he was ashamed of, that he wished he'd never done in his life. 'I don't know what happened to me, how I could stoop so low to do such a thing?'

I didn't press him, but I thought about it afterwards, and wondered whether how all these things would affect the rest of his ordinary American life, which I would never know about.

10
TRIAL OF STRENGTH

After eight months in Guantánamo I knew that the early promises by the Americans that I would get a lawyer were hollow, and that I was a man in limbo, on the say-so of President George Bush. It seemed as though my Guantánamo life could go on for ever, as I sat in my steel cell and saw young guards and interrogators come to the end of their term and be replaced by new faces. I had begun to realize the power and rigidity of the US military system, and its ability to consume any individual. Me, in this case.

One day started with the surprise of a guard telling me I was going to 'Reservation', which meant interrogations, and not in Echo. It was the very first time I had ever been anywhere near Camp Delta – Guantánamo's main prison – and I was curious, and in my typical way, hoping something positive would happen.

The MPs put me in a three-piece suit in my cell, and I shuffled out. They put me into the back of a tiny medical van, where I was squeezed in next to a guard. It felt like an oven, with a steel interior. There was no water to drink. The distance from Camp Echo to Camp Delta was only half a mile or so, I'd heard from the guards, and estimated when I climbed up the cage in the recreation yard and taken a quick look. I had seen a road snaking towards an enclosed area, Camp Delta, and even heard the call to prayer in the distance. But this journey took over an hour, sometimes stopping, sometimes crawling.

I felt myself getting dehydrated, and I asked the soldier, 'This is ridiculous. Why is it taking so long to get to this place, Reservation? It's only a few minutes' drive.' He didn't answer, but the heat was clearly troubling him too.

I had had no breakfast. The guards had rushed me out of my cell, saying, 'Get yourself ready, you have to go, somebody wants to see you.'

Sweat was streaming down my face, and I could feel it lying inside the shackles. I said, 'I really, really, need some water, please.'

'I can't open the door from inside. They won't open the door until we arrive.' He could have banged on the door, or used his radio, but he decided to wait. This military rigidity, the inability to grasp a situation with common humane sense, the absolute lack of flexibility, was something that really ground me down, although I always tried to control my fury. Suddenly, I vomited right there inside the vehicle. As it was a medical van, there was a bucket in it, which the guard managed to place near me. Eventually he banged on the door hard enough to get attention. The truck stopped, and they gave me some water, and helped me out.

I was trying to keep calm. 'This is ridiculous. Do you know how long I've been in the back of this vehicle?'

'Well, that soldier has been in there with you too.'

I was so angry I swore. 'He's not bloody shackled, is he?'

They took me to a room and shackled me to the floor with a metal loop that stuck out of the ground. I was left sitting there on a chair, but I was so uncomfortable, I could barely move my legs, even to stretch. Finally I just lay on the floor. I was there for at least seven hours, without anybody coming in at all, and with nothing to eat or drink.

Eventually, my surprise visitor arrived. It was Martin from the Foreign Office, and he had an American with him, probably an interrogator for all I knew. I sat up when they came in, and told them exactly what had happened that day.

Martin did at least ask to have me unshackled, which they did, except for the legs. It was supposed to be a welfare visit. 'Any complaints?'

Of course I had complaints. I told him, just as I had the first time he came: I was in a dog kennel; letters were not making it through regularly; the food was disgusting; recreation was a joke; and worst of all, I still had no idea about what was supposed to happen, and the lawyers I was supposed to have, had never come.

It was quite unreal, here was this Englishman, who I was absurdly glad to see just because he was English, and because he would be bringing me things from home, letters, photographs, magazines. But we were sitting in this interrogation room, across a table from each other, as though we were having a chat in a cafe.

At least he seemed a little embarrassed. 'Last time I saw you it wasn't like this, was it?' he said, pointing at my shackled feet. Last time I saw him, when he came with Lucy, the atmosphere and conditions were a lot more relaxed. I think Kim had had a lot to do with that, but also, all those months ago we had all been going along with the idea that I was heading to some kind of resolution.

'You know it wasn't like this.' I wanted him to register: this is not a normal situation I was in. I told him I was just resigned to my fate; there was no consistency in Guantánamo, nothing logical to hold on to.

He knew he'd given me letters and drawings by my children the previous time, and I could see he felt awkward when he had to tell me, 'Everything has to go through the censorship department of the US military.' He told me about a few things from the letters, which he'd obviously read. 'Your eldest daughter has had some problems at school . . .'

'What did he mean?' I asked myself. Too afraid of the answer he might give, if I asked him, 'Are my children being harassed because of me?' O Lord, please, they've been through enough; they're only children. My daughter is only eight years old. I know how children talk about their parents, often with reverence, but all my children know is that I'm in prison, and that means I must be . . .

I decided to wait until I received the letters. He said that I would get the letters once they were cleared, but I doubted that too. 'I don't believe I'll receive anything if you're not here to make sure that I get it.' He didn't want to be seen to be too sympathetic to me, in front of the Americans, as I was supposed to be a terrorist, and yet he still had to report on my mood and conditions to his superiors and forward those details to my family.

On 7 July 2003, I became one of only six prisoners in Guantánamo facing a potential trial, under President Bush's military order. I didn't know this, until that day, almost two months later, when Martin told me.

'After discussions held between the UK and US governments I must now inform you that you are eligible for trial by US Military Commission,' he read from a sheet on the table between us. 'I want to ask you if you understand what has been said to you and if you have any questions. I am not a legal advisor, or part of the military process, but my colleague may be able to answer any questions you might have.'

So this was it: trial, by military commission – a soldier's trial. 'What does that mean?' I thought. 'What are they going to charge me with? Are they going to try me here, in the US, or in England? What if I'm convicted based on the statement I signed? Will I get life? Surely they won't execute ... ? Will I get my own lawyer? Maybe I can see my family in court?' No, I couldn't bear to even think of such a thing. Even though my heart was yearning to see them again, that must never happen. They can't see me chained like an animal in a foreign court. Can I really expect a fair trial, or is it going to be a kangaroo court?' The questions raced through my mind then – and for months to come.

'So, do you have any questions, Mr Begg?'

'No. It's all perfectly clear.'

He soon left, after some trivial talk about David Beckham's transfer from Manchester United to Real Madrid, and the Queen Mother's death the previous year. I had to sit there for another two hours, still with no food or drink, before the MPs came to take me away. It was dark by then.

The next day was déjà vu. The same thing happened all over again, despite my having so specifically complained to Martin. He had told me that MI5 would want to speak to me the following day, and I asked, 'Can you make sure that the same ordeal isn't repeated?' But it was exactly the same, except that I took a bottle of water with me in the vehicle, and I didn't vomit. I shouted out to get the attention of the guards, who had left me again, chained for seven hours in the inter-rogation room. I wondered often whether these exercises were carried out with deliberate malice, or was it simply incompetence.

At last, MI5 came into the room. It was Lucy and someone else. They apologized profusely, presenting me with a book, *English Passengers*. The questioning didn't last very long; it included about ten minutes of showing photographs, and questions about people I didn't know, or had last seen many years ago.

By the time I was returned to my cell, it was late. I had missed rec and dinner. My sole consolation was a book about a fictional nine-teenth-century English quest for the Garden of Eden – in Tasmania.

I could not stop thinking about the message Martin had delivered. I felt a little foolish not having questioned him about it, but I had been afraid of what some of the answers might have been. Whatever it meant, I knew it wasn't progress. I'd understood that it wasn't what I had hoped, going to a United States court, where I would enter a normal legal system, where the onus was on the prosecution to prove that I had committed a crime.

I started asking the guards, with a nagging increase in anxiety, 'What have you heard about the military commissions?' The general consensus seemed muddled and ill informed, but they said it would include the use of secret information, the absence of a jury, and a mil-itary defence lawyer. I would have no say in the matter. It seemed quite outrageous to me: how on earth was it possible for a soldier to defend me? A soldier who'd given his oath of allegiance to the United States of America, and to George Bush, the Commander-in-Chief, who had already labelled us as killers and terrorists?

An interrogator once tried to draw an analogy. 'Have you ever seen *A Few Good Men*, with Tom Cruise and Demi Moore?'

'You forgot Jack Nicholson.'

'Yes, him too. Anyway, you know most of the story occurs in Guantánamo Bay, strangely enough. But the military lawyer tried to defend his client as best as he could.'

'True. But that's because his client was a US Marine, and he was US Navy. I am called "an illegal combatant". And you're talking about a film, this is my life at stake here.'

Months before, Kim had said, 'Once the lawyer is appointed, I, as an interrogator, am not allowed to speak to you or visit without his or her explicit agreement.' I was upset at the thought of losing her visits, and she too said that she felt guilty leaving, while I stayed. About three weeks passed while I waited to meet a lawyer.

Then to my surprise Kim turned up again. 'I didn't think I'd ever see you again. What's the occasion?' I asked.

'I was told that you had asked for me, because lawyers haven't arrived yet. Haven't they come?'

'No, I thought you would have known about that.'

'I am really sorry. I was assured that a US military lawyer had been appointed and was due to meet you within days of when I last saw you. Anyway, this gives me time to see you over a couple of weeks until I leave.'

She left after those two weeks, still maintaining that the lawyer was going to come soon. It never happened. They kept me in that limbo for a very long time. It was very hard not to lose hope, and not to let the strain show. My final farewell to Kim was quite sad. She'd been around for over six months, and I felt she took a personal interest in my welfare. I remembered one day she came just to request the NCOIC, Sergeant Walker, to allow me out of the cell to look at something weird she'd spotted outside. This was considered highly irregular, as I was only allowed out during rec times. But she convinced him. We all walked out together, I was shackled of course, and she told me to look up. It was the strangest thing: the sun seemed to be encircled, perfectly, by a golden halo. Both of us thought it quite amazing, but the others couldn't see what the fuss was about. Before she left, Kim gave me a copy of one of the photographs she'd taken that day of the sun. It had been stamped, like any other letters or literature, 'Approved by US Forces'.

Other interrogators replaced Kim, and they did behave like their job description. I'd had enough of most of them by this time. I was on edge, beginning to lose tolerance and patience with them perpetually asking me the same questions, and giving me no answers. Weeks and months were passing by without another mention of a lawyer's arrival, though they all said, 'You'll be seeing a defence attorney soon.'

Once, in a rare moment of rage, I asked a soldier to record in the log, 'If the interrogators return, and you bring me out of my cell to speak to them, I won't be responsible for what happens. I may end up hitting one of them.' Then, as the anger mounted, I raised my voice, 'They're a bunch of lying bastards and hypocrites . . .'

'Um, five-five-eight . . . How do you spell hi-po-crit?'

That evening, the night-shift SOG, having read the day's log, on a routine visit to my cell said, 'I promise you, five-five-eight, you will be sorry if you try and harm one of my MPs.'

'Your soldiers are not the problem, Sergeant. A few of them are the only friends I've got. I made threats against the interrogators. I don't want to see their faces, I don't want to be taken anywhere near them.' And still they came.

I knew there had been tensions between MPs and interrogators. The guards felt that the interrogators assumed an air of superiority over them; not socializing, or even talking to them, unless they absolutely had to. Many interrogators were thick-skinned, continually returning even after I'd flatly refused to answer their questions. Sometimes they pleaded that they were trying to save lives, and other times they threatened to harm mine.

'We won't let your letters through unless you answer our questions,' one had said.

Kim had left behind a dictionary for me with her replacement, saying I should ask for it when he came next; she'd not had time to have it stamped and approved before she left. When I asked him for it he said, 'Well, first you answer my questions.'

'No, it was left for me by Kim. You were only supposed to hand it over.'

'*I'm* here now, you've got to deal with *me*, it's nothing to do with her. Just answer a couple of questions for me and I'll bring you some cookies next time, and we'll conversate. I hear you like to philosophize. So do I.'

'You can keep your cookies, and to hell with your questions, because I am not answering them. Keep the dictionary too – seems like you need it more than me.'

He eventually did give me the Webster's dictionary in an attempt to get on better with me and perhaps to get some information. Then he began to 'conversate'.

'So, Moazzam, what's your opinion on suicide bombers?'

'Here we go again,' I thought. Sometimes I wished I couldn't speak English.

'Suicide operations are not a new phenomenon,' I began, 'and they're certainly not exclusive to the Muslim world. They are the product of extreme situations, last resorts, coupled with an unshakeable belief in a fight against oppression, with the ultimate weapon: one's own life. No person, Muslim or otherwise, knowingly sacrifices his life believing it to be an evil act – not for family, friends, country, or creed. There are differing opinions amongst Islamic jurists. Some are completely opposed to it, citing the clear Quranic injunction against taking one's own life, under any circumstances. Others have quoted precedent from the early Islamic period, when individual soldiers had charged into a mass of enemy troops, deliberately, causing their own death. Of course the enemy in these cases inflicted the death blow. How that translates to the present is also hotly debated, especially about occupations like in Palestine and Chechnya. I think, in principle, there is little difference between dropping a smart bomb from twenty thousand feet in the sky, which usually kills large numbers of civilians, collateral damage as you call it, and the person who kills civilians with a bomb in a restaurant . . .'

'So you're perfectly happy with someone, having the "right intention", walking into a shopping mall, strapped with forty pounds of TNT around his chest, looking for the right moment to kill as many infidels as possible?' he said, trying to needle me.

'No, I am not. But the issue is not one of mode. It's about the target. I believe categorically that it is wrong to target civilians in any military engagement. Just as it is wrong to carpet-bomb civilians – quite often in their own homes, their own homes for God's sake – in an area where suspected enemies are based, just because the bombers, in their B52s, do not have to look their victims in the face.'

'But everywhere you look, you see terrorism: suicide bombers are on the increase, and it always stems from the Muslim world, murdering in the name of religion. Algeria, Afghanistan, Iraq, Lebanon, Somalia, Bosnia, Israel, India, Philippines, Russia, Egypt, and Sudan – you name it. And now it's come to our shores. But we put a Texan in the White House . . .'

'Most of these places you've mentioned are occupied, or ruled by despots. And it is not new on your shores. Your world has been at war with itself for ages. You had two world wars, wars against the real Native Americans, your barbarous history with the slave trade, and the self-destructive Civil War. Korea and Vietnam too are etched in the memory of generations. I know the Muslim world is in a mess, but you tell me where the concept of world war originated? And what about weapons of mass destruction? "Enola Gay" isn't the most notorious aircraft in the world's history because of its peculiar name, now is it? Your gun lobby, the National Rifle Association, is one of the most powerful in the US. You fight for the right to bear arms, in a country that is plagued by firearms violence: juvenile college killings, shopping-mall snipers, serial killers, Hollywood-style shoot-outs with the cops, gang violence from all your races – Latino Lords,

Mexican Mafia, Crips and Bloods, Aryan Brotherhood, Ku Klux Klan;
highest crime figures in the world, especially murder in your capital
city. I've met soldiers now from almost every state in your country.
Everyone I've spoken to knows someone who's been shot or killed.
Some have even been shot themselves. They'd have been far safer in
Afghanistan.'

And so the 'conversating' ended.

Being in solitary confinement for such a long time gave more
opportunity than I could have imagined to reflect on my life. I thought
I knew so much before. I had seen my mother die when I was only six,
my sister when I was eleven, and one of my closest friends when I was
twenty-one. I'd seen corpses in Bosnia and Afghanistan – I knew
about death. I was not scared of it, but I was afraid of my judgement in
the ultimate court of the Hereafter. So I had embarked on a journey
that would help secure my fate in the afterlife, by helping the poor and
oppressed from amongst the people I related to most: Muslims. That
was what I was doing when I travelled around Europe and Asia, learning about a world that had been alien to me. This was part of the
reason I was here.

But I made a huge discovery during incarceration, about relating to
people. When I first saw Sergeant Foshee I thought, 'He's too old to be
in the army; they *must* be desperate.' And when he asked me, in his
Alabama drawl, if I was English, I thought, 'Another typical raghead-
hating, stars-and-bars, KKK-type redneck.'

Foshee was a redneck, a 'good ol' boy'. Most of the time, when he
was in my room, he sat there reading the Bible, and we didn't speak.
I'd heard from Kelvin, the Virgin Islander, and others that Foshee was
racist, didn't like women in the army, hated JFK, lost his temper
quickly and ordered people about. Back in the US he worked as an
undercover narcotics agent. But he was also a Vietnam veteran.

'Excuse me, Sergeant, do you mind if I ask you something about Vietnam?'

As a teenager I'd been fascinated by the Vietnam War, and even then I'd identified with the underdog. I felt compelled to ask this vet from Nam about his experiences.

I must have asked the right question. Foshee loved giving me his detailed recollections of Vietnam, and I couldn't get enough. He described graphically the assaults he'd been in, the friends he'd seen killed, the civilian massacres, and the stress he'd suffered on return to the US. Several of his comrades had been POWs.

Then came the inevitable comparison between them and us.

Foshee was deeply disturbed by our treatment as detainees. He couldn't understand why we weren't treated as POWs. For us he had a soldier's respect.

'I don't know if you've done anything, but they say this is a war. You should all be sent home, cos the war's over. Or you should be treated like POWs. I know there are people here who fought the Soviets for years and even *I'm* a baby compared to them – in age and experience. I get so pissed when I see those punkass kids treating y'all that way, when they ain't even done a thing for this country.' He was talking about soldiers in Echo who had soaked detainees with water, then left the air conditioning on full. 'I'm fixin' on opening one of them there cell doors to see what those young fools do when a man's not in chains.'

To me Foshee was an enigma: his attitudes were clearly Republican, and yet he did not like what he was seeing. And he wasn't the only one.

Jennifer was a woman in her early twenties, from the Deep South: Selma, Alabama. Her most striking feature was the length of her auburn hair, which she kept tucked under an army cap – following the rules – much of the time. The first time I spoke to her was about Dickens' *Bleak House*, which I was reading. I saw instantly that I was going to have some rare, erudite discussions with this soldier. Whenever she entered my room, green coffee flask in hand, she sat down, logged in, and began doodling on a piece of paper. Or so I imagined. In fact she was drawing and colouring very intricate symmetrical designs of psychedelic artwork. Simultaneously, she was engaged in deep conversation with me about anything from the Dead Sea Scrolls to cooking escargots. Or she was telling me why, in her spare time, she painted her lips and fingernails black, dressed like a Goth, and read Tarot cards. Before this, with my conservative Islamic approach to life, I would never have imagined I could find a friend in someone like her. To top it all she was a Republican.

What could I possibly have had in common with her? Well, as it turned out: studying jujitsu, flying lessons, sword collections, affinity for the English language, poetry, a taste for classical literature and ancient history. The unique circumstances produced a somewhat unique friendship.

'I know it sounds a little treasonous, but I would much rather sit here and talk with y'all than the airheads we have in the military,' she said once. 'They're only ever after one thing, no matter who you are. It's an obsession with them, even a lot of the females. And if you don't surrender yourself to them they spread malicious rumours around.'

Once, she confided, 'When we were briefed about this place we weren't relishing the idea of spending a long time here. Gitmo was home to the "worst of the worst", they said. Then a handful of us were chosen for this mission in Echo, maximum-security isolation block, where the most dangerous terrorists in the whole island were kept. I was expecting a Hannibal Lecter/Agent Starling type situation, with you guys trying to terrify us using perverse mind games . . .'

'So how does it feel, discussing *Les Misérables* with one of the most dangerous men on earth?'

'I can see now how we all bought the hype. I don't know if they've even accused you of anything, but I know y'*all* can't be guilty. The government would have displayed their strongest evidence in a sensational show trial by now . . . I expected you to hate all Americans after all you've been through, especially us soldiers. But you're wonderfully complex, Moazzam. All the things I'd expect you to be, you're not.'

Despite being very young, she was rather mature, and rare among her peers in enjoying an intellectual discussion. Jennifer only stayed in Guantánamo a few months, and left suddenly because of difficulties at home. But she left me with a lasting impression: all Americans were not the same.

Jenner, a teenager from Minnesota, told me his ancestor was Edward Jenner, who, I remembered from secondary-school biology, was the man who discovered that the prevention for smallpox lay in the hands of the milkmaids, who had contracted cowpox. Hence, 'vaccination', from the Latin for cow, *vacca*. With his round steel-rimmed glasses, short blond hair, and soft voice, Jenner could have been mistaken for a geek, especially because he loved computer role-playing games and reading fantasy novels about elves and wizards. Some of the other soldiers thought him a wimp. They named him Snap, after he'd shouted, 'It's snapped!' when in fact 'it', his ankle, was only sprained during a soccer match. Jenner also began dating the oddest, most unlikely female soldier I, or her colleagues, had ever encountered.

I had the habit of giving nicknames to deserving guards. In Guantánamo there was Saddam Hitler, because of his resemblance to one and behaviour like the other, Elmer Fudd, Killer B, Knuckle Dragger and now Jenner's new girlfriend, Mildred. 'Why Mildred?' the MPs asked.

'Because she looks like one, and it's better than Gertrude, the only other possible choice.'

I found Jenner easy to talk to and liked listening to him tell tales of his tour in Korea, and Hungary, where he guarded US forces training Iraqi insurgents for the imminent war against Saddam Hussein. I also heard about his philosophical conversations on Islam with a Moroccan detainee known as the General.*

But the most profound story Jenner told was about a letter he'd just received from a friend stationed in Iraq. Jenner said that he and six of his friends from school had all joined the military around the same time. The seven friends all promised each other to meet next in 2007, on the seventh day of the seventh month at 7 p.m. But now that promise could never be fulfilled. One of the seven had been killed in a suicide-bomb attack. I was very moved by the story, and the fact that he had shared it with me.

'Jenner, I feel for your personal loss. I know what it is to lose loved ones, more than I hope you'll ever have to imagine. But as long as US occupation forces remain in Muslim lands, slaughtering people indiscriminately, people like your friend are going to continue getting killed, until they leave.' May be it was utterly insensitive to say that, perhaps I should have said nothing at all, but Jenner's response took me by surprise. 'You're right! I don't know what the hell we're doing in a country that most of us don't know or give a damn about. It's one thing to defend your nation from foreign and

---

* Ahmad Arrachidi: a British resident from Morocco.

domestic foes, but the Iraqis have never done shit to us. Why did he have to die over there?'

I only had one direction that wasn't white steel wall to look at. Staring through the diamond-shaped caged mesh had begun to damage my eyes from day one in Guantánamo. Headaches increased and I was soon on more medication than I had been in my entire life. I developed acute pains in my ears and sometimes they felt like they were about to explode. I was prescribed sleeping tablets and antidepressants.

I find it hard to describe the sense of utter desperation and claustrophobia I often felt during almost two years, isolated in a cell smaller than my toilet at home. I spent countless nights praying, crying, thinking . . . and regretting certain decisions in my life. When I finally did get to sleep my dreams were filled with strange and wonderful visions of life far away from US soldiers and concentration camps. In fact I hated waking up. I wished I never woke up again. It was during that time I wrote 'Dark World'. Some of its verses read:

> Tormenting strain is at a height,
> Darkness blotting out sunlight,
> All has disappeared, but night,
> Eyes have shed their tears from light

> Awaiting anxiously respite,
> The noose is closing in too tight.
> Proceeding on ahead, despite
> The guiltless beings they indict

> Life is drained by parasite,
> Inflicting pain as from a bite.

End is near, but not just quite –
My world is dark, and theirs – is white

There had been a nauseating smell daily growing worse by the time my cell was infested with maggots. My complaints had fallen on deaf ears, so I scooped up the creatures and flushed them down the toilet. But more came, and kept coming until they transformed into flies. An iguana had died underneath my cell.

All that day I'd felt something building up inside me. There was only space enough to pace three steps forward, then back again, up and down. And then, I exploded. I lost control of myself, which was something that had never happened to me. Threatening interrogators from afar was the worst I'd done. I picked up everything in my cell and smashed it to the ground; I kicked the walls, I kicked the door, I punched it, I started swearing and crying, not particularly at Jenner, but at anybody. Jenner was shocked. He did not know what to do, as he was used to my being so calm. He rushed out and called the sergeant of the guard, Sergeant Lopez, a professional, decent, and empathetic Hispanic. The camp commander, First Sergeant Glenn Carnahan, rushed in too, and as soon as I saw him I began to swear. Carnahan wasn't a bad person either, but as he was the camp commander he became the obvious target of my frustration.

'Come to see the show, you motherfucking bastard? Either you come in my cell, you wimp, or fuck off! Go on, just fuck off!'

They told me afterwards he was so stunned that he walked right out of the camp.

Later I tried to explain to them, 'Listen, when a person like me starts blowing up you've got to know that there's something seriously wrong.'

When Foshee, the Vietnam vet, heard about the incident he was very upset and tried to comfort me with stories of the Hanoi Hilton, how some of his friends had survived torture and solitary – and some hadn't. I had. I made a few friends with guards over the years in US custody, but only one ever earned my respect.

I later apologized to Carnahan for having lost control – not because my complaints weren't genuine, but because it was so unlike me to swear.

The strain was definitely building up as time went on. I started getting less talkative and wasn't interested in talking to the newer soldiers. I was becoming more of a recluse.

My solace was in writing to my family, and in writing poetry. I found I could channel some of my anger into my poetry, and it culminated in a fifty-three-verse poem, called 'Indictment USA'. I wanted to write a poem with each stanza ending in 'fuck the USA' and 'damn the USA'. But by the time I'd cooled down and was thinking lucidly, it became a rhyming history of the US in three sections: from the Founding Fathers through to the Civil Rights movement; from the Second World War to the War on Terror, and the internal affairs of a postmodern US, with a personal epilogue to close.

Psychiatrists came to see me as a result of my uncontrollable anxiety attack. But it was not a psychiatrist I needed when I'd asked Sergeant Lopez to get somebody over. I had wanted to speak to a senior ranking officer and complain about still being here with no end in sight, about mail, lawyers, recreation, food, and conditions. Sergeant Lopez, of course, was very restricted in who he could call. He would have to do it through Sergeant Carnahan, because of the rank structure. Carnahan called the most appropriate person he could think of, a psychiatrist. For me that just revealed Carnahan's limited mentality.

The psychiatrist came over. First of all he was very surprised that I spoke English. And then he started telling me some drivel about the methods they use to try and help people, based on experiences of survivors of Belsen and Auschwitz. 'So at least you acknowledge what you're running here bears an uncanny resemblance to the camps your grandfathers helped liberate over a half-century ago,' I snapped. I was thinking to myself, 'This fool's patronizing me with all this nonsense . . .'

I went on, 'You see me as the enemy. You're there in your combat BDU [Battle Dress Uniform], with the US flag facing the wrong way because you're "charging towards the enemy" and I'm here in orange. I don't need your advice.'

'Look at the Auschwitz survivors, or at Nelson Mandela . . .' he went on oblivious.

'Have you ever read Nelson Mandela's life story,' I asked him, '*Long Walk to Freedom*?'

'No.'

'Perhaps you'd better before you start quoting him.'

He went on with, 'Have you read the Book of Job in the Bible? It's a very inspirational way of looking how to tackle trials and tribulations.'

'Yes, as a matter of fact I've read the Book of Job several times. My wife has named my youngest son Ayub, or Job in English, for precisely that reason. But you are the cause of my trials and tribulations. How many times have I asked for another Muslim to speak to, or even a US Army Muslim chaplain? And they give me a psychiatrist that talks of a religion that he doesn't believe in, quoting from books he's never read.'

I knew exactly why he was doing it; I was a practising Muslim, so therefore I must be susceptible to stories from the Bible, or the Quran.

'It's over two years since I've been a captive of you and your country.

Held in these conditions you should be asking why I haven't exploded before. Any sane person would have.'

In Guantánamo there was a rodent nicknamed the Banana Rat, the size of a domestic cat, with long rat-like tail. Some soldiers and interrogators would wear orange T-shirts depicting these animals as detainees. I never actually saw one (though I had seen a similar T-shirt in Bagram), but one of the guards had slipped up and mentioned it to me, and then later I had it confirmed because other people were talking about buying these T-shirts and taking them home as souvenirs.

'Tell me something,' I asked the psychiatrist. 'You're an officer, right?'

'Yes.'

'Well, what have you done about the dehumanization process that you're very much a part of?'

'What do you mean? We don't dehumanize you at all, we view you as human beings and we try to treat you as such.'

'Really? So what, as an officer, have you done about those T-shirts circulated on the island, caricaturing us as animals?'

His expression was telling, as if to say, 'How the hell did you know that I bought one?'

Later on I saw two other Hitchcocks, as they were called (a name I assumed came from the film *Psycho*). One came over after another, less dramatic, incident when my anger boiled over again. It was not as drastic as the first time, but they'd decided to call a psychiatrist again. She was an African American. I couldn't make her out, she was either really dense or she was insidiously malicious, and trying to use mind games to explore my weaknesses.

She asked me, 'Have you ever thought about harming yourself?'

'No, never.'

'Haven't you ever thought about getting your trousers and threading them with your bed sheet so that you could form a noose and tie it around your neck?'*

'No. Not until you suggested it.'

They actually sent me this psychiatrist instead of a Muslim chaplain, whom I had asked for continuously, but they'd always refused. It was so obvious to me that contact with a fellow Muslim would have helped me enormously psychologically. And that was just what they didn't want.

There was a medic, Blondie, who used to visit my cell every few days and I often used to talk to him. He asked me once if I had ever met the Muslim chaplain.† I hadn't. He told me that the chaplain had been arrested by the military and charged with providing secret information to al-Qa'idah. One of the guards overheard Blondie saying this, and within minutes the guard called the sergeant of the guard. Blondie was taken out immediately and that was the last I saw of him. I heard from the next medic that Blondie had been severely reprimanded for discussing classified information with the enemy.

I had repeatedly asked for contact with other detainees – to be taken out of isolation, but they gave me a psychiatrist instead. Dr B. visited me over quite a long period. She was fairly well read, and the weekly one-hour sessions opened a door for conversation that was increasingly being shut in my face. Since cameras had been installed, in the summer of 2004, guards only visited the cells once every hour or so.

Dr B. once said, 'One day, I believe parts of this camp will be on display in the Smithsonian Museum, just as remnants of the Japanese

---

* Since my return I have read about these types of methods being used by the US military as part of a strategy to break prisoners. The *New Yorker*, July 2005 and *International Herald Tribune*, 25 June 2005.
† Captain James Yee. In 2003, Yee was falsely accused by the FBI and US military of spying against the US, providing classified information to the Syrians and being an al-Qa'idah sympathizer. After spending seventy-six days in solitary confinement he was cleared of all charges, but never received an apology. See *For God and Country* by James Yee (Public Affairs, 2005).

internment camps are there now, a witness to our history.' She didn't seem too proud of America.

I tried to draw out information from her about other detainees, asking about the worst cases she'd seen in Guantánamo. She told me there were people who'd lost all sense of time, reason, reality; people who had been kept in a solitary cell, completely blocked off with no window, eight foot by six, like mine, but with absolutely nobody to speak to, nobody. She said some of them just ended up talking to themselves. She also confirmed that there had been suicide attempts. I had heard from the guards about one detainee who they called Timmy, who had hanged himself. They managed to get to him in time to save his life, but he had become a vegetable by the time they did, so he was always in hospital, shaking, unable to speak.

About this time I was taken to the hospital because I had toothache, which I had been complaining about for several months. They took me in that van, like for Reservations. In the hospital I was put on a military bunk bed, with one of my legs and one of my arms shackled to it so that I couldn't move. I could just about sit up. I could hear voices, so I knew there was a detainee in one of the beds across from me, though they'd put a curtain round it. I worked out that if I leant over and pulled the curtain across, and if he did the same, we could manage to speak to one another and see one another, and that would be amazing. I had never seen a detainee in all my time in Guantánamo.

The hospital guards didn't know who I was, or that I was from Camp Echo. As far as they were concerned, this was another one from Delta, and they're used to speaking to each other.

I pulled the curtain a little, and whispered, '*As-salaamu alaikum.*'

The reply came back, '*Wa alaikum as-salaam.*'

I said, 'Move your curtain forward.'

He did, and I saw him. I didn't know him. Much later I learned that he was Salim Hamdan, allegedly one of Usamah bin Ladin's many drivers, who was also held in Camp Echo, three rooms away from my cell. We started talking, and, apart from the relief of the contact with someone who knew exactly what I was going through, what he said was quite encouraging. He told me that he was in a military commission process, and had had a military lawyer appointed. With a lawyer, even though he was from the military, he had more contact with the outside world. He also told me a bit about the main Camp Delta, where he had been before Echo.

Just looking him in the face was amazing, and the whole incident really raised my morale. We were talking in whispers, and every time we heard footsteps, we stopped. Our little meeting only lasted for about ten minutes or so, and then they came along and took me to my dental appointment.

Life in Echo was boring and monotonous. Things changed as the guards changed, every few months. I had to get used to a whole new set of guards – besides those new interrogators who had made me so furious that I'd lost control. These guards were a mixture of men and women from full-time active-duty units as well as National Guard and Reservists. They were from the North and from the South, whereas the previous unit had been mostly from around Michigan and Ohio.

The new group was mixed and included people from Alabama, Arkansas, the Virgin Islands, from Puerto Rico, although there were no Puerto Rican units in Camp Echo. With each changing of the guard everybody wanted to be seen to be implementing new and improved techniques to run the camp. They all wanted to rewrite the SOP. I paid attention and noticed the marked differences between people of various cultures and backgrounds among the guards: ages, experience, and whether they were active-duty or Reservists or National Guard.

Understanding all these intricate differences appealed to me. Partly it was because I'm always interested in people and what motivates them, partly because it was an intellectual puzzle to pass the time. I noticed, for instance that the black soldiers tended to hang around and talk to one another, and keep well away from, for example, white soldiers from Alabama. The Hispanics too hung around with one another. A lot of them used to spend time with me. If one, say, Lopez, was in my room, Gonzales would walk in too, and so would Ruiz and others. People from the Virgin Islands were the same, and I got along well with them too.

When I was young, in Birmingham, I knew a lot of Jamaicans, people from St Kitts and the British Virgin Islands, and I used to listen to reggae music and eat with them and socialize. When I came across people from the US Virgin Islands – which I'd never heard of – with the same type of accent although not as strong as the Jamaicans, it was clear to me that these people were completely different to mainland US soldiers. They even looked different, more African than the average black American. We had plenty of things to chat about.

Also, they were very relaxed, very laid back, and generally they treated me more humanely than other people did. They weren't sticklers for the rules. They spoke to me as if I was just an ordinary person, and they certainly weren't interested in hiding their nametags. Other guards were pretty scornful and racist towards them, seeing them as not really Americans, but wearing a US Army uniform and having a little meal ticket to ride off the back of the United States. Some of them told me they were upset at how they were treated. They said how clearly racist the whites often were. 'They don't like black people . . . to them we're in a lower category even than you detainees, because you're still lighter skinned than us . . . we're black, and they just hate us.'

Two of them became my friends. One was Kelvin, who was a very ordinary man from the Virgin Islands, whose goals were to have the fastest cars and motorbikes, a surround-sound stereo system and the latest DVDs, and watch the latest porno movies. When I started to talk to him about religion, philosophy, and war politics, he was an example of somebody who for the first time started searching within himself to find out about the world. The first time that he'd stepped outside his island was when he went to basic training, and he was shocked to be asked by fellow trainees, 'Do you guys have electricity there? Do you have proper houses? Do you have cars?' He told me it had made him very indignant.

Kelvin had come smack up against the ignorance of Americans, and the small-minded prejudice which made them say, 'You're not proper Americans.' He, like many of his fellow soldiers from the US Virgin Islands, was homesick. Geographically speaking, their home was very close to where we were in Cuba, a flight home would take no more than half an hour. But when they looked at the detainees, they couldn't help seeing some of their own history. I used to talk with some of them about the origins of the war on terror, and I pointed out that the last time in history that people were taken over the Atlantic, en masse, and brought to the Americas, it was their ancestors.

Kelvin became one of my closest friends, and he used to talk to me about very private things, like how much he had been affected by the death of his father, who he deeply missed. When Kelvin talked in depth about these kinds of things I thought, 'I doubt he's discussing these things with his platoon sergeant.' We had a real bond, a friendship. I could read his moods from day to day. I knew that Feroz, my unseen companion, used to talk to him too, and he would sometimes mention things about Feroz, or other prisoners in Echo, such as David Hicks, or Salim Hamdan.

Kelvin asked me once, 'Why would al-Qa'idah attack America? What does Usamah bin Ladin want?' I started to explain that one of the reasons was the US presence in the Arabian peninsula . . . But then, realizing, I suppose, these issues were so disassociated with his life, he said, 'This is just above me, I don't understand any of it.' And he'd bring everything back to his own feelings. 'I hate this damn armpit of the world. I don't want to be here, damn the military. I only joined because I thought I was going to be a National Guard, I never, ever, thought I was going to get activated and sent to this damn place, I hate it, and now they're talking about possibly sending us to Iraq as well. I'm going to leave the army; I'm going to go AWOL or whatever.' He had a wife and a child back home and he told me a lot about how he met her and what she was like, her morals and manners, very personal things. Listening to him I thought, 'He really loves his wife.' I felt close to him although we came from such different worlds.

I said to several of the guards that one day they should visit me in Birmingham. Kelvin was the only one who actually invited me back to *his* place to visit his family – something I could actually envisage myself doing.

I told his chubby friend, Natty, with whom I could joke *and* be serious, 'I'd study a bit of your roots and your origins and try and work out how that relates to the situation that we're in. If you can't recognize the parallel, then I think you're blind to history. After all, the majority of slaves taken from west Africa were Muslim. Start with Haley's *Roots* if you doubt me, and do your own research.' I don't know if he ever read it, but he enjoyed those discussions. Many of them talked proudly about their own Caribbean culture, uniquely distinct from mainland America.

'You ever heard of the Caribbean dish *Moros y Cristianos*, fatty . . . I mean Natty?'

'Don't be smart, shorty. Yes, I have, black beans and rice, right?'

'Right. But did you know that *Moros* is Spanish for "Moors", North African Muslims?'

'I didn't know that.'

The war on terror, the attacks in the United States, had not affected the Islanders much, and they felt it didn't involve them. Kelvin once said to me, 'September 11th was the first day in history black people got a break: they hated you Muslims more than they hated us.'

'So if you happen to be black *and* Muslim . . .'

Amongst the Virgin Islanders there was a girl called Thomson – the only white person in that unit. But she identified herself as black. 'I'm black. Black is a state of mind, not a colour.' She referred to some of the mainland blacks as 'freshwater Yankees'.

One of these soldiers was Richardson, a kid from somewhere in Louisiana, whose aspirations were like Kelvin's. 'All you Muslims are so dedicated to your faith,' he said once, 'but it's just a waste of time.'

'Well, what is faith? In fact, what is your faith, if you have any?'

'I don't know, man.' He didn't want to get into that discussion.

'Just go and look at your history, your ancestors certainly weren't indigenous to America, have a look at where they came from, study that a bit, and tell me then what you think about my faith. Because my faith is the same as your ancestors' was too.' That was an angle he had not expected at all.

Thomson and I were discussing Marcus Garvey one day, and his impact on black people in America. Richardson came in the room, clueless about Garvey; he had never even heard of him. Thomson tore into this 'freshwater Yankee' about his ignorance. I added salt to the wounds by quoting him, 'A people without history are like a tree without roots.'

Then we started talking about Malcolm X, Dr King, the Black Panthers, and the US civil-rights movement. I found it very sad that he didn't know much about them either. Maybe he didn't even care.

A few days later, I saw Richardson come into my room, carrying a thick book. I was always curious to know what books MPs were reading, staring hungrily through the cage on the offchance they'd forget it on the table, so I could ask the next unwitting soldier if he'd 'pass me my book from the table'. More often than not though, it was a King, Grisham, or Patterson novel. I peered through the cage, trying to glimpse the title. Richardson lifted it up and began to read: *Roots* by Alex Haley.

'Hey, Moazzam,' Kelvin once asked, 'why do your pals call us *himaar* all the time?' This was something many soldiers had asked me.

'Because they like you. It means donkey. If they really disliked you they'd be calling you *khanzeer* – pig.'

Kelvin also once told me that an Arab detainee called him nigger.

'Well you are, Kelvin. "Nigger" is a derivative of the French word *negre*, which means black.'

'That man's racist, Moazzam, he don't like black people at all. I did nothing wrong to him, but he's always cussing at the black soldiers.'

I was surprised to hear this. 'Go back,' I told him, 'and tell him that his ignorance is like that of the people who have labelled us "terrorists". In Islamic history there is a particular incident about one of the companions of the Prophet Muhammad called Bilal, who is revered as the first muezzin, the one who makes the call to prayer. He had the sweetest voice. A man once addressed him with, "O you son of a black slave-woman!" When the Prophet Muhammad heard about this he was enraged. Realizing he'd upset the Prophet, the man went over to Bilal, placed his own head on the ground, took Bilal's foot, and put it on his head saying, "Please forgive me." Go and tell him that story. That story is well known in the Islamic world. It means that racism is not supposed to be tolerated.'

Another soldier, Mesadore, originally from Haiti, was very different again. He was almost embarrassed by his Haitian origins. He spoke French patois and I tried to develop the French I'd learned in Bagram with him, but he was uncomfortable. 'Look, I don't even speak proper French.'

'Well, it's better than someone who doesn't speak French at all. Don't put yourself down.'

Many soldiers saw Haitians as the lowest of all in the Caribbean. In 1991, Camp X-Ray was first used by the US to hold thousands who had attempted to enter the US.

Mesadore spent nearly a whole year guarding in Camp Echo. We had almost daily conversations about everything, from his new love life in the military, to the hardships of life in the Haitian suburbs of Miami. Mesadore was, like Jenner, an active-duty soldier based in Fort Polk, Louisiana. He could not plead ignorance, as the National Guardsmen and Reservists had. Or so I thought. Mesadore was one of the growing numbers of very young soldiers who had joined the army for job security and travel, rather than from patriotism. He had not been swept up by the patriotic fervour following September 11. Instead, he'd been constantly hounded at college by a recruiting sergeant, after expressing some interest in the army. He was told that he'd be stationed in Germany and Korea. The recruiting sergeant, he told me, had a certain quota he must achieve every month. Failure to meet it resulted in demotion – the only job in the army like that.

I told him about my capture, my experiences in Kandahar, Bagram, and with what he knew about Guantánamo he said, 'Shit, Moazzam, after the way you've been treated, if y'all weren't terrorists before you came here, you will be by the time you leave.'

It was from Mesadore that I learned something about the naked-prisoner pyramids in Abu Ghraib. He felt ashamed, because the abusers, just like him, were MPs. In spring 2004, Mesadore wrote a poem about his thoughts on us. The last verse read:

> *Fully swindled by the dream of Justice,*
> *Now I'm awake and dare not discuss.*
> *The Orange man's pain and the white man's injustice;*
> *The flock's black sheep soldier left full of disgust.*

Mesadore was only nineteen years old and often went against the grain in his unit. He told me that some detainees didn't like him. But my experience of him was positive. He was another soldier who used to confide in me, and I gave him my advice about whatever I could. He often went out of his way to get me something, like a book or a snack, that would have got him in serious trouble. (The guards were not authorized to give me books, so any I did get from them I hid openly among the ones I was allowed. Very rarely would the guards check approved stamps.)

Before he left Mesadore said something that many MPs had told me: 'Listen, Mr Begg. I've learned so much from you. I will never forget you.'

And I will never forget them.

The term 'detainee' has been used almost exclusively to refer to people held for an indefinite period, without charge or trial, by US forces in Guantánamo Bay. The guards there, under pain of punishment, were required, as they told me, to refer to us all as 'detainees', which sometimes got me upset and into a quarrel with them. I was a captive, an abductee – or prisoner at the very least.

Many of the guards refused to get into conversations with 'anyone in an orange uniform', as I heard from Mesadore and knew for myself. Some of them tried to antagonize me by slamming the cell doors late at night, or brightening the lights. Others just clicked the shackles several notches more than necessary to cause pain and discomfort during transportation. One of these, a huge black staff sergeant from Washington (I knew his rank from his arm patch and the three chevrons on his cap and collars), once escorted me to the rec yard.

'Detainee comin' through,' he yelled to the guards on the other side. 'Close that door on twelve alpha [cell number].'

As we walked along I found the leg shackles were cutting into my skin.

'The shackles are too tight, Sergeant. Do you think they could be loosened, just a little?' I asked.

He stopped in his tracks, keeping a firm grip on my arm. Looking at me directly he said, 'How'd you know I was a sergeant?'

Keeping his gaze, I answered, 'The collars gave it away. How did you know I was a detainee?'

The other guard just shook his head, while the sergeant said nothing and just walked on. He didn't like talking to detainees.

Another guard from DC asked me once where I was from. When I told her I was from England, she thought for a moment then asked, 'Y'all got lions, elephants, and shit there?'

'Only in zoos. I said I'm from *England*, not Uganda.'

My only real consolation was writing occasional letters to Zaynab. Once I wrote asking her, 'Do you remember when, many years ago, I had a dream and woke up weeping and in tears? How I described a situation that is uncannily similar to the one I'm in now; how a child was born to us, but I couldn't be there? I thought the dream, at the time, was about Umamah, but in fact, as is now apparent, it referred to our son – Ayub.'Writing on the small pieces of Red Cross paper, and never knowing how long a letter would take to arrive, was desperately frustrating. I was always asking her whether she had received my letters and poems, and asking her if she or the children had been troubled by anyone because of me. Once I told her that my faith level was low, after not speaking to another Muslim for so many months. I asked her to understand that I got depressed, just as she did. But what could I really convey to her about my monotonous life?

After one whole year in Guantánamo I wrote to her, '. . . I cannot expect you to wait for me for ever. I'm sorry if I have said something you don't want to hear, believe me, I don't like saying it . . . I'm truly sorry that things have happened this way. I love you and the children, more than my own life . . . if I have said the wrong things here, just ignore it – I'm just frustrated, and am at a loss for what to do.'

But four days later my mood had changed. 'Today I received your beautiful "heart" drawn with scented pens. It's strange, a lot of people here have been talking about Valentine's Day – and, although we don't celebrate it, I get your letter now – mid-February.' I wrote her two letters that day, one via the Red Cross, and one through the US military, hoping that at least one would arrive. I tried to explain the mood behind my previous letter. 'I have various and conflicting inner thoughts, and I feel so responsible for the difficulties you must be facing. The truth is I really can't do anything . . . And therefore I feel I don't know what to do. I feel often that my prayers have gone unanswered – due to my own weak faith. I love you, your husband, *ton mari*.'

The same day I wrote to my older daughter, my dearest Umamah, 'I am sorry I have not written for a while. I did get all your lovely letters before: the one with the "smelly" ink, the "heart" drawings, and the letter about "skunks" and "vampire" bats . . . I want to know so much about what is happening with all of you . . . I miss you and love you so much that I cry when I think about it too much. Always read as much as you can . . . Your writing is very good indeed. Also, use a children's dictionary if you want to spell and use new words. I think about you every day and want to come home so much. Remember me when you pray and kiss everyone for me.'

Just a month later, in March 2004, Foreign Office Martin visited me, and read a statement about the release of five British prisoners* from Guantánamo. My response to that was twofold: complete elation at the news that it was finally over, for some people, people from Britain; but it was made clear that although 'negotiations between the UK and US governments are ongoing' in my case, I was not going with them. That also meant four of us Brits were to remain. The harsh reality was that I had no idea how long I was going to spend in Guantánamo.

A few months later I had another British visit, this time from MI5. Matt, the one I'd met in Kandahar, presented me with what I thought was a peace offering: *The English: A Portrait of a People*, by Jeremy Paxman. Why did they choose this book? It was humorous, informative, thorough, well researched and referenced. But did it contain a message for me about my own 'Britishness', or 'Englishness'? Were they saying, 'Traitor! Your forebears fought for the British Raj, and now look at you. Look at where your home is, the people whose land you call your own. And you've joined hands with terrorists who want to destroy our heritage?'

I read that book five times, from cover to cover – searching. In the

---

* Shafiq Rasul, Asif Iqbal, Ruhel Ahmed, Tarek Dergoul, and Jamal al-Harith.

end, though, I concluded there was little ulterior motive in a nostalgic look at John Bull's disdain of 'funny foreigners', 'the breed' of public-school boys who enjoyed a good spanking, the Duke of Edinburgh's embarrassing cock-ups, or boring old ladies in tweed skirts hosting a summer tea party on what remains of the village green.

I also wondered about Paxman's assertion, 'never underestimate the capacity of the English to back the underdog'. For a moment I thought, 'Maybe I'm English after all.'

But it didn't really ring true from my knowledge of history. More often than not – past or present, right or wrong – it was the British against, or even fighting, the underdog. But it's the *notion* of backing (even if they weren't) the weaker one who's up against the odds which probably appealed to their consciences.

It made me think, but the book was nothing more than an enjoyable read.

'We've just come to ask about your welfare and see if you're OK. We happened to be in the area, just passing by.' Nobody just 'passes by' at Guantánamo. I never did understand the purpose of that MI5 visit. Surely it couldn't have just been to deliver Paxman? They didn't even ask me any questions, except, 'How are you holding out, Moazzam? Is your faith strong, or do you think you're weaker?'

I used the chance to complain, again: no Muslim chaplain, no regular mail, no lawyers, solitary confinement, and no progress . . . 'But why are you here?'

'We're concerned about you and wanted to let you know MI5 are not that bad.'

'Well, they are,' I said. 'They are that bad.'

11

THE TEASING ILLUSION

After nearly a year and a half in solitary in Guantánamo – two and a half years since I had seen my family – I had learned to live this life, keeping my dignity and humanity, but inside I was deeply angry at the huge injustice I was suffering. I still had never understood why I was being held at all, never mind why in solitary. Visits from the Foreign Office usually brought letters from Dad, my stepmother, and from Zaynab including photographs of the children, and touching drawings they had made for me. I was still in their lives, but there was no way I could convey to them my little routine of cell, exercise yard, disgusting food, orange uniform, and reading the Quran – not that I wanted to. But the British officials never levelled with me – what did they really think of me? Surely they *knew* I wasn't a terrorist, or even a terrorist sympathizer?

It was a total surprise when I got what seemed to be a clue to why I was special for the Americans – perhaps why I was alone. I was a witness to two murders by US soldiers. I was going to be used for their own internal disciplinary reasons, which of course had nothing to do with anything I personally was accused of.

In June 2004, two investigators from the Criminal Investigation Department (CID) came over to my cell and asked me about my time in Bagram. They asked me about the first murder I had witnessed, but they were most interested in the second. They were very thorough and wanted me to describe in exact detail what I saw and how close I was. First they showed me the picture of 421, and I vaguely recognized him although I hadn't see him too clearly because he was always facing away. And then they told me to brace myself because they were going to show me a picture of his body. They did. There were tubes attached to his nose and I could also see that the body was bruised. Then they told me that this was a homicide investigation. They showed me computer pictures of the guards, and I pointed out the ones I believed were the perpetrators. They asked me whether I would be willing to appear as a witness in a trial against these people.

I just said, 'It's so ironic, isn't it, that you hold me here for all of this time, and you wanted me to be a witness against other detainees, but really the only people I can be a witness against are American soldiers.'

Then I thought that perhaps this was the real reason for keeping me in isolation in Camp Echo. Of course other detainees had witnessed the murders too, but the others spoke no English, and anyway most of them had been released by then and would have been hard to contact in their Afghan villages.

Later that month, I heard from Sergeant Foshee that there was a case pending in the US Supreme Court about detainees in Guantánamo, and that it seemed the judges were leaning towards a favourable decision for the detainees. I was astonished. It seemed such a dramatic turn, after so many months of hearing nothing from the lawyer I had been promised, and having almost got used to the legal limbo. Of course, I didn't know the details of what was being argued, but I optimistically assumed that if it was the Supreme Court, then it would be a completely authoritative decision about our legal rights. Within days I heard from Foshee and other MPs that the decision had been made, 'You have the legal right to be represented in court,' though the interrogators never once mentioned anything about it.

Rumours and conflicting stories were flying around about what it all really meant, but the one thing they all agreed on was that it was positive for us, a step forward. One soldier came and told me that they had to make a decision on all the detainees within ninety days, and after that they had to release us all. This was almost too fantastic to believe, and my mind was whirling with the possibilities. I was elated.

On my birthday, 5 July, I decided to write a formal letter to the Military Administration in Guantánamo, demanding my rights, in this new situation with US law now apparently on my side. I felt good, more assured than for the whole two years I'd been in custody. I wrote in biro on two sides of a sheet of ruled paper, and gave the letter to the NCO in charge, asking for copies to be sent to the Home Secretary, and to my solicitor in London, Gareth Peirce.

I, Moazzam Begg, citizen of the United Kingdom of Great Britain [sic], attributed in this facility the number 00558, formally demand the following rights accorded under US and international law pertaining to detention:

That I am immediately and unconditionally released and returned home, to my domicile in the UK. That all personal property seized by US/Pakistani agents on 31st January 2002, from my residence in Islamabad, Pakistan, be duly returned.

Under the foreseeable likelihood that the above demands are rejected, or unnecessarily delayed, again, under the said laws, I demand:

That any and all charges are made known in writing to me.

Since I have never been in US territory prior, and was brought here by force, I demand an explanation of all my rights.

That I am given access to a telephone that is able to call my family in the UK.

That a full inventoried list, detailing all items seized from my residence in Islamabad, Pakistan on January 31st 2002, be provided to me.

That I am provided with a full and legitimate explanation as to why I have been held in solitary confinement since my arrival in Cuba on February 8, 2003.

I went on to detail how I had been interrogated under torture, threatened with worse torture, and given death threats, particularly in Bagram, and how I had witnessed what I believed were fatal beatings of fellow detainees, by US personnel.

A week later, after thinking so much about the possible implications of the Supreme Court decision, I wrote another letter – twice as long, repeating the same points, but a lot more detailed, and requesting it be copied to many more people, including the US Supreme Court, Amnesty, ICRC, European Court of Human Rights, and the media. It was a huge mental effort to recall all these points, to concentrate, and to put them down coherently. It meant so much to me, and I was afraid of it getting lost in the black hole of US military bureaucracy. So I asked the camp commander, Sergeant Low, to read it, and then make a note in both the cell and camp logs and to pass it on. 'It's your responsibility now, Sergeant, I need this letter passed over to your legal department, if you don't mind.'

I was pretty anxious as I wrote all these letters and made four hand-written copies, trying to connect with the outside world about this momentous news.

But only a day afterwards, on 13 July, a US Army officer came round with several other people and sat down in the outer room. He was going from cell to cell reading out a document called the *Combatant*

Status Review Tribunal Notice To Detainees. It was just a single typed page of paper. When he had finished reading, he slipped it through the side of my steel door. This was the first we'd heard of CSRTs, which were the Pentagon's response to the Supreme Court decision that we should have our day in court, although I didn't know enough to understand the full implication of that at the time.

The document said, 'You are being held as an enemy combatant by the US armed forces. An enemy combatant is an individual who was part of or supporting Taliban or al-Qaeda forces, or associated forces that are engaged in hostilities against the United States, or its coalition partners. The definition includes any person who has committed a belligerent act or has directly supported such hostilities.'

Back in December 2003, Sergeant Parler had come to my cell and read out the first ever official military statement to detainees. It was about the capture of Saddam Hussein by US forces in Iraq.

'And when did the US enter Iraq, again?' I asked, feigning ignorance. I had, of course, learned quite a lot from the guards about the whole conflict.

'Sorry, you know I can't discuss current affairs.'

'So why have you chosen to give me *this* little snippet of current affairs?'

'Orders. This statement is being read out to all detainees.'

'And its particular relevance to me?'

I knew perfectly well that the Americans were gloating over the capture of this man, who had tortured and butchered more people from the Islamic opposition than they cared to acknowledge. Saddam's victims included Kurds, whose training camps in Afghanistan I had supported, and which had helped land me where I was, regarded as hostile to the US, and labelled 'enemy combatant'. Parler left without answering.

Now, for a second time, the US military, in this information-starved period, had taken the trouble to read out an official military statement to detainees. It looked like a very strange process to me. I had been a law student and this did not look like any legal process that I had studied. The document also said, 'This is not a criminal trial, and the Tribunal will not punish you, but will determine whether you are properly held.' I thought, 'What does that mean, "properly held"? Being held *is* punishment.'

I began to feel deflated from the initial excitement about the Supreme Court, as I listened to him, and then read the paper. There were five paragraphs about how the CSRT would work. I would get a written 'factual basis' for my classification as an enemy combatant. I would have a Personal Representative, though he would not be a lawyer, and, he was part of the military system. When I met the representative later, he explained that he was not obliged to safeguard, or keep private, any information that I gave him.

One crucial thing the document said was, 'You will be able to present evidence to the tribunal including the testimony of witnesses. If those witnesses you propose are not reasonably available, their written testimony may be sought. You may also present written statements and other documents. You may testify before the Tribunal, but will not be compelled to testify, or to answer questions.'

The last paragraph said, almost as a footnote, that, 'As a matter separate from these Tribunals, the United States courts have jurisdiction to consider petitions brought by enemy combatants held at this facility that challenge the legality of their detention.' I had absolutely no idea how that might happen, given that we were virtually incommunicado and had no access to the outside world.

It was clear to me too that the US government was trying to link the outcome of the CSRTs with the Supreme Court decision: if they could show that we were correctly deemed enemy combatants, then there would be no basis to consider the petitions in the US courts. Despite this, I thought that I must start engaging with this process, unjust as it was, because it was at least a chance, after years with no chance, to try and present my arguments.

The officer pre-empted any questions, saying quickly, 'If you have any questions, your Personal Representative will be coming around soon enough and you can discuss that with him.'

A few days later, on 16 July, I had a visit from Foreign Office Martin. He was with two US officials in plain clothes, and we discussed a few formalities before we got to the big issue of the CSRTs. Martin wanted to make sure that I understood what the CSRTs were, and what they meant. But he quickly told me that he wasn't there to advise me on what I should or shouldn't do, he wasn't a legal adviser, and neither were these other people with him. I sat there and tried to explain to them exactly what I felt about the CSRTs after having examined the notice very carefully.

I asked them about the Personal Representative himself. 'How can this person be *representative* of me? The terminology is deliberately misleading.'

The three of them had a difficult time trying to explain to me that these CSRTs would be a fair process.

'How can it say, "It doesn't seek to punish you", when, if I am found to be an enemy combatant, that will be the reason to keep me here?' I said, pointing to the small cage. 'Being locked up for years, without charge, lawyer, or trial, in a cage like this is the worst punishment.'

I thought it would be only too easy to find me an enemy combatant, as they were not giving me an opportunity for any legal recourse. They went on to talk about how the determination of civilian, enemy combatant, non-combatant, or POW is made on the battlefield within weeks of capture.

'I don't see any battlefields around here, and I wasn't picked up from one. Secondly, it's three years late.'

After dancing around the issue for a while, I let them know that I thought it was a complete farce and there was no way I was going to get any justice from it. I told them frankly that I thought it was just another exercise in gathering information, and that they were hoping people who hadn't spoken to interrogators for one reason or another would now start speaking, believing they were possibly going to be freed.

Martin, strangely, nodded his head in agreement at my comment about the farce.

When we got on to the note about having our cases heard in the US courts I said, 'Well, how can I get some legal representation, or even apply for it while I'm kept in these conditions?'

Martin made a surprising gesture. He turned slightly aside with his index finger scratching his chest. His colleagues couldn't see, but I could, and he pointed clearly towards himself as the answer to my question.

My response was on cue: 'Can you, as the British consular representative, instruct my lawyers and family to begin proceedings in the US courts?'

'I can't give you legal advice, but I'm sure I can convey your wishes,' he said, turning towards the Americans, who nodded approval. They all got up and left shortly after, with Martin the last to leave. Pointing to his chin, again out of sight of the Americans, he turned round and said, 'Chin up, Moazzam, chin up.'

My Personal Representative did not come to see me for several weeks, but in the meantime I had some new experiences, including a visit from the overall commander of Guantánamo Bay.

The guards had been rushing around, sweeping and mopping the floor, and generally tidying up, more than usual, which only meant one thing: visiting big shot. Brigadier General Jay Hood had come to pay his first and only visit to detainee number 558, in cell number 'seven bravo'.

Entering with his entourage, he looked around my cell, and went straight for the logbook, and then faced me.

'I see you've been to the dentist lately. Was the problem resolved?'

'Yes, thank you. But I still refused to tell him if"it was safe".' One of the aides began to smirk, but the reference to Laurence Olivier's menacing interrogation techniques in *Marathon Man* was lost on the general.

'I'm sorry, I don't understand. If *what* was "safe"?'

'It's not important. Before you leave though, General, can you tell me why the Personal Representative hasn't arrived yet?' I asked.

'I'm not involved with the CSRT process, but we have hundreds of people to get through. I know they're working as fast as they can.'

'Right,' I thought, 'I'm sure. Time is of the essence and you're all eager to see justice is done . . .'

'One more thing, General. Can you explain this?' I said, producing a Red Cross message from my daughter Umamah. US Forces' censors had blacked out most of the letter. 'What can you possibly fear from a seven-year-old? I don't receive letters for months on end, and when I do, this is the pathetic result.'

'I don't know what to tell you, except I'll look into the matter,' he said, with a slightly embarrassed look, then nodded to his aide, who jotted something down in his notebook. That was the last time I spoke to Hood.

My second surprise was a letter from a firm of attorneys in Newark, New Jersey, telling me that they had filed a habeas corpus case for me on 2 July in the Federal Court in Washington, DC. They told me that my wife, my father, Gareth Peirce, and a British lawyer working in the US, Clive Stafford Smith, had instructed them to prepare this legal challenge for me in the US courts. The letter stressed that they were civil lawyers, and had no connection to the US military. I was back on the upward swing of the rollercoaster of emotion.

Because Gareth was involved, I had faith that these new legal allies were serious, and that it meant I was really making some progress. I wrote back to the lawyers on the same day, on 6 August, saying how deeply grateful I was to the whole legal team, and underlining my confidence in Gareth. I reiterated that statements from me had been taken under duress, after torture, and with death threats held over me. I was thinking about the forced 'confession' of February 2003, and I told the lawyers this could be the only thing being used to brand me an 'enemy combatant'.

Again, I worried desperately about my letter not getting through, and I asked the camp commander to read it, log it in the camp log, and make copies.

About two weeks later I got a second letter from the firm, from a lawyer named Gitanjali Gutierrez, telling me that she had received my letter and it had only taken two weeks to arrive. She said she would be visiting me on Monday 30 August, and would also be seeing me on Tuesday, Wednesday, and Thursday. She told me too that she was meeting both Gareth and my father before the visit, to prepare herself to meet me. She was going to be the first civilian lawyer coming into Guantánamo. I knew this was a milestone, a complete turning point.

I barely slept with excitement in the next three or four days. To prepare myself, I'd begun to write down pages of things that had happened; one was called *A Chronicle of Abuse*. I also wrote a list of books that I wanted my father to get for me. I wrote letters that I wanted her to take to my father, my wife, and to Gareth.

Some of the guards encouraged me to ask the lawyer for all sorts of things, because although Gita was the first civilian lawyer to be granted access to Guantánamo, she wasn't the first lawyer. Military lawyers had been appointed for the Australian, David Hicks, and Salim Hamdan, allegedly bin Ladin's driver. The guards had seen these lawyers arriving with books or other things that the prisoners had asked for, and had seen that they were allowed to keep them in their cell.

So I wrote my lists of things I wanted, including a huge list of books, mostly about history, which I planned to present to Gita when she came. And I had a little list of other things, like a few chocolates. But in fact I didn't give any request to her the first time, because I wasn't sure whether she would be able to bring anything.

I was very curious about her name, and asked one of the Hispanic guards whether he knew Gitanjali to be a Hispanic as well as South Asian name, as I knew it. He had no idea. The American guards, typically, were all desperate to know if she was 'hot'.

When she came into the room I saw she was slim, with longish dark hair, very neat, and petite. Of course I was shackled to the ground, as I was during any interrogation or interview. But the difference was that she was left alone in the room with me. There was a table between us, and to my surprise there were no guards, although I'd been told that there could be guards there at the meeting, and that they could stop any interview any time that they felt that there were state secrets being discussed, or state security was being compromised. The camera in my cell, always trained on me, was now pointing towards us both.

'Well, Moazzam, I am truly glad to meet you after all this time,' she said, with a beaming smile. 'You know this is an historic moment: I'm the first civilian lawyer that's been given access to a detainee, and obviously, you're the first detainee.'

She was right, but I was desperate to know if that meant anything in tangible terms.

'Likewise. I've hardly slept a wink all night, thinking about what all this could mean. I have a thousand questions, and some requests, but I'll let you start first. Tell me what's happening.'

The first thing Gita did was to try to reassure me as to exactly who she was. She told me that she'd met my father and had lunch with him in New York just a few days before. It seemed really strange to me, thinking of my father in New York, discussing these legal things with her. Then she told me some things that only my father and my elder brother knew, like a nickname I'd had when I was a child, Popeye, because I used to like spinach, apparently. No one else knew that name, it had never been mentioned since my childhood. She also talked about meeting Gareth and how impressed she had been after talking to her. All those details were very important, and I was fairly reassured.

Another thing we talked about, before getting on to the legal case, was her background, and who she was. She was Indian, but had been brought up in the US. Her ethnicity meant she had an air of familiarity that brought down some barriers. I asked her about news from Britain and the US relating to my own case and Guantánamo, and about related events around the world. She was clearly not in Bush's camp from the way she talked, including the way she spoke about John Kerry's chances in the coming presidential elections. She also talked about how the lives of many non-Muslim ethnic Indians, like her – mainly Hindus and Sikhs – in the US had been shattered, after some ignorant Americans, seeing they 'all looked the same', had launched reprisal attacks in the wake of 9/11.

'I am a practising Hindu, and I've been constantly praying for you,' she said, her eyes welling up. 'I'm sorry, but this is something I've felt very strongly about for some time now. It has become part of my life.' Her sincerity struck me with a sense of guilt. Here was this woman, an American, praying for me, through a polytheistic religion diametrically contrasted to my own monotheistic belief, oblivious to all the facts of my case.

'Gita, I need to tell you that one of the reasons the Americans are holding me here for is—'

'Don't say anything at the moment. They may be monitoring our conversations, and although they don't respect the client–attorney relationship, I do.'

She was a little too cautious in the first few days, I thought, and a little naive. I wasn't going to tell her some huge secret that the Americans, or the British for that matter, were unaware of, or even rationalize my own incarceration. I was just going to tell her that I had visited a Kashmiri training camp in 1993, and had sent them a couple of hundred pounds for support. I wanted Gita, an Indian American, to know that before she started.

But I could also see that she was very young and impressionable, and she said herself that she was new to the game. I was a bit upset that she came empty handed, but she was made so anxious by the strict rules – contrary even to death-row cases she had witnessed – that she adopted a 'better safe than sorry' approach. She was worried about how she should dress, whether she should put a headscarf on, whether she should dress Western or Asian. She was concerned about how she would be perceived by someone held incommunicado for nearly three years, particularly since most detainees were said to be from conservative Muslim backgrounds, and she was not only American, but also female. She felt also that it was important for her to establish a good relationship with the military, to appear non-confrontational.

Gita talked to me in very practical terms, but one of the first substantive things she said came as a complete body blow.

'We've filed the habeas corpus case for you, and it is proceeding as quickly as possible . . .' she began.

'But could I still be sitting here this time next year, next two, or three years without ever . . .'

'Yes, Moazzam. That is a very real possibility, considering the government's position till now.' She said it clearly, but I asked her again. And once I'd been given the answer to that, nothing else seemed to matter. No matter what I did, no matter how hard I struggled, or protested my innocence, or asked to be taken to court, it might never happen. It was a devastating realization, and all the more demoralizing because my hopes had been so high.

I'd spent two months hearing about the Supreme Court decision, and then trying to understand the intricacies of the American legal system. The government, or 'respondents', as they were called in the legal documents, were arguing that detainees had no legal rights in US courts, despite the Supreme Court decision that clearly stated Guantánamo Bay was under US jurisdiction. And since they *were* the government, they were under no obligation to implement the court rulings, as President Bush, Commander-in-Chief of US Forces, had exercised his authority under the military and executive orders to determine that the judiciary did not interfere with the executive. In any other case, the government would have been in contempt of court.

The legal documents Gita brought contained a quote from Justice Jackson that caught my attention. It echoed the arguments by legal counsel for the petitioners (the detainees), and summed up the enormity of how my hopes had been raised, then dashed: '. . . that truly would be a promise to the ear to be broken to the hope, a teasing illusion, like a munificent bequest in the pauper's will.'

Gita visited me over four days, staying from morning till noon each day. The rest of the time she talked to Feroz, my unseen companion next door. I always asked her about him, and how his case was going in relation to mine. She had explained that our cases for habeas corpus had been made as a joint claim, but presented under my name. On the second day she brought in piles of legal documentation: the habeas corpus cases that had been submitted to the United States Court, the affidavits that had been done by Gareth and Zaynab. I already had a three-page letter from Gareth written on 14 August, but which arrived just before Gita, that introduced her, and explained exactly what had been happening since my abduction in Pakistan. I learned so many things that I had no idea about. I didn't know that my family had initiated a habeas corpus case back in Pakistan, or that my wife had presented our rental lease as proof that I had been in the country (because the Pakistanis had denied I was there), or that the family had fought so hard to get some involvement from the British government.

Gareth's letter also told me that my family had mounted a campaign for me, led by my father, which was so powerful there was hardly a household in Britain that hadn't heard my name. That came as a revelation. Until that point I had not realized the magnitude of my case, or known of the existence of a concerted campaign for my return.

In Gareth's letter I read with amazement, and encouragement, that it was not only she who considered what she called 'the process' in Guantánamo Bay to be unjust and unlawful. 'That view is accepted by the senior legal adviser to the British government, the Attorney General,' she wrote. Best of all, Gareth's letter said that President Bush had stated that the British detainees could be returned any time the British would have them back. Apparently, Blair in turn had said that he would take us back. Gareth said that if this contradiction went on, and we continued to be held, she would seek a judicial review. She went on to say that, regardless of what happened, the proposed military tribunals were not ones to take part in, under any circumstances. I was confused between tribunal and commission. I had known for months that I'd been designated eligible for trial by military commission, or was it military tribunal? I thought they were one and the same until I saw the Combatant Status Review Tribunals notice earlier in July. I found it confusing. I read Gareth's letter again and again, noting particularly where she had said that the military tribunals are not ones to take part in under any circumstances.

I wrote back to Gareth in a letter to go out with Gita, which would have to be declassified, so I did not know if, or when, it would reach her. I told her how difficult it was to express 'the utter elation' I had felt getting her letter, and all the legal material, and tried to say how honoured I felt that she had done all this work on my behalf, and thanked her for her commitment to human rights.

I got more confused when I asked Gita about the CSRT, and showed her the document I'd been given by the military, and asked whether or not I should participate in it. Her answer was that it was going to happen anyway, with or without me, but I would get a chance to speak, and present my point of view, which might affect the decision. It was more or less what Foreign Office Martin had said, and made me lean towards deciding to take part in it. I wasn't convinced, however, because a CSRT was an unknown entity to Gita, as a lawyer, just as it was to me.

Gita also told me about a play about the British detainees, with my father depicted on stage, telling my story. She told me it had been shown in London, and that it was playing in New York as we spoke. I imagined it being shown there, in the heart of the beast, and felt afraid for my father's safety. I had read previously that attacks against Muslims in the US had risen by over 400 per cent after September 11th. It began to dawn on me that the campaign might be powerful and influential. I even talked to the guards about my father and the play in New York, and they were certainly surprised to hear about it too. I wanted Gita to take back my poems and see if they could be included in the play, so that perhaps someone could hear my voice. She said she'd send them to the women who wrote the play.

The last time I saw Gita was on Thursday lunchtime, beetroot-with-a-slice-of-cheese-melted-on-top day, or 'beets and cheese' as the soldiers called it. Every Thursday this was lunch. Just as well the portions were tiny – I could never eat it.

'An American delicacy, no doubt,' I'd once teased the guards.

'Hell no, five-five-eight. I wouldn't feed that crap to my dog, if I had one. We were told the meals here are all culturally prepared to meet y'all's needs.'

'I don't claim to know all, but I can tell you I've travelled a fair bit around the Muslim world, and have never seen this dish. No, this is American to the core.'

Gita looked at it, and looked at me, then expressed her disgust. I had showed her because I wanted her to do something about it. But I was hoping for too much. I had requested a few things from her, but I think she just got overwhelmed in the end. The stringent military rules made it impossible for anyone to function in any normal client–lawyer terms. Before she left I made light of the situation by reading her part of my satirical poem about life in a maximum security US military prison camp, entitled 'A Taste of Echo':

> *Astringent rules of process*
> *Appear to be a caper*

Requiring an Act of Congress
To get some toilet paper

The food is often tasteless,
And far from what I please;
But nothing can be more grotesque
Than beets with melted cheese.

Deep inside this wired fence
Is another added feature:
A constipation of common sense
And a diarrhoea of procedure

At night-time some one waits until
I'm no longer awake
Then brings me in a sleeping pill
Waking me up to take

Just after Gita left interrogators came to ask me what the visit had been about.

Shortly afterwards, I got the long-awaited visit from my Personal Representative for the CSRT. As usual I was taken out of the cell and shackled to the ring on the floor. I sat down on my plastic chair opposite this man across the table, wondering whether he was really going to help me, to represent me.

He was a colonel from the air force. He wore military clothing, blue trousers and a light blue shirt, and he was very tall, perhaps six foot five, bald, and in his fifties I guessed. The Personal Representatives were supposed to be neutral soldiers, from the rank of lieutenant, or above, with no prior involvement in hostilities in Afghanistan or Iraq.

They were required even to declare if they had known anyone injured or killed in any hostile engagements against the US. Mine certainly seemed unaware of the key elements of recent history. Was this general level of ignorance that I had already encountered now deliberately being put to good use?

But I found him an easy person to talk to. He certainly seemed very friendly. 'I'm here to help you present your case . . . We'll do whatever we can to let the truth be known. This is your opportunity to say your piece, and for someone else to listen.'

Being optimistic, and taking everything at face value, I believed he was genuine. Perhaps he thought it too. But soon enough I saw what a farce and travesty of any justice system the CSRT was.

He showed me a paper, which was the so-called factual basis for my detention. He let me look at it, but he didn't allow me to keep it. I made some notes afterwards, which I titled 'Fictional Basis for Detention'. The entire thing was taken from that February 2003 statement written by the FBI, which I had signed just after arriving in Guantánamo.

The two key factors were that I was a member of al-Qa'idah or the Taliban, and that I had engaged in hostilities against the US.

In the first section it said I: '. . . had recruited individuals to attend al-Qa'idah-run terrorist training camps; had provided money and support to al-Qa'idah camps; had received training in al-Qa'idah camps in 1993, including training on AK47s, RPGs, ambushes and so on; provided support for al-Qa'idah terrorists and shelter services for families whilst al-Qa'idah committed terrorist acts.'

In the second part it said I: '. . . was armed and prepared to fight on the front line against the US and its allies, alongside the Taliban and al-Qa'idah; had retreated to Tora Bora with Taliban and al-Qa'idah fighters.' Then there was something about, 'Not wearing any military emblems . . . a chain of command; had supported Usamah bin Ladin's al-Qa'idah with knowledge of the declaration of war against the United States and that al-Qa'idah had committed terrorist acts against the US.'

Seeing all this, so clearly parroting that FBI invention, I wasn't at all sure I should participate in the CSRT. However, I wanted to, because I so badly needed to rebut all these allegations.

We talked for about an hour, and then I went straight to the point about witnesses. I assumed any witnesses that I called would actually attend the tribunal, although I couldn't understand how that would happen in Guantánamo. My witnesses would include my father and friends, who would confirm why I went to Afghanistan, and they would include members of al-Qa'idah and the Taliban, who I would ask,'Do you know me, have you ever seen me?' I wanted to say to the tribunal,'You said that I was at the front line, have you got any front-line fighters who were there, Americans or Taliban, to say that I was?' I wanted my tribunal to see all this, and I wrote down names of witnesses, in Pakistan, in Afghanistan, and in Britain, even American soldiers and interrogators.

There was one person in particular I wanted as a witness. This was Ibn as-Shaykh al-Libee, who was supposed to be the highest-ranking member of al-Qa'idah in US custody, so they would have no problem finding him. In the 1990s it was alleged he had been running camps in Afghanistan. I wanted them to ask him if I knew him, if I'd visited or trained at his camp, or been an instructor or if I'd financed it or recruited for it – as was alleged.

My representative wrote down his name, assuring me they'd find him if he was in Guantánamo.

'I believe firmly that this person is in United States custody,' I told him.'It was all over the press that he was captured in December 2001.' I also remembered that in Bagram, they said'Ibn as-Shaykh al-Libee . . .

played the same games with us as you did, and we sent him to Cairo. He talked there within two hours. You'll do the same.'

During the second visit from the Personal Representative he produced a photocopied statement, and a photograph of a detainee. Under it, it said, 'I, Mohammad Noor, have never seen or met this person, Muazzam Begg.'

'This is really strange,' I said. 'I saw him only once in a photograph, but this is not Ibn as-Shaykh. The name suggests to me that this person is either Pakistani or Afghan.'

The representative told me that this person, Mohammad Noor, was very reluctant to talk, to give any statement, and my representative seemed rather proud that he had brought this to me. I told him, 'This is not the person anyway.'

He just went on, 'This is good for you, right?'

'I don't know. Maybe it is, but this is not the person I asked for. Is this man known as Ibn as-Shaykh?'

'I don't know, but this who they told me to see,' he said. The enigmatic 'they' again, I thought. But this was beginning to feel really very, very strange, and I could not work out if it was incompetence, or was it that they wanted to hide the fact that they even knew the whereabouts of al-Libee.

I'd also requested a list of several people, who were either in Britain or in Pakistan, to give witness statements: about exactly what I was doing in Afghanistan; about whether they knew I was involved with al-Qa'idah, or the Taliban; about whether I was on the front lines; or whether I'd been engaged in any acts of hostility – or anything like that at all. All the people I named would have given very clear statements on my behalf.

My Personal Representative came again two or three times, and from what I understood, he really was trying to make representations, and contact people. He told me, 'The names that you've given us, we've managed to find them.'

Of course I was extremely relieved when he said it, but it turned out later to be complete nonsense, and either he was lying to me, or he'd been lied to. In fact they hadn't found any of the names. The most ridiculous thing was that the one person he said they couldn't locate was my father, who I knew was living in his own house in Birmingham and was constantly in contact with the British government. Out of all the people I had listed, he was undoubtedly the easiest to trace, yet they were somehow able to find people living in obscure regions of the North-West Province of Pakistan, in a refugee camp with no clear address. It didn't make any sense at all. How was it possible that they couldn't trace my father?

This made me very uneasy. Alone in my cell, after he'd left, I went over and over everything in my mind, and I began mapping out what would become, two months later, on 29 October, a detailed rebuttal of fourteen pages to the whole tribunal process.

Martin returned in mid-September, a couple of weeks after Gita's visit. One of the attachments I received with Gareth's letter was a duplicate of a letter sent by the Foreign Office to my family, detailing the contents of Martin's July visit. He was quite surprised to see that I had a copy of that report, particularly when I pointed out that there had been several mistakes in it, although the content was true in general. We returned to the CSRTs again, but this time I had some very powerful ammunition. I asked Martin what the British government's point of view on this was, and he replied, 'We don't have any position on this, it's nothing that we've been involved in.'

'But I have a letter from my UK lawyer,' I said, showing it to him, 'which says that Lord Goldsmith [the Attorney General], the senior legal adviser to the British government, has stated that these proposed military tribunals are unacceptable to the British government, and I should not participate in them, under any circumstances.'

'I wonder,' he said, 'if there is a deliberate misuse of the word "tribunal" here, or whether it is the military commission she's referring to? Lord Goldsmith, I believe, was talking about the latter. He has made no remarks about the tribunals . . .'

'But a tribunal is a court of law, which by definition seeks to pass judgement, as I remember from my legal studies. Tribunals have a three-member panel of adjudicators – hence the prefix "tri"—' I began again.

'Moazzam, we are not legal advisers, as we've said. You'll get your chance to say all you want at the tribunal . . .' said one of the Americans.

'You mean the kangaroo court. The notice says that I won't have access to the classified part of the factual basis for detention. So I have no way of knowing how to challenge those allegations. It is enough for you to make them. Also, I'd really like to know how on earth the US military will allow witnesses to attend court – I mean tribunal – when I have not been allowed to see another soul, except military personnel, in over two years? And how are witnesses from around the world supposed to gain access to this place that doesn't even permit family visits?'

'We don't have the answers to all the mechanics of the tribunals, but I can assure you the process will be fair,' said the American.

'Oh, of course it will. It sounds like the epitome of justice already.'

However, I decided that despite the negative feeling I had about the process and the ulterior motives I suspected, I would write a statement for the panel. They told me, 'Anything that you write, anything you want to say, will be presented in front of the panel members. Write whatever you want, and ask for witnesses and documentation.'

Martin said, 'If you don't take part, it will still go ahead, even if you don't attend.'

Martin was usually pleasant, I'd found on his various visits, but I thought him a little shifty at times. Sometimes he was kind, but also very officious. He wasn't bad or vindictive, but he just seemed to be very cautious, calculating every word. I could see that his position was not easy.

Before we'd begun Martin had asked me, 'Do you feel comfortable about speaking to me here with Americans present?'

I answered, knowing I was putting him on the spot, 'Well, do *you* feel comfortable with them here?'

After the conversation about the CSRT, we went on to talk about cricket, and sport, and other mundane things I wasn't really interested in. At least Martin always brought things with him. This time he brought a *National Geographic* magazine, some crosswords, and a chocolate bar, a Twix. Best of all he had plenty of letters, unlike that awful visit in September 2003, when he did not hand over any. I kept asking for those letters many months after, but never did receive an explanation.

This time, however, he gave me the letters himself, as well as post-cards, pictures, and drawings from the children. I was very, very happy to get them. Zaynab had written that she'd passed her driving test, but that she'd also crashed her car quite badly. The accident had been with a double-decker bus, with the children in the car. I dreaded reading the next line, fearing serious injuries, or worse. Thankfully, the injuries had been very slight – everyone was fine. But the thought continued to haunt me: 'What if something terrible had happened to any of my family? If my children, my father, my brothers, my wife – any of them had been hurt or worse, at any time, would the Americans have withheld it from me? And if something – Allah forbid – did happen, would the Americans release me? Probably not.' I did not see compassion as something the military structure would accept, to change their rules. For many agonizing months I'd thought that the September letters were being withheld for precisely that reason.

I had often written to my father asking about his brother and sister, who had both been my childhood guardians and mentors after my mother's death, but he never mentioned them. A nagging sense told me that something was not right. (I was to learn a year later, from a tearful father, on the day I returned home, that both had died in my absence.)

But this time the volume of letters Martin brought from home, the carefully written and drawn messages and artwork, typically childlike letters brought back my confidence and hope. I felt strong, and ready for the next turn of the legal and emotional rollercoaster.

Finally I said, 'Before you leave, Martin, let me tell you that I don't wish to spend another Ramadan in solitary confinement. This is a special time for us, a time to be in people's company – company I've not had for almost two years.'

He nodded, but said nothing.

A few days later I had a visit from a lawyer from the Red Cross, a Swiss woman called Bridget. She was an expert on international law. We talked about the CSRT process that I was involved in, and I told her that it was clear to me that the Supreme Court decision, which supposedly had ruled in our favour, really meant nothing, because of the use of the President's executive power against us. Although we had the *right* to be heard, the actual physical ability to be presented in the court was not in any way possible.*

---

* Various groups, including Vietnam and Gulf War veterans, judges, and senior military and ICRC personnel had written as *amici curiae* (or impartial advisers) in our favour, warning the US against disregarding its own laws.

Gita had said that the government was, effectively, in contempt of court, but that there was just no machine to make the Supreme Court's ruling apply. Bridget annoyed me very much by saying – just after we had had this discussion:'I still have faith in this system.' This was a Swiss lawyer speaking – I could hardly believe my ears. Was she naive? Or was she trying to compare Guantánamo with other places in the world that she'd seen, like Guatemala or Sri Lanka?

I was too polite to say to her, 'How about comparing America's Guantánamo to the Western world, or even with America itself?'

I generally looked forward to the quarterly visits by Vincent and others from the Red Cross. I liked hearing about their work around the world. But I never thought of the Red Cross as anything more than glorified postmen – because it was only mail that they brought. I knew that they were heavily funded by the US and therefore not as completely neutral as I had thought.

Neither Bridget nor Gita, for all their background as lawyers, could understand the impact of some of the decidedly illegal things that were happening to me. For instance, one day in late September the guards came to my cell early in the morning and told me to get ready because I had my tribunal. My Personal Representative had told me he was coming back to see me two days or so later.

I told the guards, 'This can't be possible, we haven't even finalized anything, I haven't been able to do what I need to present to the tribunal. He still has to get responses from the witnesses that I've asked for. It just doesn't make sense.' But then I thought, 'Yes, it makes perfect sense, this is how these things are supposed to work, it's not even a kangaroo court, it's a kangaroo tribunal.'

I said, 'OK, I'll go along.'

They shackled me up as usual, put me into the vehicle, drove round for a little bit, and then decided that it wasn't happening that morning after all, so they brought me back. It was the blind leading the blind (I was even wearing blackened goggles). None of the soldiers knew what was going on, they'd just had a phone call from somebody, 'He needs to attend the tribunal today.'

I took it as incompetence, rather than malice, again. I assumed that they had fixed a date for my CSRT earlier on, but had not told me about it; then, because I'd asked for witnesses, which they were not expecting, and they had actually tried to find them, they'd had to postpone the date.

I was pretty tense in this period. It was not good having hopes raised so high and then dashed by the legal tangle. I was still having regular visits from the psychiatrist, Dr B., and always asking her, as well as the odd officer who inspected my cell, for contact with other detainees, or a Muslim chaplain. I hadn't seen another Muslim for two years, and it was getting to me. I was also generally hardening my attitude towards the military, although I got along with most of the soldiers individually. None of these good personal relations were logged.

As far as the military establishment was concerned, I'd become trouble. I had written very strong letters about my treatment, and I'd also said that I was planning to take legal action against them at some point in the future. Also I'd screamed and shouted at a few guards too, over silly little things, and they had logged it. There was a guard who, one day after my breakfast was finished, came over and saw I was still eating a piece of fruit. He told me to hand it over. He was a new guard and he had no idea who I was. Camp Echo then held two types of prisoner: the six of us who were supposed to go through the military commissions process and had been there for so long, and prisoners who were brought there for disciplinary reasons. He had assumed that I was there for the latter. That group had very different rules, much more petty and rigorous.

This guard, known as 'Tank' because he was from an armoured vehicle unit, enjoyed telling me that I had to return my fruit. I too enjoyed telling him that if he wanted the fruit, he'd have to come into the cell and get it, because I was not going to give it to him. He went on insisting that I give him the fruit, and then I lost my temper. I verbally tore into him. I started swearing at him, telling him he was a brainless twat.

'You must have crushed your brains, soldier, when you sat down too hard on that chair.'

I watched him painstakingly put all this down in the log: 'Detainee has said that I had no brains and that I'd sat on them and crushed them,' as one of the other soldiers later read out to me.

I said to him that I couldn't hear him properly when he tried to say something, because I was shouting so loud. I told him he needed to unloosen his belt and take his trousers down so I could hear him properly. He noted that down too in his log. Eventually another soldier came in and told him that I was not the person that he wanted to discipline; he'd got the wrong man. He walked off in a huff.

I laughed afterwards, but when I was shouting at him, I really wanted him to come into the cell. I would probably just have thrown the fruit at him, but he wasn't going to risk being so close to me. This was just a moment of expressing the extreme frustration I was feeling. My hopes had been so built up by the US Supreme Court, and then they'd been so smashed by the US government.

I began to read some of the reams of papers about the legal process, which Gita had brought me, including the key case, which the Supreme Court had heard, *Rasul versus Bush*.

I also read the very interesting case of *Johnson versus Eisentrager*, which was the precedent used by the United States government in denying us our rights. It was based on the World War Two case where six

German soldiers had been captured in China and handed over to the US, which had a military base in Shanghai. Because it was not US sovereign territory, they were not given access to any legal system. The government lawyers tried to equate that to Guantánamo Bay. They also argued that because Guantánamo Bay was on a lease from Cuba, the US was not the sovereign state, therefore US laws would not apply to us. We were regarded as enemy aliens who were belligerent to the US.

The arguments for our side were very powerful too, it seemed to me as I read them. One was that if a foreign national, one of the workers from the Philippines or Jamaica, for instance, who was on the island, committed a crime, he would be taken to court. The difference was that we'd been brought over by force, and we were regarded as enemies of the US. Another argument was that although the US was not the sovereign owner of Guantánamo Bay, it has had complete authority for the past hundred years. Guantánamo Bay is effectively a large, working American town. One of the lawyers even argued that the iguanas on the island are a protected species, with laws that regulate what can or cannot be done to them on the island, but we human beings were being denied these laws. I thought it was a very good analogy.

With all this law in my head, frustrations mounting, and the month of Ramadan impending, I was agitating to everyone I saw to be put in with other detainees. It was going to be my third Ramadan in captivity, and I felt I just couldn't face it. When I went through the first one, I would never have imagined that two more would pass without spending it with my family.

All sorts of people, including Foreign Office Martin, David Hicks' lawyer, and Salim Hamdan's lawyer, later claimed credit for what happened next.

On the eve of Ramadan, 15 October 2004, the guards came to my cell in the evening, and told me to get my things ready. 'You're going.'

12

CHIME OF THE RAZOR WIRE

They came for me at 2200 hours. I'd been packing all my things together in the cell ever since one of the guards in the early evening had told me, 'Get your shit together.' I put all my belongings – mostly papers from Gita's visit – into a box, and the guards recorded it all. I had a feeling it wasn't just another cell change, but what else could it be? I did not want to get my hopes up. There was an air of bustle and busyness around the cell, and I could hear the voices of guards who had been on duty all day, but, unusually, were still around.

They came into the cell to put on the shackles and they also put on goggles before they guided me out, and into a vehicle. We didn't go far, but in those few minutes I sensed that I was not alone with the guards, there was another detainee in there with me, perhaps sitting on the other side.

They took me out, guards on either side, shackles dragging at my ankles. We walked a bit, then stopped, and I heard a gate opening, then another stop while another gate opened. I knew these were sally ports. I could feel I was in the open, it was different from all the other times I'd been moved, to the hospital, or to Reservation. I could feel wind on my face, and a deep whir of fans, very noisy and blowing in all directions, and I could hear voices in the distance, too far to make out language. I knew this must be Camp Delta, the main camp, but I knew too there were several different parts, some worse than others, so I did not start getting too happy.

We came to a small flight of stairs, five or six steps, my shackles clanking on the metal as they walked me down and along some sort of metal walkway. Then they took off my goggles and earmuffs and I could see cages, nothing but cages all around. Dog kennels was the first thing I thought. It reminded me of when my father, brother, and I went to buy our German shepherd, Sheba, when I was ten years old, at one of the dogs' homes in Birmingham. It looked exactly like that, except these cages were green.

My heart sank. It felt worse, worse than where I had been. They walked me past several series of cages and they put me right in the middle. They took off my shackles and I sat down in the cell bewildered. I could see absolutely no one. I felt complete disbelief. I could not understand why, from Camp Echo, they had brought me here. The cage was smaller than the one in Echo – I could walk about two and a half paces, instead of the three in Echo. There was the same steel bunk to sleep on as in Echo, and I put my mat on it. The guards brought my box, and they marked and recorded everything as they gave them back to me.

I was very, very hot. The room I'd been in was air-conditioned. It had been cold. Now I had to get used to the raw heat of Guantánamo. I just sat there for a while, in a daze. I was utterly dejected. I felt like crying.

Then one of the guards who had come with me said, 'Don't worry, we're going to be here with you, we've been assigned to stay with all of you guys.' Those words, 'all of you', hit me like a wave of pleasure. At that point I realized that it wasn't just going to be me.

Shortly afterwards I heard the sounds of other chains scraping across the metal floor. I got to know that sound well, as it would mean some detainee was being transported across the floor to or from a nearby cell. I hadn't quite taken it in when it was me, and my chains, making the noise. Somebody walked past, but I didn't turn round to have a look. I was in my own daze. By the time I'd realized what was happening they'd opened a cage and put him in a cell three away from me.

The night before I left Echo I'd had a dream in which I saw a black person, who I knew in the dream was my neighbour. The dream was so imprinted on my mind that I felt I'd actually seen Feroz. There were a few cages that I had to look through to see him clearly, blurred through a series of meshes, but I could make out a general view of his face.

'*As-salamu alaikum,*' I greeted him, when they'd finally removed his shackles.

'*Wa alaikum as-salaam wa rahmat Ullah.*' Then Feroz, in a very relaxed manner, said, 'Oh, is that you, Moazzam?'

'Yes.'

'Oh, right, I see, you don't look the way I'd imagined you. You're a lot shorter than I thought you would be.'

'Thank you.'

It was so strange – finally I'd met my unseen companion of two years. I felt I knew a lot about him, just from the gossiping guards. They had described him fairly well.

A few minutes later the cell slightly in front of me, but to the right, was also opened and I heard the sound of more chains dragging against the ground. Again we exchanged greetings, but didn't speak. This prisoner turned out to be Uthman al-Harbi, who was a self-declared member of al-Qa'idah.

Between me and the next detainee on my right there was a green plastic barrier that they had put inside the cell itself, so that I couldn't see my neighbour, and he couldn't see me. In that cell, directly beyond the barrier, was the man I had met and whispered to in hospital so many months before. Now I could talk to him. He was Salim Hamdan.

A few cells further up from him, was the Australian, David Hicks, who I also could not see, but could hear. Opposite Hicks was a Sudanese, Mohammad Saleh al-Qosi. We were the six who had been named for military commissions more than a year ago.

By the time we were all in there, it was well into the early hours of the morning, though we weren't even sure what time it was, but I don't think any of us slept much. I certainly didn't. I lay there looking through the mesh at the stars and feeling the breeze on my face as I hadn't for so long, except briefly in the recreation area. I could also see lit-up watchtowers with guards. I could see the razor wire, intertwined with barbed wire, on top of the fences. My head was churning. I wasn't sure what to think. In the end I decided, 'They've moved us all over here, closer to the central command . . . and the common factor here is the commissions, the military commissions. So maybe they're speeding that process up.'

Early in the morning we were still sitting and talking when I heard the dawn call to prayer. First it came over the camp loudspeakers, but then I heard prayer calls from different detainees. It was so beautiful, after so long. And then, as we prayed in congregation, that first day of Ramadan, I was completely elated by the feeling of being part of this communal moment, that day, of all the days of the year. Oddly enough, although I hadn't heard the call to prayer for almost two years, or prayed in congregation, it still felt like a natural progression, from just me, to being together. With the prayers five times a day, it was something that just came naturally.

I soon found out from shouted conversations over the cell blocks that it had been a unanimous decision of the detainees to reject the prayer call the Americans had put on the loudspeakers. There was an amazing amount of distrust for everything the Americans initiated, particularly in religious matters. The detainees believed that the prayer-call timings the Americans were using were incorrect – some believed it was by design, others by ignorance. The *athaan*, or call to prayer, is recited in the same way for each of the five daily prayers, except for the dawn prayer, when there is only one small, but fundamental difference: the words *As-salaatu khayrun min an-naum*, prayer is better than sleep, are said twice. But the recorded version played by the Americans in the camp included, *as-salaatu khayrun min an-naum* at *every* prayer time. Some guards mimicked the prayer call in a really grotesque way, upsetting us all. I heard screaming and shouting. I got my first taste of the main camp where about six hundred detainees in cages faced off against US soldiers in a virtual war zone every day.

The detainees also did not trust that the food was really halal; they didn't even trust that the qiblah, or direction for prayer, was really facing east.

The immediately striking part of being there in Papa Block, in the main Camp Delta, was the ability to communicate with all of these other men. We talked incessantly from that first night. The conversations went from one person to another, and I was soon doing a lot of translating, into Arabic for Uthman, Mohammad Saleh, and Salim, and into English for Hicks and Feroz.

It was a shock to find there was suddenly hardly any time for myself. My poetry-writing days came almost to an end. I managed to write only two poems in the two and half months that I was in Papa. I stopped consuming books at the same rate too. And even letter-writing dried up. The conversations and discussions that we had with one another were absolutely amazing, both in the content and also in the very fact of real communication after nearly three years without it.

Over the first two weeks at least, a lot of the discussion between the six of us was speculating on the reason for our collective transfer. My opinion was that I'd made a point with the British, telling them that I didn't want to spend another Ramadan alone, and that they had interceded with the Americans. Feroz thought it was because we had all been designated for trial by military commission. Uthman's opinion was that it was to get us all to talk amongst ourselves so that they could record information they wouldn't otherwise get from any of us in the interrogations. Salim's opinion was that his military lawyers had successfully argued that continued detention in solitary confinement would impede his ability to stand trial. Hicks was unsure. Mohammad Saleh said very little.

Uthman was not only the most influential person in our block, but probably one of the most influential in the whole of Guantánamo Bay. He also happened to be on the side of the block that was closest to Romeo Block, which bolstered his theory that the Americans had placed us, or him, strategically so that whatever was said would be recorded. The people in Romeo were being punished either because they refused to cooperate with interrogators or for other disciplinary reasons.

Initially Hicks had told me he didn't want to be in Camp Papa at all, because he felt that he had a better time in Echo. Partly this was because as he did not speak much Arabic he did not get the satisfaction that I did from all the interaction. But also, more importantly, he declared that he was not a practising Muslim any more, and so, again unlike the rest of us, the comfort of prayer in congregation was lost to him. In addition, he was getting more legal visits than anybody else, and those visits were held in Camp Echo. Being taken there was a tedious and agonizing process, being shackled and transported, guards holding us, and everybody staring as he walked through between the cages.

Camp Echo by then was being used just for legal visits. Hearing this, I understood why I had seen a phone being put into the outer room on my last day there. I found soon enough that going over to Echo for those legal visits was a very arduous and upsetting process.

It took quite a while to really get to know each other. No one was hurrying anything. With Feroz and me it was rather different because we had had ample pre-introductions via the guards. We had plenty to talk about, but for a start we spoke about the various guards and our experiences of them. We often had surprisingly different experiences with the same guard, and Feroz disliked a particular guard who was nice as pie with me. I understood that much of that had to do with our very different personalities. Feroz was instinctively suspicious, and very cautious about opening himself too much. But he was always very receptive when I spoke to him. Sometimes we had very lengthy, serious conversations, and other times we argued passionately. Feroz could go through days without saying more than a few words, but then so could I. Often enough there was just nothing to say. But at other times our conversations were riveting. Many of them involved Islam, no matter how unrelated the subjects seemed to be.

One of the discussions followed after we'd been speaking with Uthman about the decline of Muslim power, and how it had never recovered its position in the world after the European Ages of Discovery and Enlightenment.

'In the field of technology – and almost everything else – we've never been able to catch up with the West, especially from the time they separated Church and state,' I said. 'At the height of our decline there was, and still is, a tendency to reject Western attitudes to science by traditional Muslim scholars. And yet, for example, the Quran states, "Do not the disbelievers see that the heavens and the earth were originally one mass body that we shattered and struck asunder. And we created every living thing from water." There you have the first ever description of the Big Bang theory, coupled with the fact that water is necessary for the existence of all life forms. I've heard some Muslim scholars rubbish that theory, simply because it's been proposed by non-Muslims.'

'Yes, I've heard it too. But I think that one of the most convincing arguments in favour of Islam nowadays,' said Feroz, 'stems precisely *from* its appreciation of modern science. Despite being written over 1,400 years ago, the Quran still has relevance and appeal to a world that sees organized religion as archaic. Look at the Expanding Universe theory, which is a continuation of the Big Bang theory. Astrophysicists, like Hubble, only in the last century said that the universe continues to push outwards due to the force of the original explosion. But the Quran says, "We have created the heavens and the earth and we shall continue their expansion." There are things unexplained, though; for instance, at some point the expansion will stop and the cycle will eventually reverse, culminating in – if the magnetic pull of the planets and stars was drawn to a concentric point – a Big Bang implosion, and probably the end of the world. The Prophet Muhammad said that the world would not end until "the sun rises from the west". If – and it's only an idea – that reverse cycle was in effect, it could cause the earth to spin in the opposite direction, after a very slow deceleration.'

'But wouldn't that mean the earth would actually stop rotating? And even then, wouldn't we all go flying off the earth's surface, losing gravity as centrifugal force diminished?' I asked, thinking he'd got it wrong.

'Gravity is not a product of motion, Moazzam, it is relative to mass. The larger the mass, the more its gravitational pull.'

Feeling a little foolish, I said, 'I always thought the earth's gravitational pull on us was because it was spinning on its axis, and that if it were to stop then we'd all go flying off.'

'If it came to an abrupt stop, we probably would. But that would be because of the laws of motion, not gravity. Einstein wrote clearly about the definition of gravity, and it is based on mass.'

'You know also,' I went on, 'the Quran says, "And then we made the earth spherical in shape," in the chapter an-Naaziat. Western Europeans were still convinced the earth was flat well into the seventeenth century, although this concept wasn't new to the world, or exclusive to Islam. The Greek geographer Eratosthenes calculated the circumference of the earth to within fifty miles of its actual size, in 200 BC. But the Andalusian scholar Ibn Hazm said almost a thousand years ago that anyone who believes the world is flat becomes apostate for rejecting a clear Quranic verse.' And so it went.

Other conversations revolved around the Quranic understanding of the atom, and the acknowledgement that something could be even smaller, or how electrons orbiting an atom's nucleus were just part of Allah's design for creation, just as the earth orbits the sun, or as pilgrims circumambulate the *Ka'bah*.

Feroz told me he embraced Islam after initially setting out on a search for Buddhist enlightenment. He had decided to walk all the way to Japan. The journey led him through Switzerland, where he met a man who told him about Islam, which Feroz in fact knew was part of his own family heritage, but had known very little about. His quest then brought him back home to England, but the odyssey and his thirst for knowledge were not over. In 2000 he left the UK again, this time to enhance his knowledge of Islam by living in a Muslim country. Sadly, as is the case for many young idealists reverting or converting to Islam, the expectations contrasted with the stark realities of life in the Third World. The saying of Prophet Muhammad, 'There is no difference between a white man and a black man, or between an Arab and a non-Arab; except for the one that fears Allah,' is known to most Muslims, and is particularly appealing to people from African families, like Feroz. But ignorance, he discovered, knows no religion, race, or state.

Many of those ideals both he and I had were lost in the practicalities of life: why had tribalism, nationalism, and racism permeated Islamic society when these things were abhorrent to our way of life; why, with all the emphasis on moral and clean living, was the Muslim world rife with corruption; why did it seem that life was cheap and often meaningless, compared to life in Western nations; why was the Muslim world in a steady spiral of decline over the past three centuries; why was the Muslim world, in spite of all its attempts to mimic the West, always demonized, attacked, and humiliated?

These thoughts hounded not only Feroz and me, but also Uthman, who became increasingly involved in our discussions.

Feroz was very self-sufficient, content to be in his own little world, and dealing with things in a very philosophical way. Before Echo he had been held in Camp X-Ray, which was the worst of Guantánamo, and where some of the most horrible abuses had taken place. He was one of the first people to be brought to Guantánamo, so I heard from him some of these appalling accounts for the first time. Some of the stories I was told sickened me. My relatively uneventful experiences with guards brought home the reality of most detainees' treatment and their feelings about Guantánamo. The word on Juma al-Bahraini, was particularly nasty. Soldiers in an IRF (Initial Response Force) team had entered his cell, and despite his assuming a compliant position, threw him to the floor and smashed his face repeatedly to the ground. The whole place was covered in his blood. Other stories included how one detainee had had menstrual blood rubbed over his face during an interrogation, and how another was sexually enticed with a female interrogator straddling his lap while he struggled frantically to remove her.

Feroz had met some of the other four before. Uthman, Hicks, and Mohammad Saleh had been in X-Ray with him, and compared to me they were all veterans. Fairly soon I began having most of my conversations with Uthman. Many of the conversations I had with Hicks tended to be at night, when almost everybody else was asleep, and he could get a word in.

But during that first month, when it was Ramadan, everything was different, and in the air of celebration most people stayed up late talking. We all fasted during this month, except Hicks. That Ramadan was absolutely unique. It was probably one of the best ones that I have ever spent in my life. Despite the extreme circumstances that we were all sharing, the cheerfulness and spirit of everybody was unforgettable, and is hard to communicate to anyone who did not live it. The highlight was the congregational prayer, particularly Taraweeh, the final evening prayer, exclusive to Ramadan. Most people opted to do it, although it was very long. The usual noises of loud talking and shouting reverberating across the blocks was replaced by a solitary voice, melodically reciting verses of the Quran, which brought tears to my eyes. Who knows what those hundreds of others were feeling, remembering, contemplating, at the same time as me? But I knew one thing: everyone there had a reason to weep. And the sadness was almost sweet.

During Ramadan, Muslims abstain from food, drink, and sexual relations from dawn till dusk. There is particular emphasis placed too on not upsetting others, and not sinning during these times. It is when the spirit of Islam, involving extra-devotional worship, helping the needy, being neighbourly, and hospitable, is supposed to flower.

Mealtimes are simply readjusted: we usually eat three times during the dark hours, the main meals being pre-dawn and after sunset. The Americans had by now understood most of this, and handed out some dates every evening for us to break our fast with the traditional food. At these times the shouts in Arabic, of '*Hanee-an maree-an* or *bil aafiyah*' ('bon appetit') would ring through the air. People shouted from across the block, usually Romeo, mentioning everyone in Papa by name. Feroz and I found it somewhat awkward to initiate, or even return the greeting with as much enthusiasm. Perhaps, as I said to him, it was because of our cool British style.

'How can y'all go without food and water for so long? Hell, I could-n't do that if you paid me. Love my hamburger, my Bud, and my cheese fries too much,' one of the guards in Papa once said, as he handed the evening meal through the bean-hole.

'You know you fast every day, and you don't even realize,' I said. 'You break-fast every morning, because you fasted during the night.'

'I never thought of it like that.'

'If you look in the Bible, you'll find Jesus and the disciples used to fast all the time. I don't believe, as some people do now in the month of Lent, that simply refraining from having mushrooms on your pizza for forty days is fasting.'

Ramadan is marked with a festival called Eid ul-Fitr, or the Festival of Charity, when Muslims are required to give money or food to the poor before the Eid prayer. We had no access to any of that; but there was a jubilant period of song and entertaining each other, that lasted for three days. Although everyone is usually eager for the start of Ramadan in normal life, where lavish and exotic meals are prepared and eaten every evening, this time we were glad that fasting was over. Our food situation had improved a little, but we still had no choice in what was served through the bean-hole. As the guards said when we tried to complain, 'This ain't the Holiday Inn; and it ain't no country club.'

But this day was special: the Americans dished out baklava. People began to sing spontaneously, or to recite poetry. The whole place went quiet, to hear a lone voice echoing around the whole of the camp, sometimes in Pashto, sometimes in Farsi, sometimes in Arabic, and sometimes in London cockney or Jamaican street rap. I knew that was Martin Mubanga, who I had never met, but I had heard about, as one of us Britons. I occasionally tried to sing some Arabic songs, which I knew a few words of. I also recited some of my own poetry, which nobody understood except for Hicks, Feroz, and the guards. One I recited out loud with some relish was 'Indictment USA'. It ended in Cuba, with the verses

> *And on this rented Cuban patch*
> *The abductees all pray*
> *For justice, and a safe detach*
> *From the clutches of the USA*
>
> *Vulgarity is not my style,*
> *But still I have to say,*
> *This occasion causes me revile*
> *So f**k the USA!*

I didn't think the Americans liked hearing it.

The blocks each held a maximum of forty-eight prisoners: twenty-four on each side. My cell was number 15. Romeo Block held many more prisoners than ours, so they led the prayers, and we followed. Aside from prayer times, though, we communicated a lot with these people. There was a high turnover too, with people brought in sometimes for a few weeks, sometimes for a few days. But this turnover also brought regular bits of gossip, rumour, and genuine news. This was how we learned, that December, why the US flag in the distance was at half-mast: the tsunami.

Just like at mealtimes, every single morning somebody shouted across, and individually passed each of us greetings and salaams. They greeted each of us with *as-salaamu alaikum*, repeated with our names, from the whole of the block, which had as many as thirty or forty different people. I was always moved by the sense of them taking care not to leave anybody out. It was as though by common consent we were all trying to make sure that each person felt he counted, each person felt that he was not alone, that people were praying for him. They told us, 'We knew you were in Echo, there's not a day went past that we didn't pray for you, because we know that you must have had it harder than us, because you were isolated from everybody else.' I heard that echoed from detainees of various nationalities, and in many languages. I hadn't really thought till then about how many different nationalities there were in Guantánamo, just as there had been in Bagram.

Each day at sundown, even after Ramadan, and particularly before the prayer call was made, everything went quiet. Only the hushed tones of Quranic recitation by several detainees could be heard humming in the background. I used to look out at the sunset; sometimes it was gold, and sometimes red, setting behind one of many guard towers, visible through coils of razor wire. In a bizarre way it was quite beautiful. Usually there was a breeze blowing from the sea. Strangely there was a complete calm. The only thing I could hear was the sound of the razor wire. I wrote a poem about it in early January 2005 after nearly three months of listening to it and thinking about it. The razor wire rubbing against the barbed wire almost sounded like wind chimes. The final verse read:

Ensnared within this steel quagmire,
Our view holds little to admire,
So to the darkness we retire
Amidst the chime of the razor wire

Conversations and messages were the background noise of every-day life these days, along with guards barking orders at detainees, and detainees hurling newly learned abuse at guards. There were always conversations to listen to shouted across the blocks between one person and another, and sometimes messages were relayed across to very distant blocks, which you couldn't reach directly with your own voice. Sometimes I would hear somebody saying, 'Oh so-and-so says, salaams to you, Moazzam, from so-and-so-block.' Sometimes I couldn't place the name, was it someone I had met in Kandahar, or Bagram, in all those changes of cells? I never said, 'I don't know the person,' but just, 'Send my salaam back.' It didn't matter whether I knew them or not.

It was such a pleasure to think it was a way of information being exchanged which the Americans could not prevent. In theory the rule was that there was no talking between blocks. Technically we were not allowed to shout between blocks. Our windows in the cells were open mesh, but they had steel shutters too, two in each cell, and if the Americans decided that they wanted to shut us up, they closed those shutters.

They used to do that more to other people than to Uthman. This made me feel that maybe his theory was right. They did want him to talk. He had always refused to speak to the interrogators. He'd also said openly in the military commission that he was a member of al-Qa'idah, and he'd sacked his military-appointed lawyer, asking either to represent himself in court or be allowed a Yemeni lawyer to come over and represent him. So he'd thrown a big spanner in their works. He told me a little about this incident later on.

It took some getting used to having these new kinds of conversations, when I had got so used to the guards and with some of them I had quite a lot in common culturally, from speaking English and reading the same books, watching the same TV shows and films. I didn't have any such mundane things in common with most of my new companions, Mohammad Saleh, Salim, or Uthman. Anyway, by then I had a lot less to say to the MPs. And with changes to the guards, and some more Marines brought in, that brought a sour taste. The Marines had been responsible for a lot of the maltreatment of people during detainee movement; Feroz and Uthman both remembered them very, very clearly. They weren't at all happy about the Marine presence.

In our early days we all used to discuss the guards we had known. Those were easy conversations for all of us, and what we knew we had in common. We didn't start asking about where and how one another was seized. We all took it for granted those were things we didn't ask. It could have easily been interpreted as attempting to glean information for the Americans. That, I later heard, is exactly what happened to my old companion from Bagram, Sa'ad Iqbal. He was here in Camp Delta, and despised by almost everyone who ever mentioned him. They accused him of working for the Americans. The Americans, for their part, had stripped him of all his clothes and placed him in isolation, apparently for disciplinary reasons. At this point we all felt we didn't know who anybody else was, and people were on their guard.

I talked to Uthman about Yemen, and the details of daily life, and my favourite topic, history. History was also his forte, as well as religion, politics, literature, physics, current affairs, media, computing . . . It was like those long, long whispered conversations in Bagram where we new prisoners had passed the time telling each other about our very different homelands. Here too I tried to put myself into Uthman's world, and tried to feel what Yemen would be like. It was delicious, complete escapism, just listening to his words washing over me.

I did the same thing with Mohammad Saleh, asking him every detail about Sudan, focusing on the British involvement with the Mahdist movement of the 1880s, Gordon and Kitchener of Khartoum – as seen by the Sudanese.

And then with Hicks, I asked about Australia. Hicks loved to talk about his days as a rodeo rider, or a kangaroo skinner, and other quite exotic things he had done. They all had such different backgrounds, and I wanted to learn as much as I could from each one.

Uthman was married, with four children. He told me he had worked in Iraq in an oil field, during or just before the Gulf War. He had studied at university in Baghdad. He told me he had not always been a practising Muslim, having lived and studied in Bucharest, but that he returned to his faith as a result of various political events.

It was very similar to my own story of seeing Bosnia, the Gulf War, Afghanistan, and changing so deeply. In contrast to Feroz, Uthman had not been searching for spiritual enlightenment, neither had he 'seen the light' nor taken a 'leap of faith'. I was fascinated by Uthman's knowledge. I'd met people from Yemen in Bagram, but no one had been at all like him. He was very well read for one thing. He'd even read Tennyson and Dylan Thomas and some of the other great British poets. He knew some English, but a lot of this poetry was translated into Arabic. I read some of my poetry to him, although he couldn't understand a lot of it, but he did understand its context. I liked explaining it to him in Arabic, as it helped me to improve mine, and it increased his English range.

I had heard Uthman ask, when we first arrived, if they would put him in a cell by himself on the opposite end, near where the guards were. I asked him why. He said, 'One of my problems is I talk too much, I enjoy speaking. And these days of Ramadan, or anyway the last few days of Ramadan, are supposed to be spent in meditation and contemplation, and I won't be able to do that if I'm around anybody.' But by the time that they actually made a decision on his request, Ramadan was over, and he'd become well settled into the place, happy to be where he was, almost in the centre. Everybody could speak to him. When they came to move him, he refused, saying he didn't want to go any more. He wanted to stay where he was.

Inevitably our discussions led to Usamah bin Ladin, al-Qa'idah, and the justification for the September 11th attacks on America. I soon discovered one of the possible reasons for his vast knowledge. It was alleged by the Americans that he was a media person for al-Qa'idah, involved in publishing visual imagery. He had clearly spent a lot of time looking at the news on the Internet, on TV, on radio, and analysing news reports. He also sounded quite competent in the use of computers, which, surprisingly, many of the detainees still knew fairly little about.

Many subjects interested us all, from US politics, to Israeli prisons, and then more personal things like what we would do once we were released. We debated and argued on some issues about Islam, and sometimes Feroz got quite upset. Once we two were talking, and we asked Uthman's opinion, because he was more knowledgeable than both of us on Islamic issues. I translated the answer to Feroz, and he thought for a long time, but eventually accepted. We were both very ready to end a discussion with, 'Oh, you know, I think you were right about that.' When we talked about Usamah bin Ladin and the various attacks, Feroz said he was very upset that we had to suffer for what had taken place. On the one hand he felt convinced that what the Americans were doing was totally wrong, and he hated them almost as much as I did, if not more, but he also felt that what al-Qa'idah had done, or were doing, was really damaging the name of Islam.

Uthman's position on bin Ladin was different: he said he knew the man personally and had no doubts about his sincerity and genuineness; that he loved and cared for Muslims and only wanted their welfare. He even suggested that the September 11 attacks had been supported clandestinely by several leading figures from around the world, and religious edicts were given by some of the highest ranking clerics in the Arabian peninsula. He offered Islamic justifications for the attacks, which both Feroz and I argued fiercely against. We said that it was unlawful in Islam to target a place where there are women and children, or uninvolved civilians.

Uthman began, 'These Americans have been killing our people for a long time – even the Marine anthem mentions the "shores of Tripoli", which is about a US naval raid on Libya in the nineteenth century. Every time and everywhere you look in recent history, you see them interfering in our lands. The entire world knows that the establishment of a Jewish state in the Occupied Territories was only made possible by US support. They have committed genocide on Muslim people in Libya, Iraq, Somalia, and all but occupied the Arabian peninsula. From there they launched continuous attacks, which, along with the sanctions and trade embargos, caused the deaths of more than five thousand Iraqi children every month. The sheikh sees these innocents as our own children, and grieves for them, as we should all do. "The Muslim nation," the Prophet said, "is like one body: when one limb hurts it affects the rest." The sheikh did not go to America until America came to him. He had no desire to go there; he only wanted to set our own house in order and change the corrupt, apostate rulers that have imposed themselves on our people, or remove them by force. Look at Algeria. We don't believe in democracy, although it is the better of the two evils, in comparison to Arab Socialist Nationalism, but still the Islamic movement, the FIS, chose to use the democratic process. What happened? They were poised to win the election, but the government, with the full support of America, cancelled the elections and outlawed the party. A similar thing happened in Turkey with the very moderate Islamic Refah party: outlawed, and the West is silent.

'They do not want to see a unified Islamic bloc; it would be worse for them than the USSR was. They are siphoning the people's wealth from their own lands, and making sure their puppet leaders are in power so that they don't have to occupy *every* Muslim country to do it. We have it from the most authoritative sources that they plan to economically and militarily strangle the Muslim lands into submission. And they have no qualms about killing millions of us in the process.'

'Listen, Uthman,' I said, 'that is not the issue here. I agree with most of what you've said. But the Prophet, peace be upon him, prohibited Muslim armies from deliberately targeting women, children, old men, priests, and civilians in general; he even forbade the burning down of trees. He outlawed the use of torture, causing death by fire, and the mutilation of enemy dead. Prisoners of war were freed, or ransomed, if they could teach Muslims to read and write. I have no doubt that what we had at that time was the first ever set of military rules of engagement in human history. There is no argument between us about defending Muslim lands from aggression and military occupation. Allah says, "Fight those who fight against you, and do not transgress. Indeed, Allah does not like the transgressors." That verse is addressing Muslims, telling them not to overstep the boundaries of war . . .'

'So what about the verse,' he said, '"And whoever transgresses against you, transgress against them the way they transgress against you"?'

'But that verse finishes with, "And fear Allah. Indeed Allah is with the God-fearing,"' I quoted. 'There's nothing conducive to fearing God in killing women and children, Uthman. The criminals, Muslim or not, are not our teachers. When they commit rape against our women, like in Bosnia, are you now telling me that we also should rape their women in retaliation, "transgressing against the transgressor"? Each time we begin an action we say, "In the Name of Allah, Most Compassionate, Most Merciful". The Messenger of Allah whilst being unflinching in battle is called "A Mercy unto Mankind" in the Quran. And Allah Himself says, "And His mercy supersedes His wrath." I don't claim to know all the classical explanations of Quranic verses, but the meaning you've extrapolated here cannot be in tune with the spirit of Islam.'

'This is war. They didn't target a nursery or infants' school. Firstly, it was their Defense Ministry, the Pentagon, where the apparatus of making decisions to strike our countries is held. Then it was the World Trade Center; they struck at the US economy, just like they usurp ours. And the White House was the head of the dragon, even though that attack was unsuccessful. Furthermore, the American people voted for their leaders, and knew full well the foreign policies they were implementing in our lands. They are not all innocent.'

'But you know that most people elect their leaders based on internal policy; many do not agree with everything their government does. And what about those who voted against Bush? The sheikh's strikes do not discriminate.'

'Just like their bombs don't discriminate.'

I knew I'd ignited a passion in Uthman. He continued, 'Not innocent from guilty, not man from woman, not child from adult, not even human from animal. But at least the sheikh aimed his strikes; he knew the targets and hit them accordingly. When America bombs our countries with 1,500lb loads, from thousands of metres high, do you think they care about accuracy? If young children are left with no eyes, or severed limbs, or horrific burns with half their faces hanging off, crying for their mothers, who in turn scream in agony for their offspring, "What crime did my child commit, that they punish him like this?"– the lucky ones that didn't die – they call it collateral damage; a casualty rate that they're more than happy to inflict. On September 11th, they too suffered collateral damage. They were so busy hitting every other small child in the world, that when one small child hit back, the giant stumbled. Next time he'll fall. Muslims have always been the reactionaries to agendas set by them. Whether it was indirectly, like the jihad in Afghanistan against the USSR, or directly when they invaded Iraq or Somalia. This time we've set the agenda; they're playing to our tune.'

'And was it part of your tune that they destroy Afghanistan too?' I asked. 'I understand when you hit military targets, even though it makes no sense to me that you take on the US, since the Muslim world was plagued by occupation forces in Bosnia, Chechnya, Palestine, and Kashmir already. You managed, in one single swoop, to undermine the struggles for freedom in these places, by shifting world attention, and importantly, opinion, because bin Ladin decided what was in the interests of the Muslim world. And now we all have to pay the price.'

'You are not part of al-Qa'idah,' he said, 'and neither are all of the others here. But you should make no mistake: the only reason you are here is because you have some feeling for the Muslims, and America has declared a war on Islam. It is the Americans who are responsible for this,' he said, spreading his arms apart towards the blocks.

'Sheikh Abu Abdullah [Usamah bin Ladin] has made immense personal sacrifices for this cause. Nobody can question his sincerity during the Afghan jihad, when he physically fought against the Russians, abandoning the luxurious lifestyle that was his for the taking, sleeping instead in trenches, eating dry bread and tea, making his home in caves and battle-scarred mountains, giving his wealth freely to the poor and the mujahideen. Tell me of just one Western, or even Eastern leader who is like that? Most of them are too afraid to walk in the open, for fear of assassination by their own people.'

'Or by your group.'

'We *are* from among the people, the ordinary people.'

America and September 11 was one of the main fault lines of our disagreements with Uthman. Feroz knew a lot more than I did about the bin Ladins and other Saudis flown out of the US immediately after the events, and he went so far as to say that he believed the conspiracy theory that Bush and his regime had, if not been involved in it directly, certainly knew that it was going to happen, and did nothing to stop it. He was convinced that somehow the Bush and bin Ladin names were linked. Uthman really took exception to that theory, and said, 'I don't know how you can make such an accusation against the sheikh without proof. I know him personally and have no doubts about his integrity or his objectives.'

Some Afghan locals, who eventually handed him over to the Americans, in December 2001, had captured Feroz in Afghanistan. I had heard from the guards that he had written in a confession that he was himself part of al-Qa'idah, that he was fighting coalition forces, that he was the highly trained and committed Special Forces-type operative they claimed he was back in Kandahar. But Feroz told me the harrowing story of how he wrote that confession under the influence of drugs administered by US military medics, and that he had never engaged in hostilities against the US or coalition forces. I did not press him on the exact circumstances of his capture, just as I did not with anyone else, but if Feroz was al-Qa'idah (something I did not believe for a moment), he made for a very contrary member.

Feroz's Arabic was not fluent enough for him to manage these conversations with Uthman without me translating, which sometimes put me in a difficult position, so I refused to translate a couple of times when things got very heated. I found it very hard to be objective at these times, particularly when I had my own opposing opinion.

Relations between Uthman and Hicks soon worsened partly because of miscommunication. But Uthman could be really dogmatic too despite his intelligence, knowledge, and relative wisdom. And he was ready to pronounce the verdict of apostasy on someone who had, for all intents and purposes, abandoned Islam. This person was Hicks, and things really came to boiling point.

There were already rumours that Hicks had agreed to a deal with the Americans. But Uthman did try to be objective and fair in his judgement about that. He said, 'We don't base any of our judgements of anybody else on what the guards have spread around about them. First of all, forget about anything that anybody's heard. But what I can say now is that we have been with Dawood [David] now in this place for seven, eight weeks. During the month of Ramadan, he didn't pray with us, he didn't fast with us, he didn't celebrate the day of Eid with us, he didn't partake in any of the Islamic duties.'

Part of the problem was that Uthman didn't know Hicks very well, and there was a problem of communication because, although Uthman understood my English, he didn't understand Hicks' Australian accent.

I used to talk to Hicks more than anybody else did. He felt more isolated than he'd been in Echo, not surprisingly because over there he'd had fun chatting with guards about the kind of things they were all interested in – motorbikes, drinking, and girls. Now he had to speak just to us five. Feroz was so quiet; Salim didn't say much either, though he loved to joke around when he did. Then there was Mohammad Saleh, the softly spoken Sudanese, who it was hard to understand on the rare occasions when he did speak. Uthman, who was so obviously a leader, dynamic and intellectual, overshadowed Saleh. Uthman was talking all the time, if not to me, then across the blocks. People were always asking him one question or another, about Islamic jurisprudence, or history, politics, engineering, the oil industry, or even the astronomical movement of heavenly bodies or something equally abstruse.

Uthman and I used to talk about religious differences quite often. We discussed numerous topics, like how Islam regards the Ahlul Kitaab (People of the Book: Jews and Christians), compared with Mushrikeen (polytheists) or Mulhideen (atheists). How do we deal with them, and what is their status? Do they all, according to Islamic belief, go to heaven or hell? What is the evidence for this? We had discussions and sometimes arguments about those things. A lot of the time he was more open-minded than I expected.

Once, when some of the new Marines were shackling him, one of them pulled him hard, and put the shackles on very tight. Uthman asked him to loosen them, but he wouldn't. Uthman looked up at him, and he said, in his Arabic-English way, 'All this security do you no good September 11. Where is it?' He looked the Marine in the face, and I could see that the guard tried to stare him out, but was lost for words. 'Your Defense Ministry could not defend himself from little attack.' I couldn't believe the way he was antagonizing them. But he didn't cause any trouble and generally seemed compliant with the guards. Uthman was very confident, and in fact I think some of the soldiers had a grudging respect for him, because he was completely unashamed, and said what he thought.

Another of Uthman's abilities was the interpretation of dreams. He was chief dream interpreter in the whole area. Daily, even nightly, someone would ask him to explain some obscure-sounding dream. At first it was a little intriguing, but I soon lost interest and got really sick of it. Feroz did too. He used to say to me, 'Some of the Arab brothers are always dreaming.' I had had two dreams in my entire life that were worth recalling, and I have mentioned them in my story. But there were some people who were always having amazing dreams. I could see that Uthman tried to be very careful about the interpretations. Some people would make important judgements and decisions about others, based on a dream. People would decide that somebody was an agent of the Americans, or some such thing, based on a dream. I heard Uthman tell people that they had got to put a stop to this, that it was all nonsense. Other dreams he would just interpret as a good omen, or as a bad omen.

But one day, when all this was irritating me, I said, 'Uthman, you know what the problem is?'

'What?'

'You know why people dream so much?'

'Why?'

'Because they sleep too bloody much.'

He replied, in all seriousness, 'No, no, no, it's not that, it's because of the situation and people want to see things, and thoughts come into their subconscious.'

Hicks had some very powerful dreams, and he wanted them interpreted by Uthman, so again, I translated. There was one, which involved him seeing a very pretty woman, who was in a burka, and he ended up really liking her in the dream. And in another part of the dream he saw some sort of an idol spinning out of the ground and rising up, and he went over and said something to it in Arabic, a pronunciation of a prayer, which smashed the idol. Uthman interpreted that to be a good omen, meaning that Hicks would eventually return to the fold.

There was so much talking going on these days that sometimes

Hicks, or anybody else, would have to wait all day long just to get a word in edgeways with Uthman.

Salim often read out transcripts of his own case, which I translated for the others. One in particular was the most important case in determining that the CSRTs were incompetent, as a US District Court had rejected them. In addition the court said that until a competent Article V hearing under the Geneva Conventions had been held to determine our status, we should all be regarded as prisoners of war. We all knew what POW status meant: they could not ask us questions; we would have to live in similar accommodation to what they lived in; we would have to have access to regular mail; we would have to be put in compounds where we could live a reasonable, decent life. After that decision in Hamdan's case he was taken out of Camp Papa, and I never saw him again. We were told that he was allowed to wear his own clothes, which had been sent by his family. On paper he was a POW, but in practical terms he was just another Guantánamo detainee – who was allowed to wear his own clothes.

Something happened one day that triggered a breach between Hicks and Uthman. Uthman spelled it out, through me of course, which was pretty uncomfortable. He said, 'Tell Hicks that we have been praying, fasting, and remembering Allah all throughout this blessed month, and yet he's done nothing to show his Islam in all the time we've been with him.' I suppose Hicks knew it was coming.

Things got worse because Uthman decided that Hicks would be publicly excommunicated. I completely disagreed with this. Uthman said that a person who had abandoned the prayer completely, who never prayed at all, who never had any semblance of Islam about him, was out of the fold. He had plenty of evidence for this, quoting verses from the Quran, prophetic sayings and opinions from the major schools of Islamic jurisprudence. He told Hicks, and then he made his statement to the rest of the blocks. 'I want it known this day that I have tried to speak to the man who's no longer a brother, Dawood, and he has not responded to . . .' going through the whole litany of accusations. 'No praying, no fasting, and he has confirmed for me that he is more with the Americans than with us. I bear witness to all this before Allah. I will not respond to him, I will not send my salaam to him, I will not talk to him.'

The effect of that on Hicks was going to be huge, and no doubt painful, because it meant that now in the morning when everybody said the *salaam, hanee-an maree-an,* or *kayfa haaluka,* no one said it to him.

I said to Uthman, 'Look, you know what you've done. You might have been getting through to him, by having discussions with him, it doesn't matter how long it takes, and, even if in the end he decides that he doesn't want to be a Muslim, that's his free choice. But you've now turned him away.'

I came to realize, that for Uthman, Islam wasn't the only issue here. It was the fact that he suspected Hicks was being used as a pawn, or was purposely relaying information to and from the Americans. That was what Uthman was worried about.

In Hicks' defence, I told Uthman that he'd been offered a plea bargain by the Americans to take twenty years if he testified. Then, desperate for a deal, they cut it down to eight, and finally they had it down to two years, which he could serve in Australia. But Hicks maintained that he would never, ever, turn state's witness – since he had not witnessed any crimes to begin with. After that I tried a number of times to heal the breach. 'Look, Hicks, you chose Islam of your own free will when you started practising. Don't abandon it now, just because of the hardship. If you're abandoning it now it means that you were weak to begin with. We have all felt weak at some point.'

Feroz tried to speak to him about other things, because we didn't want him to exclude him, which is what began to happen. 'Hicks, I'll always speak to you, regardless of whatever you choose, it makes no difference to me. Right here and now we all need help.'

All these intense conversations and relationships going on in Papa Block were pretty different from much of what was happening in the rest of Camp Delta. We heard many things from Romeo. Some of the detainees had just refused to cooperate with the interrogators at all. There were people there who had refused even to give their names to the Americans. They tried all sorts of tactics to get them to break. The punishments included being held there without anything in their cell at all. All they had was a pair of shorts and a prayer mat, that's it. No toothpaste, no toothbrush, no toilet paper, no soap, no papers, and no books. I'm not even sure they all had the Quran. It was very distressing to hear about their situation. Once Uthman told me about a case of a detainee in there being wrapped in an Israeli flag and made to bow in front of a woman soldier. There was a general call to pray for Mohammad al-Qahtani,* a Saudi, who we had heard was being very, very badly assaulted. At the time I did not put the two together.

I once spoke over the wire to a friendly old Palestinian,† probably in his sixties, married with several children. We talked, shouted really, across the cages. I told him that my wife was also Palestinian. His response was so typically Palestinian, 'Oh, you're one of us; you're part of our family! You have to come and visit us, we live in Jordan now, but, you know, when we have our own lands back in Palestine you can come and visit us there.' I realized that he was the same man I had seen in Bagram, two years before.

---

* Said to be the twentieth 9/11 hijacker.
† Khalid al-Asmar, released August 2005.

My world was full of people like that; lovely warm conversations with faceless voices, like the Iranian who I'd also met in Bagram. At last I was with my peers – in faith. My patience had been tested in solitary, but here I was with men whose life experiences had taught them the patience and stoicism I aspired to.

Our neighbours in Romeo were always being punished, and some had stayed there for quite a long time. One of them was Rashid al-Jowfee. He was from the north of Saudi Arabia, and I had seen him once with the old Palestinian, in Bagram. They had been held in the same cell with Richard Belmar, next to the cell where I was first brought. I only vaguely remembered what Rashid looked like, and I tried to conjure up his face as we talked. He began to talk about that time, and confirmed for me something, which I had hoped was only an illusory ploy by my tormentors.'Do you remember when they took you for interrogations in May, upstairs?'

'Yes.'

'We heard sounds of screaming.'

'Yeah, I know.'

'You know, we were all praying for you, because we thought it was your wife.'

I found it so moving that they had tried to be with me in that awful time. They had all known, through our whispered conversations in Bagram, that I was desperate for news about my family. Hearing the screams they had assumed the worst, just as I had done. It had never occurred to me that even they had thought that too.*

---

* In July 2005, four men escaped from Bagram. In an interview with the Arabic TV channel, Al Arabiya, one of the men spoke about a female prisoner, number 650. He said she had been held in Bagram for over two years and had lost her senses after being constantly interrogated, abused and isolated. Many prisoners went on hunger strike in protest, and she was removed a few weeks before the escape, he said.

There was one incident with Rashid that I heard, and which upset me very much. The prisoners in Romeo didn't have sheets like we did which we put up for privacy when using the toilet. They had to do everything in front of each other, and in front of the guards. It was really humiliating.

Once, Rashid asked for a bar of soap after using the toilet. He was supposed to give it straight back, but he just decided that he was not going to hand it back because he wanted to wash a little more. The guards then decided that they would order the Initial Response Force team.

I'd heard a lot about IRFs before, from guards who'd always threatened me with them, sometimes joking, sometimes seriously. In the earlier days they'd used pepper sprays on people before they entered the cell. The IRFs were carried out by about five or six guards, and, apparently, always videoed. I had a good idea of the force involved, because whenever I was taken out from the main camp, from Papa Block, I passed the other blocks, and at the entrances I saw the riot gear all neatly piled and ready for use, with helmets and chest guards, leg guards and ankle guards, and big shields. The very sight of it was quite intimidating, but in use it sounded really intimidating. First there was the sound of stamping feet in unison, very, very loud on the metal floor, and with a hollow echo because the whole block was raised.

They entered the block, marched towards Rashid's cell, with the sounds of the six pairs of feet stamping altogether, threatening violence, as it was meant to. Then I heard the shouts and screams of all the other detainees who had seen what was going to happen. By then the days of prisoners being intimidated were over. A sort of familiarity with the guards had set in, we knew what they were like, and all the prisoners made sure the new ones would be given a hard time.

The guards opened the cell, charged at Rashid, shouting that he should get down. I could hear detainees shouting too, a lot of them were swearing at the guards, calling them names in Arabic and Pashto, calling them dogs and pigs, and all sorts of curses. My own screams were lost amongst theirs. They were giving us a running commentary too. Rashid did not get down on his knees and put his hands on his head, waiting for them to throw him down to the ground as IRF teams always did. He just sat there. When they threw him on the ground his nose hit the edge of the steel bunk, and it started bleeding. The person in the cell next to him shouted that his blood was all over the place. They physically carried him out in a prone position, and they took him to another isolation cell.

I heard the IRF team a few other times as well. Martin Mubanga decided one day that he was not going to leave the recreation yard until he'd finished talking to Feroz in the other recreation yard. I'd heard that Martin was physically very fit, strong and tall, with a fantastic six-pack. From the rumours I'd heard about him, the guards were afraid of him. Instead of bringing five guards, apparently they brought in ten. Martin was then in Quebec Block, next to Romeo, on the other side from us. So I could hear it all pretty well. They carried him out, but he didn't put up a fight. He said that he couldn't be bothered to walk back to his cell, and wanted a lift. And that's exactly what they did: they lifted him back – to an isolation cell. Martin made me laugh quite a bit that day, and that was just the first time. In every shouted contact I had the feeling he would be making me laugh in the future too.

By now everybody in our cell was being taken out for recreation daily for about forty-five minutes to an hour. It was a great improvement over Camp Echo. The recreation yard was almost three times as big and the floor here was concrete, not mud and stone. Also I could see the moon very clearly, and feel the breeze a lot better too. In fact,

I even saw more of the famed Guantánamo wildlife than I'd ever seen in Echo. I saw geckos, iguanas, and vultures. Once, I was actually chased by a snake in the rec yard – the first time I'd ever encountered one face to face.

But of course it was still the old story of having to exercise alone, one at a time. I made a slightly different training programme and it made me very fit. I used to run about five laps, very fast, then do thirty press-ups, then run another five laps, then do the same amount of sit-ups and squat thrusts, and then star jumps. After that I would carry on running for a while. And every single day, just before sunset, I did a workout in my cell. I learned a technique from Hicks, who had tied one of his two sheets into one of the corners of his cell near the door, attaching it so that there was a place where he could pull himself up. I copied that, and I made sure that I did it every single day. In fact that was something I pretty much looked forward to.

Every evening, at exactly the same time, we heard the call to prayer, and the US national anthem. Trouble often flared up at sunset when both these things happened simultaneously – no one wanted their right overshadowed by the other. Everyone stopped whatever they were doing – detainees and guards. Hicks once, in a matter-of-fact way, summed up what we all felt. 'Isn't it amazing? One group of people stop to worship their God and another group stop to worship their flag.'

13

MOCKERY OF JUSTICE

In mid-November 2004, with Ramadan just over, I received another legal letter, written at the beginning of the month, from a new lawyer, introducing himself as now assuming the primary responsibility for my case, and announcing he would be seeing me in the next few days. It was from Clive Stafford Smith, a Briton. Gita had explained in a previous letter that Clive had had vast experience working in the US for over twenty years on death-row cases. Most importantly, he told me clearly not to take part in the CSRT process. He said that Gareth too felt strongly about this, and described it as 'a farce' – exactly my sentiment, as I'd told Foreign Office Martin.

I had a letter from Gita too the very same day, which told me that she'd been to Britain, she'd spoken to Lord Goldsmith, and she'd met Gareth, my wife, and my father, and even my younger son. I was really looking forward to seeing her again to hear about all this. She also said that after having spoken to Gareth, they all agreed that I should not take part in the CSRTs.

The CSRT, however, was going to be held the very next day, Saturday 20 November. And here I was with a two-week-old letter, telling me not to take part, and which warned that the Americans would use information gathered in the CSRTs as they had for people who were being held in Britain. That completely baffled me. I didn't understand it. I read that sentence several times over, and then to Feroz and Uthman. 'What do you think this could mean? Is this saying that the British are using information from Guantánamo? For what?'

At that time I knew nothing about Belmarsh, the high-security prison in London, and the Muslim prisoners held there, though I soon understood from Clive. I felt pretty unsettled by all this, and a little upset that after all the preparations I'd made for the CSRT, it was the wrong thing to be doing. And in fact I had already had submitted a fourteen-page document I'd written with great care to my Personal Representative.

Among the many arguments in it, I quoted from my legal documents, 'Another leading British jurist [Lord Steyn] describes the proposed military tribunal as "a mockery of justice" that "derives from the jumps of the kangaroo".' I quoted this British lord's description often to the Americans and included it in the rebuttal to the CSRT with some relish.

My representative had copied my document, and then returned it to me. I had asked for witness statements, and I had mentally prepared myself to answer questions and argue my position against their basis for my detention. Feroz had attended the tribunal already, so I was constantly seeking advice from him about the proceedings, and about how the officials reacted to his arguments. He told me, unsurprisingly, that they were unimpressed about some of his contributions to the proceedings, such as when he'd read them a passage from Malcolm X: 'I am not anti-American, and I did not come here to condemn America. I want to make that very clear. I came here to tell the truth and if the truth condemns America, then she stands condemned . . .'

Feroz had received his CSRT transcript from Gita, and he read the whole thing out to me. 'Unlike the greatest terrorist attacks known to history, the atom bombings of Nagasaki and Hiroshima, there has not been shown any adequate, sufficient and substantial evidence to establish the guilt of al-Qa'idah as the very perpetrators of the terrorist attacks of September 11th, 2001 . . . Therefore, based on the wholesome principle of "innocent until proven guilty, without a shadow of a doubt", al-Qa'idah can be said to be innocent . . .' So, he said, it stood to reason that 'the Taliban cannot be guilty of harbouring terrorists', and 'Congress' Joint Resolution authorizing the use of necessary and appropriate force . . . against Taliban and al-Qa'idah . . . not only does not have a leg to stand on, it does not even have buttocks to sit on . . .' I found this argument quite amusing, and correct, but it was when he told me about the tribunal president's interruptions that I got a clearer picture of the process.

'This is your last warning . . . this is not a matter of al-Qa'idah . . . It is a matter of what you did in Afghanistan.'

'I believe this is a matter of my classification as "enemy combatant".'

'It is not. I am here to tell you it is not.'

'I want to address my designation as "enemy combatant" by international law and Geneva Conventions . . .'

'Once again, international law and Geneva Conventions do not apply. You have been designated as an enemy combatant . . .' the tribunal president retorted. And so it went on, until Feroz was removed from the tribunal. This really confirmed my decision not to take part.

On the day of my CSRT the guards came to take me, but I refused to go. 'You can go back, and tell them that I've been advised by my legal representatives not to take part, so I'm not going to.'

They had my document by then, but I never heard whether they held the tribunal, and whether the CSRT did rule that I was an enemy combatant or not. But I soon heard what we all knew would happen: out of several hundred CSRTs conducted, only one person was declared *not* correctly designated as 'enemy combatant'.

Meanwhile, Hicks, who was seeing several lawyers about his military commission hearing, had lodged a serious complaint about how they treated him when they took him back to Camp Echo for his legal meetings. Camp Echo by then was under a completely different chain of command. Hardly any of the MPs there knew us. Hicks told me the feeling of being back in Echo was horrible. He said he felt the place was intrinsically evil. He felt that the camera in the room was like an eye watching him all the time, and the place seemed to be closing in on him. Being back in a completely closed room with no windows felt unbearably stifling after Camp Papa.

We all noticed that when he left to see the lawyers, the process that began at about eight in the morning ended only at about ten or eleven at night – for just an hour's meeting.

I soon found out all about it for myself. The first day I went to meet Clive, they took me very early, about six o'clock in the morning, and put me in the old cell with absolutely nothing. When I wanted to attract the attention of the guards, I had to wave to the camera, and if nobody happened to be looking in that direction I was stuck. After a while I started banging and shouting in the cell, and one of the new guards eventually walked in saying, 'Who do you think you are, shouting in your cell?'

I was amazed. I said, 'I can't believe this. I've been in this cell, waiting and waiting for somebody to come along. I just need some water to drink. I've been trying to get someone's attention for two hours . . .'

'Well, you can't be shouting with our superiors walking around.'

I shouted again, 'I don't care about that. How am I supposed to get somebody to get me some water? What if something serious had happened and no one was looking at the camera as they're supposed to?'

We got into a staring match, but he broke the angry silence. 'Listen up. *I'm* the MP, *you're* the detainee. You do what *I* say. You've got to learn to behave yourself first before you get what you want . . .'

I was enraged. 'You're full of shit, soldier. I don't recognize your terminology. *I'm* the hostage, *you're* the kidnapper – let's get that straight. And don't make it appear as if you're doing me any special favours. I'm asking for drinking water, not duck *à l'orange.* You're new to this place, but I've spent nearly two years in this nightmare. Despite that, I don't create problems for you, if you care to check my record. But then, I don't usually have to deal with reprobates like you either.'

Being back in Camp Echo had been unbearable enough, as Hicks had rightly said, but this new attitude made it worse. Of all the places to bring us – Camp Echo was the worst. I wondered whether they had done it with malice, or was it just complete insensitivity? Nobody cared, of course. That was the point: nobody cared. Perhaps, also, leaving us for hours on end was an attempt to deter us from wanting to meet lawyers.

Little would have deterred me from wanting to see Clive, once I'd met him. He walked in, and I saw a very tall, very English man, dressed very casually. He was so rumpled I thought he looked as if he'd just got out of bed. He was different to Gita in every way. The fact that he was British made a big difference too. The only other British people I had spoken to were either MI5 or Foreign Office, and I'd even had a sense of familiarity with them. With Clive, I felt I was meeting someone who I knew was for real.

He said straightaway, 'Look, in my experience, you have to embarrass these bastards into making a move, because otherwise they don't care.' His approach was completely different to Gita's. He had some more habeas corpus documents for me to look at, and told me the government was still arguing against our right of audience in the court, which I thought was already decided by the Supreme Court.

He pointed to the papers and said, 'I don't have much faith in this crap. What we have to do is embarrass these people, and that means start talking about things that maybe you don't want to talk about, like the abuses. We have to start logging them, and making sure you're getting them all down.'

So we went through all the sordid details that totalled my experiences over the past three years, which was painful at times, but I could see was necessary. (A few days later, 24 November, using the notes I had made, and from what I had told him, he produced a thirty-page report on me, which, with typical Clive panache, he called, 'One thousand days and nights of torture: the systematic torture and abuse of Moazzam Begg, a British citizen, by the United States of America.')

He even said, almost casually, 'Look, as far as you're concerned I think it's all done, it's in the bag, you're going home. It's the other people we have to start considering.'

He wanted me to get actively involved with helping out the others, which I was more than willing to do. 'We have to get the names of other people who don't have lawyers, and see if we can help them. Most of these guys have been abandoned by their governments and it's going to be a harder job getting them somewhere safe from torture.'

Clive also gave me the news that he was seeing Richard Belmar, one of the four remaining British detainees, and that he planned to see my old friend Shaker, as well as Omar Deghayes and Jamal Kiyemba – all British residents. He was not representing Bisher and Jamil, though he was well aware of their cases. I felt so at home with him that I asked him to bring me some junk food when he came the second day.

When I first heard about Clive being a 'death-row' lawyer I remember thinking, 'Oh my Lord, things are not looking very good.' But now his attitude intrigued me.

He spoke about seeing people that he'd represented on the notorious death rows, in the Deep South, being executed, and how traumatized he had felt. But I wanted to know why he cared about them, and even more, why he cared about us.

'The treatment of prisoners on the US mainland is probably worse than you guys have it, although your conditions are much poorer than anything I've ever seen on death row in the past twenty years. But now they've moved clearly into the realm of torture, and I don't mean just psychologically. I've spoken to detainees who've been sexually abused, raped, and tortured. And God knows what's happening to the ones held as "Ghost" detainees, in places like Egypt and Diego Garcia – and who knows where else.

'In the US they have always hated black people, but never feared them. During the Cold War, they feared the Soviets, but never hated them. With the Muslim world, they fear you *and* hate you.

'It's argued,' he went on, 'that to stop the "ticking time bomb" in New York City, it would be fully justified to resort to torture in order to extract vital information. But there is no precedent for this. Nowhere in history has it ever worked. In fact, Guy Fawkes' seventeenth-century plot to blow up the Houses of Parliament is a good example. Fawkes was ready to die himself – a potential suicide bomber. When they tortured him to reveal details about further plots, he suggested Jesuits – whom the English were looking for an excuse to kill – were responsible. But the hatred increased and the problem did not go away.'

Later on, Clive said, 'Forgiveness is a very important concept for society, not retribution. You too will have to think about forgiveness, if you want to put this behind you.'

I didn't know how much of this I agreed with, especially when I thought about my own family and how I would react to any – God forbid – serious crime against any of them. Yes, Clive got me thinking for a while about these things, but those words, 'You are going home,' so confidently uttered, were ringing too loudly in my head to dwell on anything else too long. It was totally stunning for me, repeating them to myself, sitting there in Camp Echo.

And it chimed with something Feroz had heard recently in the recreation yard, from Martin Mubanga, that his lawyer had said he was going home in February. That news had spread like wildfire all around the camp. So when Clive told me this, I was trying to say to myself, this makes sense, this fits in with what Martin's been told. But I thought that probably Feroz and I would be staying, because we'd been designated for military commissions. There were all sorts of unanswered questions pounding in my head, especially 'Am I to face charges in the UK if we do return?'

'What's the worst that's been said about me in the media, Clive?' I had asked him earlier.

'Well, apart from President Bush's statement, about you and Feroz – "I don't know what these men have done, but I know they're the worst of the worst" – reports leaked to *Newsweek* claim that you designed and were planning to fly unmanned drones loaded with anthrax into the Houses of Parliament.'

'That's insane, I can't believe . . . you're serious, Clive?'

'Absolutely. In fact, I was hoping that you really did confess to something as ludicrous as that. We'd have a field day hearing them explain how you were planning to get these military aircraft that cost millions of pounds each – and even more so if you were accused of designing and building them. And why on earth, if you wanted to spread anthrax about, would you crash a planeload of the stuff into a building, rather than, say, put it in the ventilation system?'

Clive seemed almost upset when I told him that I wasn't even questioned about anything like that.

I had heard once from PFC Lopez, in Camp Echo, that he'd read I was accused of planning to carry out attacks with remote-controlled helicopters, but I really thought he was joking. Now it was more than just a rumour, or a joke – but I didn't understand where that one came from.

'Apparently a former schoolfellow of yours from the Jewish school . . .'

'King David?'

'Yes. I think so. Anyway, this chap works for *Newsweek* in the US, and he came to see your father when he heard about your story. He said he was an old classmate of yours and wanted to help very much. He met Zaynab and the children, and was at your father's house quite often. Then he went back to the States and printed this story, which he says was from FBI sources.'

'I can't believe it. I haven't seen anyone from King David in more than twenty years.'

'Are you sure there isn't something that could have given them the fuel for this?'

'Well . . . I told the FBI about flying lessons I had taken eighteen years ago – when I was eighteen. Maybe that's—'

'That must be it – anyone can make up the rest.'

The *Newsweek* correspondent, Richard Wolfe (who I hadn't remembered), was not the only former Jewish classmate from King David to write about me.

I was near to tears when I received a year-old letter from my brother telling me that Mischa Moselle, now a Hong Kong journalist, had not only remembered me, but also shown his solidarity after all these years. I hadn't seen or heard from him since 1979. He wrote to the *Guardian*:

I feel it is impossible that this organizer of a charitable school in Afghanistan took away none of the liberal ideas imparted by the King David Jewish junior and infants' school in Birmingham . . . I would urge all those in a position to do so to put as much pressure as possible on the relevant authorities to see that my old mate 'Mozambique' gets a fair trial. My thoughts are with Moazzam and his family.

After arriving in Papa Block, two unprecedented things had happened. Firstly, our orange clothes had been replaced by tan ones. This had a profound effect on how we regarded ourselves. I detested the orange uniforms we were forced to wear for so long, and the new clothes were a pleasant surprise. It was a matter of speculation amongst us all as to why we'd been apparently singled out for this: perhaps because of military commissions? We found out later though that all level-one detainees had had the change. Secondly, Feroz and I were each taken out of our cells one day – without any shackles – and a soldier we'd never seen before, accompanied by the guards, took our measurements. 'Why would they need our measurements?' we asked each other.

'It's for the commissions,' said Hicks and Uthman. 'We were given specially tailored clothing for the trials.'

When I asked Clive, though, he said, 'Maybe they're going to give you tailor-made clothes for your return. You're not going to any military commissions, I can almost guarantee that.'

Uthman wasn't seeing any lawyers at all. He'd sacked his army lawyer at the beginning of his military commission, saying, 'This person does not represent me and I don't want him acting on my behalf. He's from the US military and regards me as his enemy, and I regard him as mine, so how can he defend me? I want to represent myself, and if I'm not able to do that, then I want a Yemeni lawyer.' He

went on, 'I am a member of al-Qa'idah . . .' His words had been immediately struck off mid-sentence from the commission record, and the
proceedings halted. Uthman did not trust the lawyers, whom he
termed 'interrogators masquerading as lawyers'.

After our first meeting, Clive asked me to gather names of any
other detainees who wanted legal representation but were not able to
get it – the majority of people detained in Guantánamo at the time. He
needed their next of kin, name, address, telephone numbers,
Internment Serial Number (ISN), and details of languages spoken.

I knew by now there was an atmosphere of great scepticism
towards the lawyers, part of it coming from Uthman. After Feroz and
I had got lawyers, several others also received visits from legal teams
in the US. But other detainees had refused to see lawyers at all,
because they didn't believe they were properly representative of them,
or they didn't trust them, or they found the notion of American courts
incompatible with their beliefs. Much of this was due to the perception
that seeking judgement in a non-Islamic court was not permissible.

There was a much-respected Chinese student of Islam, who also
spoke fluent classical Arabic, whose sermons I could sometimes hear
in the distance. He was asked for a ruling on this issue. Once I listened
to him give a discourse on the permissibility of seeking judgement in
a non-Islamic court. He quoted Islamic references, almost like a legal
brief, from the Quran, the Sunnah (prophetic traditions), various
books and scholars, both classical and contemporary, describing the
various rulings, before finally opining that it was not legal. 'In conclusion,' he said, 'pursuing legal judgement on a matter in a non-Islamic
court is not permissible for a Muslim,' although, he added, it would be
permissible in the most extreme circumstances. 'And if this situation
doesn't amount to extreme circumstances, then I don't know what
does,' I thought to myself.

Uthman had maintained the position that he would not participate. But I'd asked him anyway if he could call across for me, because of his proximity to the other blocks. I wanted him to let them know that I was asking for the names of people who wanted lawyers, and then he could relay the names back to me. But he said he couldn't do it, because he didn't agree with it in principle, and he did not want to be a conduit for it. I was annoyed, but not particularly antagonistic. However, it was one of the times when Feroz got quite upset with him.

'I don't know what's wrong with some of you people. Do you expect the angels to descend from the heavens and help you, while all you do is raise your hands in supplication? I see no difference between this and the Sufis.'

Although his comment may have been unfair, it struck a nerve. Many who practise Islam according to the *Salafi* (early) way, like Uthman and even myself, regard parts of Sufi mystic doctrine as heretical. I was in the middle of the argument, trying to diffuse it with selective interpretation, and finally, a blatant refusal to participate.

But I did say to Uthman, 'Listen, brother. There has been no real working Islamic state since the demise of the Ottoman Empire, and even then it had departed from many of the fundamentals. Tell me, how, for the past eighty years or so, have people in the Muslim world been getting their rights, in the absence of Islamic courts? In your own country, Yemen, tribal law is most common. And in post-colonial countries like Pakistan we have a mutation of British and Islamic law, all in one. If someone were to commit a crime against me, are you saying I have no recourse to justice, simply because I cannot seek judgement in a court that doesn't rule by the Shari'ah? If some unscrupulous non-Muslims, or Muslims for that matter, were to discover this belief of yours they'd be robbing you day and night.'

But Uthman did have a point. The habeas corpus ruling had produced no tangible results; the Supreme Court decision meant nothing. It was just as Uthman used to say, 'Décor – America trying to feel good about itself, at our expense.' However, the way I saw it was how Clive had described it. We weren't even counting on the habeas petitions; we just needed to find a conduit to expose some of the realities of the war on terror and Guantánamo Bay. Maybe lawyers could be that conduit.

Anyway, I shouted across the blocks myself, and the first answer I got was from the Russian, Saeed,* my old companion from Bagram. As soon as he heard my voice he shouted across a dozen different greetings in Russian, broken Arabic, English, and Pashto. His Arabic was still a struggle, but he just plugged on, making himself understood somehow. It was so good to hear his voice.

I asked Saeed whether he wanted legal representation. He shouted back, giving me his bio-data, which I transliterated. After him was a Tunisian who gave me his details and said he wanted a lawyer too. Then there was Rashid, the Saudi, who they had recently 'IRFed'. Finally, there was an old Algerian who wanted a lawyer, but he had no next of kin. These four, out of a cellblock of about twenty-five, were the only ones whose names I managed to collect.

There were other people who wanted lawyers, but they felt peer pressure after two knowledgeable people had spoken out against it. It would have been hard for them then to say, 'Yes, I want to take part in it.' Nothing could be done secretly. They had to do it openly and everybody would hear that they had given me their details.

Feroz was very pleased with the four having taken this stand. We knew that it was Saeed's reaction which really broke the ice, although

---

* Ravil Mingazov (Saeed's Russian name): the last remaining Russian in Guantánamo.

I didn't think he realized that he'd contributed to the hottest issue of the day.

At the same time as I had been with Clive the first day, Feroz saw Gita, as she was still his lawyer, and afterwards we went through everything they had both said, comparing notes. We read the legal documents meticulously, sometimes to one another, if he'd received them first, or vice versa. And we discussed, almost like lawyers, various parts of the case. One of the most astounding arguments we came across was the hypothetical example of a little old Swiss woman who had unknowingly donated money to al-Qa'idah. 'Is this woman an enemy combatant?' the presiding Judge Green had asked. The government lawyer said, 'Yes, I think she would be in this case.'

By now in Papa, day in, day out, together, in the tan uniforms which marked us out from the other prisoners, we had built up quite a deep and unusual comradeship. It was a bit like I imagined death row, from films I'd seen. All in our own cells, but sharing this special, unbelievable experience. The only time we ever got to see one another directly was when someone passed our cells going to or from recreation or interrogation. Sometimes guards would allow us, when we were walking past, to stop and put our fingers through the cage just to shake hands. But even without that touching, there was always the salaam, always given with the brightest smile. Nobody ever walked past my cell without acknowledging me, and asking me in ten different ways, as people do in Arabic, how I was doing.

I'd learned by then to appreciate how much people's culture was the factor in these habits. We Brits were a lot colder, a lot more reserved than the others. I would often pass Feroz's cell with little more than a nod, and he passed mine similarly, but neither of us would ever fail to greet the others in the proper, extended, careful way. I felt I had a lot of cultural catching up to do. When I went past Hicks' cell we would have a mutual exchange of grunts, very crude compared to the politeness and warmth of the standard string of greetings.

There was one incident in this period which well illustrates the state of mind that I was in. We all wanted to antagonize the guards a little. I came up with the idea of writing a page full of words and sentences from different languages, appearing like coded messages I was attempting to pass on. It was complete nonsense. I wrote a page of words and sentences in Arabic, Urdu, French, Spanish, Hebrew, Greek, Mandarin, Hindi, Russian, and Latin. I even changed the motto of the US Marines from *Semper Fidelis* to its opposite, *Semper Infidelis.* Then I drew flags of different countries. I folded it up and put it in my top pocket and went out to the recreation yard. I hid it in the recreation yard, knowing they would find it. When they found the paper, I laughed to myself, wondering how many interpreters it would take to translate it.

Within an hour, General Hood came walking around, inspecting things and talking to the sergeant in charge of the block. I was sure it was my little trick that had got them worried. After that every time anybody went in and out of the cells we were searched thoroughly. I apologized to the others for that, but I had enjoyed my little joke on the Americans.

By now I was in a different mood as far as the military were concerned. Almost since my arrival in Papa in October, there had been a new phase of interrogations, and a kind of trial of mental strength between all of us and the interrogators. The authorities certainly showed a new interest in interviews with me again. It was months since I had refused to speak to them. But I was taken to interrogation from Papa at least twenty-five times in less than three months, much more than at any period in Echo. This time around they started playing mind games.

Uthman, very perceptive, as always, said that this was a sign that I was going home. This was what had happened to the Tipton boys, a year earlier, he said. Feroz and I were not sure he was right, and did not want to get our hopes up. But I began regularly dreaming of my wife, and my mind was running on home more than I quite admitted even to myself. I did not write home much, and when I did, I gave little hint of the enormity of the change that seemed to be hanging over us, and just concentrated on mundane details like the improved size of the exercise yard. Although once I wrote to Zaynab more deeply, trying to remind her gently that after two and half years in solitary I might seem unfamiliar at first whenever I did get home.

Feroz was also getting interrogated quite regularly, though not as often as me. I thought it was probably because Feroz is a very reserved person who would just say to them, 'Look, ask my lawyer, speak to my lawyer . . .' But I would get involved in polemical debates and arguments with the interrogators.

Military intelligence, and many other different agencies such as the FBI, CIA, and NSA, who didn't always identify themselves, came to interrogate me. It was intense, sometimes twice a day. Feroz used to shout across two recreation yards – to get messages to Martin Mubanga. We wanted to know whether these interrogations were also happening to Martin, because if so, therefore there really was something going on. But if it was just Feroz and me, then it was something different. At that time Martin was not having any new interrogations.

I soon realized that some of the interrogations seemed to be related to my legal visits. After my first visit from Gita, at the end of August, there had been an immediate visit from the interrogators. I spent hours afterwards wondering if there was a deliberate purpose behind its timing. Were they trying to give me a subliminal message, 'She's really with us'?

It happened too the day before Clive came. The interrogation took place in Gold Building, just outside the sally ports, within walking distance from Papa Block. One of the interrogators, Ian, was a very short man with a huge beard and a moustache, reddish hair. He sat down in front of me and offered me a bottle of water.

'Do you think I drink urine in my cell?' I asked with indignation. 'I hope this isn't your attempt at hospitality?' He was a little taken aback by my attitude; I was trying to disorient him, throw him off guard. How many games had they played with me before?

'Look, let me show you an equation here,' he began. 'You understand algebra?' I felt he was CIA from the way he operated, trying to intimidate and socialize at the same time.

'Well, not really. I'm crap at maths, especially algebra. But I can tell you jihad isn't the only Arabic word to strike terror into the hearts of the West. The word "algebra" comes from *al-Jabra*, to repair or fix. In mathematics it comes from the title of Abu Ja'far al-Khowarizmi's works, from whose name we also get the word *algorithm*—'

'That's all very interesting,' he interrupted. 'Now listen. X plus Y equals Z. OK, that's the equation. X is the knowledge that we have on you. Y is the information that you may or may not give us. And Z equals terrorist. You are Z. X is what we have, Y is what could change the equation.'

'Thank you, Einstein. Now explain to me what it is you're trying to tell me. Are you offering me a cooperation deal, again? If so, you can take it, and stick it "where the sun don't shine". My answer is no. It's not happening.'

'This is what you are,' he then said, pointing to the word he had written on the piece of paper, TERRORIST.

'You people really believe that if a word is said often enough, it actually becomes true, don't you? What is it that Hitler said? "Great masses of people will more easily fall victim to a big lie than to a small one. Especially if it is repeated over and over." I should sit here calling you "donkey" until they come and take me away.'

This thick-skinned man went on, oblivious, 'We know about the complaints that you've made to your lawyers. We know all about your lawyers' visits, your complaints and when they're going to come.' He was obviously referring to the letter that I'd written in July, which had been in the media. 'The American public doesn't care. And American public opinion is what counts, not British. And as far as your government is concerned, they are impotent to do anything, the same as your lawyers.'

It seemed as though he was trying to find a new approach to me. He told me they had information on me, which they had got from other detainees. 'You have not been cooperating or answering our questions for a long time. I'm here to try and make you change your position. How would you feel if you were to be here for many, many years to come?'

'Well, I've been here for three years, and three might not be many, many, but it's enough. And I've not seen anything take place that you have promised or threatened, like sending me to court. I really don't care any more. Actually, you know what? I quite like it here now.'

In fact I did like it, compared to Echo, though 'like' might seem a strange word. I liked being able to hear the call to prayer, I liked to pray in congregation, I liked having discussions with other detainees and I liked a larger recreation yard.

'I'm an optimist, Ian. I think this situation will resolve itself in one way or another, and I don't need your help with it. I already know from my experience of having signed that FBI statement exactly what happens. Nothing. They told me then that I was going to court, but I didn't. There is no way on God's earth that I will trust people like you ever again, whatever you threaten me with.'

As I talked, I remembered how I was in tears the first time the CIA interrogated me, threatening me, frightening me, back in Islamabad, and in Kandahar and Bagram, but not this time.

This went on for about two hours, with his approach and methods appearing very slimy, almost laughably so. I could see the anger on his face, even though he tried to act calm. He had not realized that by this time I wasn't afraid of the CIA or any of the interrogators like him.

It was quite comical when I went back to the cell and told the others about it, and everyone started enthusiastically to make an analysis. There was always an analysis of American actions. We tried to analyse the purposes of each question: why was he playing this game, why was there just one interrogator?

And after my two days with Clive, they took me out to interrogation again. This time it was a new interrogator, who came from a different angle.

He started off trying to make it seem like a friendly chat. 'I've heard you like talking about history and politics . . .'

'I like talking about Greek mythology too . . .'

'Oh, come on, Mr Begg. Do you mind if I call you Moazzam? Is it Mozzam, or Mo-azzam?'

'Say it however you like. It doesn't make any difference. I'm sure you can't pronounce Urdu, or Arabic words correctly . . . If you want to talk about those things, fine. But I'm not answering any of your questions about me, or anybody else.'

They weren't allowed to discuss current affairs, but they would talk about things in general terms, such as the war on terror, and allude to the war in Iraq, without specifics. This particular interrogator made a bad pretence at understanding Islamic culture, alluding to the history and politics of the Middle East, saying he really wanted to understand more. After a long conversation I realized that he had the same tunnel vision that most interrogators had.

He asked me about Tablighi Jamaat – the biggest Islamic missionary organization in the world, originally from India. Then he asked me, 'Why do you think al-Qa'idah and Tablighi Jamaat would have a working relationship?'

I was irritated and said,'Oh my goodness, you're all obsessed, putting Muslim groups under al-Qa'idah's umbrella, struggling to prove they're all linked, somehow.'

Then he spelled out his theory.'We believe that al-Qa'idah is trying to infiltrate the governments of sub-Saharan Africa, and they're doing it through missionary organizations like Tablighi Jamaat.'

'OK, but as most sub-Saharan countries have small Muslim populations, how are they going to possibly do that?'Then I realized what he was getting at: Tablighi Jamaat, being a missionary organization, was going to miraculously convert all these people, and then al-Qa'idah was going to move in with some sort of bloodless coup, or blood-filled coup, and take power.

He was also trying to link all this with aid organizations. He asked me,'You've worked with Muslim aid organizations: they always have some sort of link to militant Islam and—'

'Al-Qa'idah, I suppose. I thought I'd say it before you did, that *link* or *association* we all have to the ubiquitous al-Qa'idah. What you really mean – but are too afraid to say – is what links aid organizations, missionary groups, and militancy to al-Qa'idah is Islam. So you're potentially investigating 1.6 billion enemy combatants. Good luck.'

'Why don't you answer our questions?'said another man.'You have family, people could get hurt.'

Was he trying to threaten my family?

'Don't you ever mention my family again. You've accused me of being a member of al-Qa'idah, right?' Then I said, as menacingly as I could, 'What about your family?'

He said nothing.

I wrote to both Clive and Gita immediately after this interrogation, describing what had happened, and how I felt there was definitely a pattern of the interrogations being timed to undermine me after the legal visits. It was the same interrogator who had seen me immediately after both visits. I also put the list of the four detainees who wanted lawyers, in the letter to Clive, trying to focus on others' needs too. I wrote to Clive again two days later, telling him more about Ian and how I had managed to keep up my 'cordial but non-cooperative approach' after he had told me I was a terrorist. I asked him to try and get the books and magazines that he had brought, released by the authorities. We had had no books from the library for more than three months, and I badly needed intellectual distraction.

A few days later they called me yet again for interrogation. This time it was two men from the Department of Defense, who were investigating allegations of abuse. They were only interested in physical, not psychological abuse.

On 28 December they came for me again, but they also told Feroz to get ready.

In the room were six guards, three chairs, and one table. There were three interrogators, sitting on top of the table. One of them I recognized: Ian, minus his beard and moustache. Richard Belmar and Feroz were already there. I sat down with them. There were two guards to a person, plus some guards in front.

I hadn't seen Richard for a long time, and even when I did, in Bagram, we only spoke once. He looked good. He has very dark, ebony-coloured skin, a sharp contrast against the bright orange he was still wearing. Strangely, this was the first time I'd seen Feroz face-to-face, and not through mesh.

Everyone was dead silent. I looked over to Feroz, and got a funny smile. Richard was very quiet, not saying a word. I looked at Ian, and it had taken me a couple of seconds to register who he was. I said, 'Oh my goodness, Ian, you have no chin.' That was probably why he'd kept a beard when I saw him first.

One of the interrogators said, 'Look, you haven't been cooperating with us, but now we're here to give you a privileged and unique opportunity. We're meeting you on behalf of the British. If you co-operate with us your country can act in a favourable way towards you because of what we tell them that you've done for us, i.e. you've cooperated. We want to ask you some questions now. We're giving you a golden opportunity so that the British government has a reason to ask for your repatriation.'

They took us all to separate rooms, and they began the interroga-tions. I sat alone in my room waiting for them. I was chained to the ground and seated on a swivel chair. There were cameras recording my every move, and everything I said. I moved myself closer to the wall, as much as the chain would allow, and I tried to listen to what was happening next door. I could hear, 'Please, please cooperate with us, it's very important that you do, this is fundamental to your future.' I could hear a muted voice, 'Speak to my lawyers, speak to my lawyers . . .'

After about an hour or so they came to my room, and they began the questions with me. They were asking me about things in Britain. They asked me about a Pakistani man, Abu somebody.

'I don't know what you're talking about. You know how long I've been here, I don't even know the price of a pound of bananas – or is it kilos now? – in Britain.'

They also asked me about a British guesthouse in Kabul, saying it was linked to something very important that was going to happen in Britain. 'Is this part of something that they want to offer the British?' I thought. 'A game maybe, like they played with the Tipton lads? Is it because we're coming up to the end of the year, and there really *is* some threat of an attack in Britain?' But what if they were telling the truth? I asked myself all these things, with my mind completely confused. I didn't know the answers to the questions that they were asking anyway, but I wasn't going to tell them that.

I just said, 'Look, I don't want any innocent people to be hurt, anywhere. But I don't trust or believe you. You have lied to and tormented my family and me for three years, and now you expect me to believe you?'

'But you could be saving thousands of lives.'

'How? How am I going to be saving thousands of lives? You're always trying to put this kind of thing onto me, as if my saying a few words somehow will save someone . . . what about the thousands of lives that you've taken? You could be saving thousands of lives by not killing them in the first place. And what about the lives of my wife and my children that you personally have destroyed?'

There had been a time when I used to say to them, 'Look, I don't hold you personally responsible, it's the system.' But by this time I was saying, 'You personally as an individual, you are responsible, you. And you need to look at yourself and see what you've been doing.' I said it in a very angry way. I don't think I've ever been so abusive to anybody in my entire life as I was to those three. I swore, I cursed them. I had had enough.

After all this, they said, 'Look, something really could happen in your country. You have your wife, you have your family over there, and you wouldn't want anything to happen to them.'

'Listen, I've told you people never to mention my family. Never, ever mention my family.'

Amazingly, one of them started apologizing. 'I didn't mean to get you upset about all of that.'

Then I said that if they really thought something was going to happen in Britain, why didn't they call MI5, and let them speak to me directly? Very oddly they said, 'No, there's just no time for that.' Then I thought, 'This is rubbish, I don't believe this, MI5 could be here in a day if necessary.' I actually quoted to them from the book MI5 had given me, earlier in the year, *The English*. The point was that more than twice as many people crossed the Atlantic between the US and the UK, than between the US and the rest of Europe.

By the end of that interrogation I'd come to the conclusion that this was more of a game than anything substantial. I asked Feroz what he thought, afterwards, when we were all taken back to our cells. He said it had been the same questions for him. They asked him too about this Abu whoever, the Pakistani, and about some British guesthouse in Kabul. But his way was not to get into any discussions with them.

I, on the other hand, had been round the circuit of recent history – Iraq, Afghanistan, Chechnya. One of them was obviously ignorant.

'We helped your people and Muslims in Afghanistan, look what we did over there. And we helped in Chechnya too.'

'What?'

'Yeah, yeah, we were there.'

'Really?'

'No, I think you mean Afghanistan,' said Ian.

But the other one persisted. 'No, no, we were there in Chechnya.'

Ian just had his head in his hands.

Writing to Clive about this interrogation – the sixth since his visit – was a way of trying to calm my anxiety. I wrote him my fourth letter, five closely written pages, telling him all about that evening, and how the interrogators seemed to me 'almost desperate'. There were so many odd aspects about that meeting, and one of them had actually said that the people involved in terrorism against the US were not in Guantánamo, and we were there instead. I was baffled too about how they thought my stale information about Britain could possibly be useful, and how after three hundred interrogations they had not had their fill of me. I had to tell Clive too that I was feeling extremely anxious that I had not heard from him at all, though Feroz had had several communications.

The interrogations went on, two more nights running, and I wrote to Clive again on 1 January, spilling out that I was 'sick and tired of this tedious, theatrical performance'. There had now been eight interrogations since I saw him. I apologized for bombarding him with letters, and asked him whether I really had to write down all the details of my abuse, which I was finding 'painful and disturbing'. I knew Feroz was diligently doing it, but that didn't make it easier to do it myself. I told him again how worried I was not to hear from him. I told him I knew he must be very busy, but also that I wondered if I was making a mistake with the address. I ended by sending him 'Best wishes for the New Year', as though it was just a normal letter.

I wrote to Zaynab too, the following day, with greetings for the approaching Eid-al-Adha, and saying, 'I realize that the children have grown and changed much since I last saw them. I don't know exactly how I'll react on my return, but envisage it to be, probably, the happiest day of my life. May Allah hasten its coming.' I half believed it might be soon.

When I was called out yet again, I thought, 'Perhaps they're taking me out more than anybody else because they want to sow seeds of doubt about me amongst the other detainees.' I thought about refusing and not going, but I never knew where I was going, so I might have missed a lawyer's visit, or a British delegation. Of course the guards knew what I was going for, because they knew the destination: lawyers, Camp Echo; interrogators, Gold Building.

On the way back to my cell from the last interrogation, I heard one of the two guards say, 'Don't worry, it'll be over soon.' I thought I'd caught part of a conversation between them, but he had meant the remark for me.

One day, the guards came into the cell and started doing a full inventory of everything, like they did when I left Echo. Was Papa Block going to be reshuffled? Normally they did cell checks when we were in recreation. But this was different, they were doing it while I was in the cell, they were asking me to produce each item that I had, and then marking it off a list. This meant that something urgent was happening, and they couldn't wait until recreation the next day. I could see too that Feroz, and everybody else, was getting the same treatment.

I was taken out the next morning so early that everybody was asleep and I didn't get a chance to say a word to anybody, apart from Feroz. I thought that they were taking me to Echo, imagining that it must be to see Clive. I thought, 'The only reason anybody goes to Echo is to see their lawyer.' But nobody turned up for the whole morning, and into the afternoon. I had nothing at all with me. The cell was empty.

This was actually much worse, in some ways, than the old system, although if I had had the Quran, I would have been all right. I had learned by now how to deal with the solitary life. I found it very easy to be by myself. That day I sat there, remembering those guards who used to be here, the ones I used to get along with, Foshee, Kelvin, Mesadore, Jennifer, and all the others I had known through those years. It was an odd feeling, but evocative of the human contacts we had made, despite the inhuman conditions. Now they were gone, but I was back in solitary.

That feeling didn't last very long. Sergeant Low, who was in charge of Papa, and everyone in it, even those who had been moved to Echo, came over with a major, and stood in the cell, looking very military in the way she held herself. She didn't say a word, but the major with her said, 'Mr Begg, I am here to inform you that the United States . . .' And as soon as he said that, I thought, 'Oh God, it's going to be the charge, now they're going to charge me, and they're going to put me through this process.''. . . military has decided to hand you over to the British authorities, and any charges that we had pending have been dropped.'

Sergeant Low was standing there in the Parade Rest position, with her feet spread almost shoulder-width apart, hands behind the back with her head up, and back straight. She was stood there in the Parade Rest position, while the major said these extraordinary words.

'I don't believe you, Major.'

'I'm not in the habit of telling lies. You've never seen me before, and I'm confident you'll never see me again.'

Sergeant Low showed no expression at all, though I had spoken to her a couple of times before, and had seen her smile and laugh. Not this time. Her predecessor, Carnahan, would probably have shown a lot more expression. But Low just turned and walked out, and that was the last I ever saw of her.

Shortly afterwards someone brought a box with my things. These were new guards, and I didn't know any of them. I really wanted to ask them about Feroz.

Then one of the MPs came in, and said, 'Hey, Saif says hello.' That instantly told me that Martin Mubanga was there in Echo. And it told me, 'Hold on, this thing that the major was telling me could well be true.'

There was a female soldier working on the block, and she used to help me pass the time by secretly reading to me from a book called *Tuesdays with Morrie*. I asked her if there were any other Brits in Echo, and she told me, 'Feroz is here, and so are Martin and Richard.'

Then I really knew that something very big was happening. It was a very, very long two weeks. Clive came about three days later, and that was the end of my being unsure. I had started thinking beyond the end of Guantánamo. 'What's going to happen in Britain? Are they going to arrest me, are they going to put me through a court system, what sort of conditions will there be over there?'

But Clive made it absolutely clear that I had nothing to worry about. As usual he was thinking about others. He brought me some things from Zaynab, cashew nuts, snacks, chocolates, and when he told me he was going to see Shaker, I told him, 'Look, just give it to him.' Shaker by this time was in Camp Five, which I'd watched being built from my recreation yard where I could just see the watchtower. The soldiers had told me that it was a permanent facility, and that sounded like really bad news for Shaker. I had asked the guards why people were kept there, and I was given two answers, one, that it was for people who had refused to cooperate or answer questions, two, that it was for people who were considered troublemakers or ringleaders. I knew Shaker would always be considered influential wherever he was; he was such an outstanding person, as even the guards had told me.

Two days before I left, a very unexpected visitor turned up. I had written Gita quite a harsh, though polite, letter, saying, 'You've seen all these people and you haven't come back to tell me about it, you haven't even written to me, in fact you've only written to me once since I saw you. If you say you're going to do something, then either do it, or write to me saying that it's impossible, I can't do it, I made a mistake. But don't keep me in this limbo condition that I'm already in.'

Gita had actually come to apologize, and then also to express solidarity and happiness for us. She even knew the exact day we were going, which was more than the guards did.

I was preparing myself as best I could. It all felt so unfamiliar, thinking about the future, instead of just each day. I went through my papers, and some I ripped up, because there were things I'd written down that I didn't want the Americans to have. Some were very private and personal thoughts. Some were skeleton notes of the book that I wanted to write, and I passed those to Clive, although I knew they would have to be declassified, and I didn't know if I would ever see them again. I had no idea what they would allow through.

Just before I left, the same man who had taunted me, mentioning my family, came in again with some other people, but this time all they were doing was fingerprinting. This time round they took me out of the cell with no shackles. It felt weird.

Before he left the man said, 'Are you sure you don't want to answer any of my questions?'

'Surer than I've ever been in my life.'

Shortly after that, guards came to take my measurements again. In a moment of madness I thought they were going to make me some tailor-made clothes. But they came back with a horrible, thin, white made-in-Bangladesh T-shirt, and jeans and a denim jacket that I wouldn't be caught dead in. There were some shoes too. I tried them on, and of course they were too big. In fact everything was too big. They gave me a black carry-all bag, and in it there was a little 'goodbye package'. There was a toothbrush, toothpaste, deodorant, a comb, and baby wipes, a blanket, and a few other little things for us to be getting on with when we got back to normal life.

One of the *National Geographic* magazines that Martin gave me advertised a 'Great Escape Exhibition' at the Imperial War Museum that was beginning next week. I just had to go.

As I packed away all my papers, including the poems, I thought about the first time I ever wrote one, here in Camp Echo. It was called 'Homeward Bound'. The final verse read:

> *Still the paper do I pen*
> *Knowing not, or ever when –*
> *As dreams begin and nightmares end –*
> *I'm homeward bound to beloved tend*

My final act in Guantánamo was memorizing chapter 17 of the Quran, al-Israa, which is about the Prophet's journey to Jerusalem. I had made it my goal to memorize it in those two weeks. It is a long chapter, but I completed it on the last day, the last hour, before I left that cell and Echo for the last time.

I was wearing the new clothes, in anticipation, when they came and took me out of the cell at about one o'clock in the morning. The guards had told me, 'Normally when we move people, it is late, or very early in the morning.' I was just waiting. I was going home. I wasn't asleep; I had been reading Sherlock Holmes. I made a particular last prayer, a prayer of thankfulness, 'Thank you, O Lord, for giving me the strength to pass through this trial,' and I prayed for Him to make it easy for my family to accept my return, and to make things even better for them.

The guards came in to shackle me, even more than usual, and with an additional padlock too. They felt stupid about doing it, and one muttered, 'I don't know why we're padlocking them boys, what are they going to do, escape on the way to the plane?'

They put me into a truck, with goggles over my eyes. But to my surprise I heard the familiar voice of a female soldier. She took my goggles off, and said, 'Told you I'd see you again.' Smith was a young Californian I'd last seen in Echo, back in October. The other guards had ousted her there after a leg injury playing soccer, which they said impeded her ability to perform her duty effectively. So she was sent to the main Camp Delta, paradoxically a lot more physically demanding The fact of the matter, she confided to me, was that they didn't like her. She was a lot more friendly and talkative than most among the new guards, a fact that many of them resented.

'You're finally going home now, aren't you? I knew you would.'

'Yes. It's hard to believe, but I think it's true. Although, as I've heard from many a soldier, believe—'

'Nothing of what you hear and half of what you see,' she finished the sentence and we laughed. 'I'm really happy for you, though,' she continued. 'I get to stay here for another six months.'

'Even now,' I thought, 'how bizarre it is that she can relate her life in Guantánamo to mine, even equate the two in some ways. Yet we all know the reality: I'm the prisoner – the bad guy; she's the US trooper – the good guy.'

'Maybe we'll meet some day,' she said, as the vehicle started off. 'I've wanted to go to England for a long time.'

'So have I, my dear, so have I.'

I went off then in the truck. It was horrible, just like every other time, although I had got used to it because I'd been transported so many times. It was very claustrophobic in the back of the all-metal vehicle. It had a series of loops in the floor, and they threaded my chains through them. The only consolation was that I was not there alone. There was a guard, and there was space too for somebody on the other side, and I had the feeling that Feroz, or somebody else, was there.

They took me to Gold Building, and put me in a room there, by myself, chained to the floor again. I was wondering why, and then I thought, 'The British are going to come now and take this chain off.' But no, they were handing us over from one group of MPs to another. They took me from there and what I saw in front of me was a huge coach, with blacked-out windows. I climbed on board. Feroz and Richard Belmar were already on there. It was packed with soldiers. I saw the three Brits sitting there shackled, each one next to soldiers. I walked on and sat down. I saw Martin Mubanga, with his dreadlocks, hair all over the place, Feroz looking as serene and calm as ever, Richard just quiet.

Martin Mubanga was the first to start speaking to me. I knew his voice from the rapping he used to do in the blocks. We started speaking in Arabic. Martin's Arabic was broken, but it was understandable. The guards seemed a little disturbed by this. One of them got up, walked over to the front, had a word in somebody's ear, and that person got up and came and sat at the back. It was obvious that he was an Arab. Quick as a flash Martin changed to speaking fast in Jamaican London street slang, which I found almost impossible to understand. It was funny looking at the interpreter's face.

Then we came to a stop, again, and the vehicle began to rock and move slowly. We must have been on the ferry to the other part of the island. After about an hour or so we arrived on the other side.

Martin and I were chatting. Feroz was very calm. Richard was quiet. Nobody was really ecstatic, because we all felt we didn't know what was happening. And we were still shackled. Finally we came to a stop and Foreign Office Martin walked on board. He shook everybody's hand, and asked if we were all OK. Then a woman came on board who he said was from Scotland Yard. She was rather stern-faced, quite tall, brown hair, and seemed a little dazed by her surroundings, and among all these soldiers. Martin looked out of place, but she was even more so.

Then came my last memory of Guantánamo Bay. They asked me to stand up: 'You're going first.' They wanted to undo the padlock around my waist first, before the handcuffs, but they couldn't, because they didn't have the key. All the MPs were looking at each other, one person asking another and everyone accusing the next person, 'I haven't got them.'

'You've got them.'

'You had them.'

'No I didn't, he had them.'

So I said, 'Do you mind if I sit back down again, please?'

I heard the senior officer, a captain, outside, reprimanding his guards, 'How could you do this, it's so embarrassing.' Eventually they walked in with a huge pair of wire cutters. 'Can you stand up again?' I was worried, as they were really big and they had to put them close to my stomach and my hands. The soldier tried to cut the padlock, but he couldn't do it, the top part of the cutters bent. They cursed at one another a little bit again, and then another pair was brought, even larger, and I was even more frightened this time. I turned my head to the side and closed my eyes, and I heard the snap. It was a big, big snap. The chains were off, and they took me out.

The last thing I said to them was, 'Have you ever had a soup sandwich?'

'No.'

'Try putting soup in a sandwich and see what happens.'

They didn't find that funny at all, but the other Brits laughed.

As I walked out with the guards, I saw what looked like some sort of parade. The back of the British military transport plane was open and outside there were so many police officers standing in line – without their hats. There were some other civilians hovering around too. I walked up with the two US soldiers, and two or three police came to meet me. The American soldiers had put some plastic flexicuffs on me after the chains came off. They took out some scissors and cut the flexicuffs off, asking the police, 'Do you want to put shackles on him now?'

'No,' one answered, 'thank you, we'll take it from here. Come this way, sir.'

The British didn't touch me at all. They escorted me into the plane, and I walked in and sat down. It was so strange to be sitting in an aeroplane after all this time. I was trying to read every face and every person who was walking past. As I sat down, I turned to my left, and I saw Feroz coming in. He too sat down. The police came and introduced themselves, showed me who was the person in charge, and the two officers who were going to be sitting with me on either side. They told me that if I needed to go to the bathroom, just to tell them, and they would escort me. If I needed to pray then they had got a mat there for me, they said. There were prayer mats, Qurans, books, newspapers, halal food, snacks, and drinks.

'We've got a Muslim liaison officer, and if there's anything that you need to talk to him about, he's over there. Is there anything you want?'

'Just the newspapers, please, I haven't read those in three years.'

'What would you like?'

I asked for every broadsheet they could give me. I didn't sleep at all in all the hours of that journey. Not for a second did I close my eyes. The din of the engines was too loud anyway.

But I was quite excited.

I began devouring all the papers as fast as I could; even the *Sun* and the *Daily Mail*. I saw articles with pictures of the others, and me. 'Unbelievable,' I thought, 'I'm on the front page of every newspaper in Britain. Is there much support out there, or do people hate us?' Then

I read about the Belmarsh detainees, how, after three years, the House of Lords was going to rule on the legality of the detentions. It sounded like something I'd done recently: challenge the legality of my detention. I also saw reports of abuse by British soldiers in Iraq, which came as a shock.

Then the police told me they had new clothes for me, as I would probably want to get out of the American ones. But I didn't bother to change – clothes were the last thing on my mind.

One of the officers from the Met came and sat next to me and began speaking in a Liverpudlian accent. 'I've seen your face on the telly a few times. This is the second trip like this I've done, last time we got those lads from Tipton.'

'And how were they?'

'All quite dazed, a bit like you lot.' Then he said, 'So did the Americans treat you well, mate, or did they torture you?'

It was hard to answer a question like that, but I soon realized it was the question on many lips. 'A bit of both, I think.'

'You're all right now, though? Glad you're coming back?'

'Oh yes. I've been dreaming of this day for three years.'

I looked around to see if there was anybody I recognized. The only one was Foreign Office Martin. He went over and said hello to everybody, then he came and sat down next to me and shook my hand: 'We did it. I told you we'd do it!'

I thought, 'That's bull, Martin. But say whatever you want, it doesn't matter.' He started talking to me about things that he'd never spoken to me about before, presumably because he'd been with the Americans all the time. He talked about my father's campaign, and how dignified it had been. He told me that he went to see the play with my father and me in, too, but he didn't think it was very good.

Then he went on to talk about what really seemed to be on his mind: 'There seem to be some reports by your lawyers that I actually advised you to take part in the CSRTs and . . .'

'Look, Martin, to be fair to you, I remember when you came to tell me about the habeas corpus case, and I wanted to know how I was going to handle it, you scratched your chest so that they couldn't see it, and it was an indication for me to ask you in front of them for a lawyer. I appreciated that. But at the same time, Martin, I remember equally distinctly, that when I asked them about the CSRTs you said that they were going to take place anyway, so I might as well take part in them.'

He didn't say anything more about that, but he did start talking to me about the other detainees, and he said, 'I must say to you that out of all the people I visited, I actually enjoyed our conversations. Compared to the other guys, some of whom would hardly even speak to me, you were fine. One of the others, for instance, when I came, he just sat under the table and made funny noises. He wouldn't speak to me. And some of them even refused to come out of the cell.'

I asked him, 'Tell me, what's going to happen when I get back home?'

'I don't know. My job ends when we land in Britain. I don't know what's going to happen.'

The RAF transport plane began its descent and final approach to somewhere in England. This was it: my constant prayer for all those years, and it was about to be answered.

14

DO YOU KNOW WHO I AM?

Sunset. RAF Northolt, 25 January 2005

The plane landed, taxied to a stop, and the doors opened. It was freezing cold. I'd forgotten all about English winters, after all those Caribbean ones. Then someone from immigration, a middle-aged woman, dressed in a fur coat and heavily made-up, came and asked me if I was a British citizen. 'What a silly question,' I thought. The woman from Scotland Yard came over soon after and sat next to me.

'I have something to read out to you,' she said in my ear, over the roar of the engines. 'I am placing you under arrest under the Prevention of Terrorism Act . . . Do you understand?'

She read this to all the others too, and the police handcuffed us all. 'Strange,' I thought, 'why handcuff us now, after a sixteen-hour journey without them?' Was this thing never going to end?

I heard the sound of a vehicle driving into the back of the transport plane. Martin and Richard were taken off first, and I heard the vehicle drive off. Then another drove on board, taking Feroz, and then me. I was utterly dejected as I walked into the back of the police van.

There was no seat for me. My place was in a cubicle at the back on the right, and they locked the door once I was inside. Throughout my entire three-year ordeal I'd never been put in something like this. Clive had told me to expect questioning, the same pattern as what had happened with the five Brits first released – but why this whole charade of high security? After three years of it . . . they still hadn't had enough?

I tucked my knees into my chest and resigned myself to the next stage of my fate, hoping – praying – this was not the shape of things to come. The only good thing was that my silent companion, again, was Feroz Abbassi.

The whole area was not more than two foot by two. As the van sped off, almost nothing was visible, except flashes of light from outside, dulled by the blackened window.

'Those lights are from all the media outside,' said the officer from Liverpool, who was also in the van. 'You're all big news today.'

After a seemingly endless journey around the streets of London – which I assumed was to shake off the media – the agonizing journey ended at Paddington Green Police Station. The relief I felt, leaving that cubicle, was like resurfacing after staying under water for too long.

It was a strange feeling, walking on British soil after such a long time; I hadn't imagined it being like this. In fact I'd expected something a lot more worrying. The one good thing that had come out of the police tactics was that they had evaded the media, which had first hovered around at the airport, and then at the police station.

Having had some experience of police stations, I was pleasantly surprised with the manner of the police officers. They were certainly accommodating, and on their best behaviour (or perhaps I was comparing them to the US military). I was escorted to a room where my handcuffs were removed, and I was offered a cup of tea. Then a duty sergeant took down some of my details and explained the process, and what would happen next. Finally he asked, 'Are there any members of your family you'd like to call?'

'My family,' I thought. 'Just like that, after three years, not hearing their voices, or seeing their faces . . .' I couldn't control my emotions, tears rolled down my face.

I said in a shaky voice, 'No, thank you. What am I supposed to say over the phone after all this time? I waited for three years – I can wait a little longer to talk in person, when I'm free. Besides, I don't remember their phone numbers anyway.'

I was escorted to a cell – without handcuffs or shackles – where I found a whole set of new clothes waiting for me, with a Quran and a prayer mat neatly laid on the bunk. The cell was nearly four times larger than anything I had experienced in Guantánamo. But now I was preparing myself for the worst. Even though I'd been assured it would-n't happen, prison seemed to be a lurking possibility. After all, why would they go through this whole procedure, unless they wanted to put me, us, away for a long time?

Dinner was awful: it was a very spicy Indian curry, with nan bread, both drenched in oil, and yet it was the most exotic dish I had tasted for a long while. Straight afterwards I performed the ritual ablution, and said my first prayer. It was well after sunset, and I was exhausted from the journey. I could hear muted, but distinct sounds of shouting or chanting outside. I could hear muffled sounds of footsteps on con-crete, doors opening and closing. And I could hear the familiar, soothing hum of Quranic recitation echoing from the next cell down, which sounded like Feroz.

Shortly after, I was asked if I wanted to speak to the Muslim liaison officer, which I declined. My cell door opened later and I had a visit from someone else, asking me about treatment and conditions. Finally, I was told that my lawyer was there to see me.

The last time I'd seen Gareth Peirce was in the spring of 2001, when I had consulted her about whether it was wise to travel after the hassles from the intelligence services. She had told me that things would probably get worse for Muslims, judging by the misconceptions that were already around at the time. I had thought about going to Saudi Arabia, for the lesser pilgrimage, or umrah, with the family, but was concerned about misinformation being passed over from British to Saudi intelligence, and how that could be misused.

'You're probably better off not going there, or anywhere that has a poor human-rights record at present,' she had said.

There she was suddenly, in the police station, the very first familiar face, welcoming me back to England.

'It's good to see you, Moazzam,' she said, with her warm, sympathetic smile. 'I'm so glad you're back, finally.'

'It's good to see you too, Gareth. How are you?'

'I'm fine . . . it's *you* that everyone's been worried about. You've lost so much weight. But you look relatively well. Are you?'

'Oh, I'm fine, just glad to be back. You probably don't recall, but I should have taken your travel advice. Anyway, what's going to happen next?' I asked, still feeling a certain nervousness.

'There's nothing to worry about. The government is just putting up a show for the Americans, as they did with the five before you. They'll ask you some questions tomorrow in an interview, but you don't have to answer – I'm sure you've had quite enough of that . . .'

'Over three hundred times, Gareth.'

'I can't imagine, I'm so sorry . . . and they've timed your return perfectly with the pending House of Lords' decision on the Belmarsh detainees. Have you heard?'

'Yes, Abu Qatada, and others. I read about it on the aeroplane, and Clive told me something about it in Guantánamo. Sorry, you were saying . . .'

'Oh yes. The elections are coming up in May, so people are competing for votes. The House of Lords will decide on the legality of the Delmarsh detentions tomorrow, and it's almost certain they will rule against it. So I might not be there tomorrow during your interview, but Hos – Hossein – from our office will be with you, if I can't make it. In any case, they won't keep you longer than that, it would be ludicrous – after all you've been through.'

I was so relieved to hear that from her. Although I would believe nothing completely until I saw it, I could see that even this chapter of imprisonment was finally ending.

'That's fine,' I said. 'How are my dad, and Zaynab and the children?'

'They are well. They've missed you very much, and are looking forward so much to see you. Your father's been amazing; he's been working tirelessly for your return and release, so it's taken its toll. But it's also given him a very powerful sense of purpose and commitment. He's outside now, but they told me you didn't want to see him here.'

'That's right, not here, not in this place.'

'Don't worry, as soon as you're released tomorrow you can all stay at my house, if you like.' It was so comforting to hear the word *tomorrow* again. 'I'm sure the media will be all over the place and you'll need time to readjust, away from people . . .'

We sat talking for a while, but were soon interrupted by an officer, who said they needed to take my fingerprints. Gareth said she'd see Richard in the meantime, and talk to me later.

I began some cordial conversation with the detectives, who produced some very archaic and dysfunctional-looking instruments.

'You know, in Birmingham they took a complete set of my finger-prints back in 2000, and your American colleagues have taken them more times than I can remember over the past few years. I think you're flogging a dead horse here, mate?'

'Procedure. You know how it is. You're probably an expert at this by now,' he said. I was. As page after repetitive page of prints were taken, they made some inevitable errors, sometimes restarting the whole sheet – which had numerous prints – for the sake of one print.

'I don't mean to criticize, but your FBI counterparts were a lot more efficient . . .' I was only joking, but I think one of them got a little frustrated with my constant reference to the FBI's fingerprinting tech-niques, contrasted with his constant smudges. After almost two hours I finally washed my hands and was taken to meet Gareth again. It was fairly late by now, I was exhausted, and I didn't want to keep her any longer.

'They seem to be in an awful muddle here,' she said. 'I spoke to Richard, and someone brought Martin in to see me, so I spoke to him for a while, even though I'm not his lawyer. They all seem rather con-fused. Anyway, *Mr Begg*, I think it's time to get some rest. You look shattered.' I was.

When I returned to my cell an officer brought me several messages from well-wishers outside: Guantánamo Human Rights Campaign, Islamic Human Rights Commission, Amnesty International, the Muslim Council of Britain, and others. I was even told that the actress Vanessa Redgrave was among them. Their message to the police was, 'Let them go.' And to us, 'Welcome home.'

That night I fell asleep imagining what was next for me . . . I slept well, but with all my clothes on: the cell was biting cold. I woke to the sound of the *athaan*, called by one of the others, and performed the dawn prayer. I read the Quran for a while, and returned to my bunk for a nap. After breakfast I went for a shower and brush up. Then I was given 'recreation' time in the car park outside. The cold was unbelievable, almost unbearably so, but I decided to stay out to witness another incredible sight. At least fifteen police officers wearing protective vests, and two police dogs, were all there waiting for me. The British had managed to outdo the Americans in overkill. 'All this trouble they've gone to – just for me,' I thought as I walked around, passing each officer – and dog – trying to appear unfazed. But the fact was that I was shivering. The cold was keeping me alert, but was biting into my face. Finally, I relented and asked to go back in.

'Don't blame you, mate,' said the escorting officer, 'but your time was up anyway.'

Shortly afterwards, Gareth returned and we talked for a while longer, before the first set of questioning began. The questions were a complete replica of the last three years: Was I a member of al-Qa'idah, did I fight against coalition troops on the front line, was I responsible for training in and funding terrorist camps?

We broke at lunchtime, and Gareth had to leave then for the House of Lords' decision on the Belmarsh cases. Hossein stayed with me to complete the second and last interrogation. I wasn't sure about him initially, but I soon saw what he was like during questioning. I had not answered any questions in Gareth's presence, but had been bursting to make some comments to the officers. One in particular, who had a strong Scottish accent, managed to get an occasional nod in disbelief from me, and even a burst of laughter.

'We believe that you have had associations with al-Qa'idah, or associated groups in the past. Can you tell us the whereabouts of these people?' he asked. I looked towards Hossein, holding my laughter in, but when I looked back at the detective I couldn't control myself.

'I see you find this amusing, Moazzam. You think it's funny?' said the Scotsman.

Then Hossein interjected, 'Well, I think it's funny, hilarious in fact. Think about what you've just asked my client. He's been held in a military prison for three years, much of it in isolation. How on earth would he know the whereabouts of these people, even if he did accept your inference about association? He didn't even know the whereabouts of his own family!'

I really felt I wanted to talk to these two – not as police officers, but just as men. But I could see they were following orders, and were not interested in too much analysis. At the end of the questioning, which had certainly been more amusing than gruelling, and which clearly demonstrated Hossein's ability to unflinchingly confront London's finest, they told me that I was free and not going to be charged.

As everyone got up to leave the room, I said to the Scotsman, 'I really hope you didn't take offence at my outburst, but your question was quite silly. But please don't take it personally.'

'None taken. You know, we have to ask these questions. We have people breathing down our necks, often setting these questions, which sound as meaningless to us as they are hilarious to you. Anyway, I have a load of property to hand over to you so we'd better get started; I'm sure you don't want to spend a second here longer than necessary.'

'True, can I just ask you though, some property was seized from my house in Pakistan, in 2002, including a laptop, my wife's purse, and several thousand pounds of our savings. Have the Americans given you any of that?'

'I know there was a computer interrogated here, and I'm sure the money was here too. I'll have to check on it and get back to you, or your lawyer,' he said.

'Strange words,' I thought. 'How do you interrogate a computer? Was it read its rights, and was a lawyer present?'

I was free to walk out of that police station from the front door.

A policeman in civilian clothes came in and introduced himself as my community liaison officer. He had come down from Birmingham to arrange whatever I wanted – to go up to Birmingham, or to bring my family down to London. He spoke with a strong Brummie accent, which made me smile; it was so long since I'd heard that voice, but it really meant home to me.

'We can arrange a hotel for you and you can stay for a few days with your family, whatever you want, it's all up to you.' I thought this was amazing, it felt as though I really did have a very new status. I politely declined his offer, expressing my gratitude for the gesture. I didn't want a hotel. Gareth had already arranged for me to meet the family at her house. So I waited in a room, unattended for the first time, while Hossein went through the same routine with Richard.

Once that was over, the police said they would take us wherever we wanted. I'd thought about leaving through the front entrance, but was worried about getting swamped by the media, and having an emotional reunion with my family seen by the press. So we asked the police to take us to Gareth's house. They sped through the traffic in a marked police van. Richard Belmar sat in the back with me. Suddenly it all felt really, really horrible. It was like being back in one of those Guantánamo oven-like vehicles, in chains. But of course we were no longer held by anybody. We were free. It didn't take long to reach our destination; Richard said it could have been a hundred miles, but nothing mattered. I was impressed to see how strong he was after all that time: 'Nothing makes any difference any more. It's over, it's all over.' The van stopped at Gareth's house, and the police got out and helped us with our bags. Then I heard somebody say, 'Al-Qa'idah, al-Qa'idah,' from the flats opposite. I thought, 'Oh my God, I can't believe this, will this never end?' That blurred the pleasure of finally entering a friendly house in England. But Hossain was still with us, a reassuring link to Gareth.

We walked into Gareth's house, where I went into a corner of her lounge and made a prostration and short prayer: *sajdah us-shukr*, or the prostration of gratitude. Soon after, the doorbell rang, and my father walked in with my two brothers and cousin.

Richard's father and his sister Jeanette were downstairs waiting for him, but before he went to them, he said, 'I want to do something first.' He got a towel out of his bag, and wrapped it around his head, Arab style. A lot of people did that in Guantánamo, and I supposed that idea must have been with him all along. Richard's family did not stay long, they'd already arranged to leave for somewhere else. As they came up, ready to go, all of the Belmars greeted the Beggs warmly, and vice versa, and finally Richard Belmar said goodbye to Moazzam Begg, both former prisoners of the United States of America in Guantánamo Bay, Cuba.

I had thought so much about seeing all my family again. But I had had no idea what I would really feel like. In fact, it wasn't hugely emotional. I wasn't a bag of nerves, or in tears, and it wasn't that we were restraining ourselves. It was just a very civilized, polite, affair – that's how we are. We usually laugh off things that are too stressful or emotionally demanding. The one thing was that my older brother, Azam, had tears in his eyes. I looked away. It was hard to see him in tears. I had never seen him cry, except when our mother died (or when Dad had given him a walloping, but that didn't really count). We were kids then.

First, my father and I embraced. It seemed like only yesterday we had sat down and had one of our debates about religion and politics.

This man had struggled so hard for the past three years, against the injustice of the US government, and the apathy of the British, to see his son returned. Life had changed.

Suddenly my cousin, Mukarram, just grabbed me. 'I love you, Moazzam *bhai* [brother] – I have the maximum amount of love for you, bro.'

Then my huge younger brother, Asad, grabbed me, saying, 'Enough respect, brother, enough respect. I'm glad you're back home. We all missed you badly, things weren't the same without you.'

All went quiet for a few moments. My family probably looked more relieved than I did. I didn't know what to say. I really didn't know what to say, to any of them. It seemed so awkward. The silence was finally broken with a typical Begg-style reference to dinner. Asad was given the honour of scouting the streets of London for food, a task we teasingly accused him of relishing. He soon returned, with over £300 worth of halal takeaway meals.

Pizzas, kebabs, chips, curries, fried chicken, humus, salads, soft drinks, fruit juices, chocolates, cakes, and ice cream were all a little too much after my diet of boiled vegetables and cold tea in Guantánamo. I found that everyone had a mobile phone – not uncommon, even before I had left, except that my dad now had one. In fact he had two. And they were all ringing incessantly – five or six phones at once. My father seemed completely drained with the calls, saying politely, but firmly, that he was tired and please would they leave him alone.

Zaynab called on my brother's phone. At last, after almost three years to the day from that terrible night in Islamabad I heard her sweet voice. Again, our conversation was calm and civilized, though partly because of all the other people who were around. And that was the problem that my well-meaning family had apparently not considered. She was the last person I'd seen before all this happened. She and my children were the only ones here who did not get a goodbye from me, and yet she and the children were not here. I had envisaged a meeting with her and the children first, and then everyone else. And I felt that she wanted the same. It made things worse when she said she wanted to come, and I said, 'Look, I don't think that is a good idea.' It was almost midnight, and it would have meant my brother would have to drive up to Birmingham, and come back with her, and then do it all over again some time later to drop us off. She was clearly upset, but she just accepted it. I couldn't bear to hear her sounding so sad and dejected, but the real reason I did not want her to come was because I was so worried about being in that place where people outside had shouted, 'Al-Qa'idah, al-Qa'idah.' I was also worried about a siege by the media, or worse if there were some crazy people waiting for the chance to hurt my family or me. I thought about it for a while, and then decided finally that it was not right to make her wait and suffer like that. So my brother went to collect them from Birmingham.

Gareth's poor husband, Bill, had been very accommodating, but careful to leave us to it. Soon Gareth came home and sat with us for a while. We discussed the various options about speaking to the media, who were swamping my father with calls. Gareth, in her usual very quiet voice, said I should not be making plans, but just concentrate on calming down, and getting myself back into normal life. But I said, no, I felt strongly that I had an obligation to speak to the press, exposing Guantánamo, for the sake of the ones left behind. We were none of us clear about exactly how to deal with the whole media circus that was apparently waiting for me. My father, who to my amazement seemed very comfortable talking to all manner of journalists, told me I should just take the largest amount of money I could get, to give me a start back with the family. He told me he had had offers of more than £100,000 from the tabloid papers, but we all cringed at the idea.

Gareth explained the difference between different papers' approach, to money, and to me. Finally I decided to do an interview with one of the broadsheets the following day, after which I would go straight back home.

Then Zaynab finally arrived at about two o'clock in the morning, with the kids. As soon as I saw her, I put my arms around her and hugged her, but with all those people there it was very, very difficult. I was hoping we'd be given some time alone. There was so much we had to talk about, but I knew, *in Sha Allah,* God willing, that we had the rest of our lives to catch up. I went over to the children, who were half asleep. Zaynab told me they'd been awake well past midnight, waiting for when they'd finally get to see their father, but they had fallen asleep in the car. They had woken up tired but excited when Zaynab told them, 'Come on, kids, wake up, Baba's here.'

I picked each one of them up, and then picked all three up together, as I used to do. '*As-salaamu alaikum,*' I said.

'*Wa alaikum as-salaam,*' they all said in their little voices.

I hadn't seen a child in three years, let alone my own. What I most wanted was for them to recognize me, to relate to me, and to feel like a father again. Nusaybah, my younger daughter, gave a little smile, not looking me directly in the face.

I asked, 'Do you know who I am?'

'Yes, you're Baba.'

Then I turned to my eldest son. 'Do you remember me, Abdur-Rahman?'

'Yes,' he answered, half asleep, 'you're Baba.'

'And what do you remember about me?'

'I remember when you used to read us bedtime stories and take us swimming. And that time in Afghanistan when we hid in your car, and you didn't even know we were there for a long time. And you used to call me "a little monkey", because I liked to jump around and climb a lot,' he said, getting a little more animated.

'He still does,' said Nusaybah, still refusing to look at me.

My older daughter, Umamah, who I was always so close to, was very emotional. She had started crying as soon she saw me. I sat down with her and we talked for a while, with me holding her like I used to do, but she wasn't the little person of three years before. I was wondering what she was thinking about me, her Baba; did I feel different to her?

Then I saw my little son for the first time ever. It was quite strange to see him – my son who'd never known a father. I was never an outwardly emotional person, but I was tumultuous inside then. There were all kinds of thoughts going through my mind about this child. I picked him up, thinking, 'He won't even know who I am, and he's going to start crying.' I could not have borne that. I held him, and kissed him, though he was still asleep. Then I handed him back to Zaynab. My wife had named him Ayub (Job), inspired by the Prophet's tests of faith, mentioned in the Quran and the Old Testament. But my father wanted Ibrahim (Abraham), so he is Ibrahim Ayub.

Gareth and Bill packed some things up and soon left. I felt very bad turning them out of their house. Much later on I learned that they took a hotel room. I already knew that Gareth was in a category of her own for selflessness and total commitment to her clients, but right then I felt so deeply grateful that she was with us, on our side, and a real friend.

My brother and cousin went off to sleep downstairs. I stayed quiet for quite a while. My father was sitting beside me, but he was shattered himself, and had another interview to do at seven in the morning. I got up and walked about. I went downstairs and started pacing. I just knew there were too many people there for me to deal with so soon. I was thinking how just a few hours ago, perhaps thirty-six hours ago, I was sitting in a cell, in solitary, isolated from everybody else, and here I had all this space to walk in. The strange thing was that all of those things that were routine to me from before, all those things that I'd done before in my normal life – which was not Bagram and Guantánamo Day – came back to me in a flash. I saw all the books on Gareth's shelves as I was walking around. I started reading bits of them, flicking through. Then I thought, 'I'm being antisocial, I don't know what I feel, but . . . this isn't right.'

I played with the children for a while, and then Zaynab took them up to bed. Upstairs, tucked up in bed, my daughter Umamah was waiting for me to come and talk to her and kiss her goodnight. I hadn't realized that she was still awake. When I came upstairs she was crying, and saying, 'Baba doesn't love me any more,' and Zaynab was a little upset that I had asked her to stay in Birmingham, and then that I wasn't paying her any attention. 'This is just too much,' I thought, 'I can't handle this, what do they all expect from me?'

Everybody had fallen asleep, except Zaynab and me. At last we were alone in a room and able to speak about all that had happened and how we'd really managed without one another. We talked for a couple of hours, and then decided that we both wanted to go home. I didn't want to stay in London another moment, it was just wrong for me. I felt so grateful to Gareth for everything, but now I just needed my own house, and I needed as few people as possible around. I called my brother Azam, who'd gone back to his house in North London. I woke everyone up and told them we were going home, to Birmingham

When we got home Azam and Asad stayed with me all night. Asad was going to be security, for a couple of days, and deal with the press or anyone else. I felt confident he'd deal with all of that, whatever it was going to be. So this was my return home. It seemed as if I'd only been here a few days before, that the last three years were an illusion. We arrived home at 5 a.m. and I found the gas heater in the living room out of order. The room was very cold, and the central heating took a while to warm up. I asked Zaynab if she had any tools. Then I set about the repair job. Of course, after dismantling the whole thing, it still didn't work, until my nine-year-old Umamah came down and inserted a loose wire back into place.

Everyone thought I was in hiding somewhere out in the country. Some of the tabloids had put out a 'contract', offering 'wads of cash' for readers who would lead them to us. One of my cousin's friends arranged for multiple reported sightings in places as diverse as Aberystwyth, Land's End, and the Mull of Kintyre.

Another cousin of mine also came, Sami, a lawyer, who I hadn't seen for many years before I was incarcerated, though he had helped my father regularly with the campaign. He turned up every day, and very kindly took the kids to the cinema, brought food for the house, and so on, but I couldn't handle even those small interactions. I found it very hard to tell people to go away. People just didn't seem to understand that I didn't want anybody around. Sometimes I just didn't open the door when they knocked, although I knew they would not understand and would feel hurt. Everybody expected to get a piece of me. I didn't want to see people. I just wanted to spend time at home alone, with my family. At times I didn't even want to be with them, and locked myself alone in a small room. I wished I could be a hermit, and just vanish into some remote and beautiful place by myself, or with Zaynab. I wrote to her about going away together like that, when I was in Guantánamo. But within a few days, I had a letter from the Home Office, saying that my passport facilities were being withdrawn, so we obviously weren't going too far. I did not bother to think much about it – it was another battle for Gareth.

There were little things too, which were not easy. I thought I would sink into my own bed with relief after those years on the thin mat on metal. But I couldn't sleep. The bed was too soft. I had to make poor Zaynab sleep on the floor with me. I worried about finding my role in this family, which seemed to have got so self-sufficient without me.

There was unexpected sadness that I had to deal with too. My father had not wanted to tell me by letter, when I was alone in a cell, that he had lost both his brother and sister in the last year. Dad told me that these two had been constantly praying for me in Guantánamo, asking about me, and always thinking and wishing the best for me. Those two deaths came as a very big shock. I felt very, very sad. Hearing about them brought tears to my eyes – for the first time.

My father talked to me for hours about the family, and I discovered that the extended family had been changed enormously by my absence. Old feuds between my father and his siblings had stopped, and they had come together. People who hadn't spoken to one another for years had turned up to my father's house and offered him their complete support. I had come home to a united family. The cousins and others were meeting regularly, and all sorts of family get-togethers were taking place, which had not happened for quite a while in the years before my abduction.

It took me a while to appreciate how my father had changed too, not only with his family, but also in handling the outside world. He had kept clippings of newspapers, bundles of whole newspapers, documents, and videos, of all those conferences, and talks, and news programmes that he had done. I spent one whole day just going through all of those cuttings, and I saw the campaign he had led was a much, much bigger affair than I had realized. I felt impressed by what he had done, and terribly touched to see how he had spoken about me, with so much public emotion. This was not a side of my father I had ever seen.

Slowly, over a few days, I began to meet people. My old friend from the bookshop, Shakeel, came to see me. I drove up to London with him – to the Imperial War Museum. God only knows how many times I had fantasized about my own Great Escape.

Shakeel and I went to visit Gareth at her office too. It was quite amazing to see the response of everyone there. Some of those people had worked hard on various aspects of my case, for the past three years. I got the feeling the people here were so genuinely committed to the preservation of human rights and the protection of the legally oppressed. (Often since I have had the feeling that I should have finished my law degree and joined Gareth's team.)

The sensation of driving after all this time still came instinctively, and gave me a great sense of freedom and autonomy. Seeing Zaynab drive off, taking the kids to school, getting the shopping, or driving to see family and friends, was a pleasant surprise. I thought a lot about how hard she must have struggled without me. But she justly pointed out that many people had helped her: her parents and mine, her best friend from Italy, her brother, and scores of other friends – even some people she didn't know. Some had taken the children swimming or to karate classes, and bought them toys. Others had brought appliances for the house, when my family returned to England with nothing, after spending a month with Zaynab's brother, in Oman. Someone had installed a new laminated floor in the house, and refused to accept payment, while another had replaced a radiator. And others still had helped financially. And further back still, in Pakistan, friends and well wishers had helped them immensely, until they were safely on board a flight to Oman. Zaynab often said that she praised Allah for all the help she received; even the media had been kind to her. But she expressed sadness for the families of other people, who did not have the kind of family and community support that she enjoyed.

After a couple of weeks I saw a psychiatrist, Dr McKeith, someone who had worked closely with Gareth (and former prisoners wrongly detained) and who had even been prepared to come to Guantánamo with my father to see me, if the Americans had ever given permission. I was very interested to hear about some of the people he'd dealt with before, like the Irish prisoners who had suffered such very long years in prison for something they never did. He was very understanding, and well aware of what I was going through. I felt, initially, that I had not suffered any lasting trauma from my ordeal. But readjustment to society, and at times, family life, became a great struggle. I did not like to socialize much and found I needed to be alone, in complete seclusion at home, sometimes for days on end. I found too that I had two very different lives – one for the home and one as a campaigner.

But there was one person I really wanted to see soon. I read some things about Feroz in the papers, which said he was having psychological problems readjusting, and that bothered me, although I didn't know if it was true. I got his phone number through his solicitor, and came up to London to meet him. I also really wanted to meet the people who ran the website cageprisoners.com. Zaynab had told me about it, and it had become my daily reading since I got home, because it had so much detail about men I knew only by voice in those strange, warm relationships shouting over the blocks in Guantánamo, or in glimpses in Bagram or Kandahar.

When I saw Feroz I felt pretty excited. 'This is the first time I've seen you properly, out of a cell.' Feroz seemed as casual as I'd expected. We went to a Korean restaurant and had lunch together, with Tariq from Cageprisoners. Feroz seemed a little paranoid that people, perhaps the

CIA, were after him. There was a lot in the news then about cases of 'rendering', when Muslim men were kidnapped by the CIA from countries like Sweden or Italy and taken to countries like Syria, Egypt, or Jordan to be tortured and imprisoned without trial. Feroz was very particular about where he sat, and would never sit with his back towards the door in the restaurant. He said to me, 'I don't know what's wrong with you, don't you realize they could be coming for us any minute?'

We talked for a while, and Feroz seemed just the same to me as he was in Guantánamo, apart from how he was dressed. But I could sense that he was a little uneasy, and looking for some sort of direction in what he was going to do next, work, study, or whatever. Unlike me he didn't have the framework of a wife and young family to be responsible for.

He told me he had problems with getting his papers in order, because of some of the things that had been taken by the Americans. I told him I was going to meet Gareth at her office around five o'clock, and suggested he should come too. I spoke to one of the girls at the office, an Arabic speaker, who had previously translated for some of the Belmarsh detainees who had just been released. One of them was Abu Qatada, the Palestinian sheikh, whom I bumped into as I was leaving. We exchanged greetings and spoke for a while about the hardships of detention without trial. Before I left I asked him one final question. 'Sheikh, what's your opinion about the September 11 attacks?'

'Listen, brother. If I had known anything about it beforehand I would have done all in my power to prevent them.'*

*

---

* Abu Qatada is the subject of an extradition agreement with Jordan where he could face torture and execution.

There was another visit I needed to make in London. I had to see the family of my friend Shaker Aamer, the Saudi whose family had lived in the same house as us in Kabul back in 2001. Shaker was still in Guantánamo, in Camp Five. I really wanted to go, but I was also dreading it, wondering what I could find to say. I had already spoken to his wife on the phone, and I found her quite weak after a spell in hospital, and I had to do all the talking. A friend offered to drive me to their place in South London. On the way I suddenly thought, 'I can't arrive empty handed, I've got to get something.' He didn't know the area, and we couldn't see any place selling toys. So I ended up just stopping at a newsagent and buying boxes of chocolates.

I had met Shaker's father-in-law and his brother-in-law, Adeel, back when Shaker was in England. Adeel said, 'I've been praying for you every single day.'

Shaker was my close friend, and we knew each other so well. Seeing his family here in London, after all they had suffered, broke my heart. I just didn't know what to say. But Shaker's eldest daughter, Juhayna, began to cry when she saw me.

'Why is she crying,' I asked, turning to Adeel, 'what's the matter?'

'She remembers the last time she saw you, when you evacuated from Kabul, and her father was still with her.'

I didn't know what to say. A silent moment passed and then I started talking to her and her brother. By the time I'd left that evening, they were all over me, jumping on top of me, fighting, pulling my hair, bringing out their books from school, reading poetry, reciting the Quran, and telling me what they'd learned. I was really sad to leave. Zaynab had been to visit them, and they'd been to see her too, so they'd been in contact.

Before I got up to leave, I found it so difficult to know what to tell them. I didn't want to give false hope, and at the same time I could not leave them without any hope. I had to strike that balance. Shaker's father-in-law had been the imam of a mosque nearby, a very respected person, and I wanted to tell him everything I could about his daughter's husband. I had to say that I never did meet Shaker during my time there, but there were two things about him that I wanted to tell them. One was about how the US soldier in Kandahar had been so impressed by Shaker that he'd almost converted to Islam, and the other was how a soldier told me he was brought to tears listening to Shaker speak about the dearest things in his life.

Of course, Shaker's family know what he's like. He's a larger-than-life character. He never stops talking. He's big, he's generous, he's influential. I loved teasing him, and our relationship was full of that kind of thing. The saddest part of all this, which I didn't tell them, was that I knew things had got harder for him there in Guantánamo, because the Americans perceived him to be very influential, and thus a threat. He spoke Arabic and English, and he was vociferous in his demands for justice. I was told the guards had nicknamed him the Professor. Shaker was no professor, but that just demonstrated the Americans' mentality. This was why they had put him in Camp Five, the super-maximum-security prison.

I couldn't stop thinking about Shaker's family; I knew that both he and they would remain in my thoughts until he was returned home, as I had been.

I thought often too about the various others I had left behind, like Jamil el-Banna and Bisher al-Rawi from London, about Hicks, Mohammad, Saeed the Russian, and even Uthman. And I thought about their families and what they were going through. These thoughts would never go away for long, and remain one of the most painful parts of my return.

Many things were confusing too. Walking through Birmingham

with the kids, going into shops and showing my credit card, or on the Underground in London, people recognized me. They wanted to shake my hand at least. In the mosque people were always hugging me, telling me I was an inspiration for them.

I went to a huge Amnesty International regional meeting, and the whole hall got up to welcome me. Afterwards people came up in droves to speak to me, grabbing my hand, telling me how they felt for me, but I had no idea who they were. They weren't Muslims, and they weren't too aware of things. At the Amnesty meeting I met an American who said, 'I'd like to apologize to you for what my country did to you. I am thoroughly ashamed of its actions.' Putting out his hand, he said, 'And I'd like to shake your hand. I wonder if you'd like to join me for a pint of beer?' Well, I hadn't heard that in a long time.

'No thank you,' I said, 'I don't drink, but I appreciate you asking.'

Realizing his mistake, he apologized profusely, adding, 'Oh hell. I bet you just think it's another ignorant American, again.'

'Not at all,' I said, almost agreeing with him. But I knew better. I really respected Amnesty's activists' wish to fight injustice, when they could have just been happy with their own lives, not caring about obscure Palestine, or Iraq, or Guantánamo. But it was strange that they had an idea of this person, Moazzam Begg, who they felt involved with, despite not knowing him.

The media rang my mobile phone constantly, asking me for interviews, but I decided to do just one major TV interview in the UK, with Jon Snow, for *Channel 4 News*. Shortly after that, the press inundated me with interview requests. They called my father, Gareth's office, friends, and relatives. As the general elections approached I also gave lectures and speeches around the country. I spoke at a Muslim unity rally in London, using it as an opportunity to highlight the plight of those left behind. This generated even more media interest. I was also moved and disturbed by the case of Babar Ahmad, a British Muslim whose extradition was being demanded by the Americans. His wife and father mounted a brave campaign for his release. They told me they were greatly inspired by my father's tenacity and his unrelenting campaign for me.

International interest was almost equal to the local and national. I talked to Brazilians, Iranians, Pakistanis, Canadians, South Africans, Italians, Germans; to ABC news and Al Jazeera. As events further unravelled with stories about religious abuses against the Quran, the media began to call me again, as they did when the US finally admitted fault in the deaths of Afghan detainees in Bagram. In fact it got to the point when I had to refuse any more interviews. I had promised myself in Guantánamo that my family would always come first.

After a few months I began to feel I had control over my life again. All the old pleasures came back, like going to the park with the family, visiting my parents on Fridays, playing badminton or indoor football with my brother. I enrolled myself and the children in jujitsu classes, began teaching them Quranic recitation, helped with homework, and read bedtime stories. I took the family for outings to Warwick Castle, Sherwood Forest, West Midlands Safari Park, and camping in Snowdonia, as I had intended, as I had promised, back in solitary confinement.

Then came 7 July, and the bombs in London two days after I turned thirty-seven. My brother Azam called to ask if I'd seen the news. I turned the television on and there was every channel reporting the bombings on the Tube, and talking about a simultaneous terrorist attack on a bus. My heart sank. I felt overwhelmed by the news. It was utter shock. My mind flashed back to the United States interrogators, back in December 2004. They had continually asked me if I could help them prevent any attacks in Britain, and they really believed, or they made out that they believed, some attacks were imminent in Britain. I didn't believe them. I thought it was not real interrogation, but some kind of testing. What could I have possibly known after three years? I have never known anybody who has carried out bombings.

As reporters and television images continued to describe the scale of the attacks and the growing numbers of dead and injured, while the emergency services desperately tried to help and bring order, I felt suffocated. Any one of my family or friends in London could have been on those trains. I made several calls to check that none of them had been hurt. None were. Even I could have been on one of those trains myself, especially since I was coming to London so often to work on my book at that time.

When I saw an interview with one of the wounded taken to the Whitechapel mosque I was moved to tears. This ordinary-looking man could have easily made wholesale statements condemning Islam, or just refused the help offered by Muslims, and probably helped shape public opinion in the process. And so could any of the other survivors. Instead there just seemed to be a sense of bewilderment, and relief. I really felt like going and offering my personal assistance, but I didn't know what to do, and even more than that, I could not have faced someone telling me, 'Get lost! We don't need the help of terrorists!'

As I sat there watching, I thought back to the time when September 11 had so affected my life. This time I thought, with dread, 'This is going to cause such a reaction in Britain that the whole face of the country will change.'

I thought about the British residents still in Guantánamo. Who was going to want to hear about them, or Babar Ahmad's case? All these things were racing through my mind. Then I thought, 'Somebody is going to try and make a link and say, "You're that type of person, the Americans were not holding you for no reason at all, you probably also subscribe to this type of thing."' How was I going to try and explain myself in an atmosphere of sheer terror, with people being full of emotional reaction? I didn't move out of the house for almost two days. I watched the news every single minute.

I felt angry and upset that someone had done this, not only because of the killing, but also because of the setback it had undoubtedly caused for Islam worldwide, as well as in Britain itself. From the days of Bosnia and Chechnya, it was crystal-clear to me that Britain was a special place where Muslims from all over the world were able to come and speak out. They could mobilize support for their causes within the framework of the law, they could even criticize the British government to kingdom come if they were honest about it. But after this tragedy, like after September 11, there would be a serious setback for any positive Islamic movement.

When I went to Afghanistan, I believed the Taliban had made some modest progress – in social justice and in upholding pure, old-style Islamic values forgotten in many Islamic countries. After September 11 that life was destroyed. After London, that would be the theme again, in many places.

The press were continuously asking me to give them my opinion. I thought perhaps they wanted to hear that I didn't condemn the bombings, so that they could turn on me as just another terrorist. But I unequivocally condemned them. I tried to analyse who could have done it, and why. Before knowing the full story I wanted to reserve judgement. And if Muslims did it, then I wanted us all to analyse why it happened. I agreed with George Galloway's brave statement, linking it with Iraq. He was hounded and attacked because he said it before anyone else, but the reality for me was that he exactly echoed how I felt. And that was what I told the press. To me the answer to why these people did it was simple: it was rage.

Looking at the media coverage I found quite often that the people they brought in were frustratingly unrepresentative. I felt I had a lot of insight into some of the things that they were talking about and I wanted to speak out. I had to educate people. This was not a time to stay quiet. So I regularly spoke to the media in the hope of creating a little understanding. After all, I was someone who had felt the extreme brunt of some of the types of proposals for combating terrorism.

There was so much talk about disenfranchised Muslim youth falling prey to a type of Islam that has no regard for innocent life, but I knew otherwise. I met several former Lynx members at the funeral of our friend Sam, a few months after I returned. Although most were settled, some were still womanizing, clubbing, taking drugs, and getting into the odd fight. (In fact one of them phoned with his commiserations from prison.) They were very in touch with the local Muslim street culture, which still looked back at the Lynx with admiration. But their political views had been formed in the wake of the war on terror and in an ensuing atmosphere of Islamophobia. A couple were now practising Muslims, though far from radical, but the majority were not. They didn't have anything good to say about radical Muslim clerics, but, predictably, they all detested Blair, and Bush even more.

Still, I also knew I had to speak to my own community. We had a local meeting about the 7 July events, just a few days afterwards – about what we could do about it to maintain our position as Muslims, but also to condemn the violence and prevent anything more taking place. I was invited. Most of the meeting I stayed quiet. But, without being arrogant, I knew that people were waiting for me to speak. And as soon as I did, it was almost unanimous that the burden was going to be on my shoulders. They wanted me to be more than an analyst. They wanted a voice, a spokesman.

I already felt that the Muslim community was looking for heroes; it was looking for people to put on a brave face for all of us. Almost everybody I was speaking to was saying now was my time to speak to people. I also felt I must address the Muslim community about what I felt was the way forward for us here in Britain. But I held back too, because I really didn't know. I didn't know what the way forward was. But in the short term I did know that it was not planting bombs on trains.

I thought, 'Each time something happens, are they going to start implementing more draconian measures? And if so, how far will it go? What is the future for us in this country? And what if the non-Muslim people who have been on our side just changed sides because of all this?' All this weighed heavily on my mind.

Things felt very hard again, psychologically. I did not want to go to London, or to go on the Tube. What went through my mind was, 'Suppose something happened when I was there, they might think it was me behind it?' I was suddenly as paranoid as Feroz had been.

About three days after the bombs, I had a phone call from Lucy, from MI5. I really knew then that I was not going to be able to just put this London thing to one side as nothing to do with me.

'Hello, I'm Lucy, I don't know if you remember me?' Of course I did, I don't know any girls called Lucy in my world. She went on, 'You're probably expecting this call.'

I said, 'Yes, I was, a long time ago, in February.'

'I heard you speaking on the radio a couple of times about what happened and thought that maybe you'd speak to us.'

'Yes, of course. I've never had a problem talking to you. The problem has always been your perception of me.'

I asked them to come over to my house, but she said, no, it would be better, more discreet, somewhere else. She called again later and said we should meet at Birmingham airport. I said yes, but I was really worried, in fact more than worried – paranoid. Should I really be going to an airport, or a train station at an airport? I was less worried about rendition or something like that, than about moving out of my predominantly Asian area, my little world where I felt safe.

I'd heard stories about even Sikhs and others being attacked, and I really did not want to go to the airport and walk around there. I thought someone was bound to say something or do something. I was feeling paranoid. I got there, waited in the car park, and didn't get out of the car. I thought, 'What if somebody sees me sitting in the car, and they report it?' I got very fidgety; I didn't know what to do. I had a book, and I tried reading it. I was trying to look normal, hoping there wasn't somebody there thinking I was doing something suspicious.

Then Lucy called, to say, 'We've had a little bit of a hiccup, we can't meet at the airport, we'd arranged a room in an hotel, but something happened there, so can you just wait a few minutes while we get sorted out?'

I sat there waiting, wondering, should I get out of the car and walk around? No, I couldn't walk around, what would I be walking around for? Then she called again, and asked me to get to the airport departure lounge, catching the monorail.

As I walked into the airport I saw some other Asians and I felt a little more comfortable. Nothing was happening. Everything was fine. Then as I was walking upstairs, a young girl came and stopped me. She said, 'Excuse me, sir, can I interest you in a store card?' I was stunned, she actually wanted to speak to me, things were normal. I started talking to her and she began to take my details. But I said, 'I really have to go, I'm really sorry, I'm late for an appointment, can you tell me the way to the monorail, please?' She pleaded that she needed to get this done today; couldn't I just quickly do it? She looked so dejected, I felt bad, but I had to rush.

When I got to the monorail I was still worried about what other people might think, and glad I wasn't carrying a bag. I phoned them at the end of the monorail. 'Where do I go now?'

Lucy gave me some directions through a huge deserted corridor, where there must have normally been hundreds of people, but there was absolutely nobody. My heart was going fast, and I was thinking, 'Why have they picked this route, where it's so quiet I can hear my footsteps echoing? The cameras are on me, everything is on me, if something happens now . . .' Eventually I reached the outside and I saw a car drive up. There was Lucy with a driver. I got into the car, and they took me to a hotel.

As soon as I walked in I saw a black Muslim friend who I hadn't seen in many years, but I remembered from when he became a Muslim in Central Mosque. He came straight over to me, and grabbed me really tight, saying, '*As-salaamu alaikum*, Moazzam, how are you doing, brother?'

'*Al-hamdu Lillah*, I'm fine.' He said he was working there.

Lucy stood there, watching, and I thought, 'What is he thinking I'm doing here with this woman?'

Then he said, 'Well, I can see you're busy.'

I walked off with her, and I felt a little embarrassed. I said to her, 'There goes your idea of trying to be discreet.'

We went upstairs to a room where a colleague of hers was waiting. We had some mundane chat about how Andrew and Matt and all those other MI5 people were. They asked me how things had been since I'd been back, and what had I been doing. I joked with Lucy telling her I'd just finished a chapter with her in it. She seemed pretty surprised, and somewhat flattered. I warned her she might not like it too much.

Then they began asking me about the bombings, my ideas about who was behind it, and my general perspective.

I hid my anger, and said, 'I spend most of my time at home with my family, my kids. I don't have close friends. I know lots of people, but I don't socialize. The rest of my time is coming up to London, working on the book.'

They really pressed me to help them analyse what was behind the bombings. I told them what I felt, who seemed to gain most from all of this. I tried to analyse it. My perception at that time was 'Who stood to gain the most?' I suggested the extreme right had just been waiting to say, 'Look, we've been telling you all along that these people are diametrically opposed to our way of life and here's the proof.' But at that time the facts hadn't even been released. I reminded them of the 1996 Oklahoma bombing, first attributed to Muslims. We talked for about an hour or so. I spelled out exactly what I thought. 'I feel what they've done is totally wrong, not just because it's in Britain and because I happen to live here, but because I don't believe in attacks on civilians anywhere, whether it's by suicide bombs or by B52s. They are both indiscriminate.' I told them I would be trying to find out everything I could about what was behind this, 'But it won't be for you, it will be because the impact on our community is going to be very, very heavy and I want to try and stop that.'

Then I asked them about Bisher al-Rawi, the British resident I'd met in Bagram. 'The press has reported that Bisher was helping you before his arrest, and yet he's sitting there in Guantánamo. You're complicit in that. Aren't you ashamed?' Then I went on, 'Your colleagues, *and* you, Lucy, were all there, and part of what was taking place, a very real part of Guantánamo and Bagram. This means that you were complicit in abduction, in trying to extract information by torture. Before I was taken into custody, I had told my friends to tell your colleague Ian that I was ready to speak to him, that he could come to my house any time and have some Pakistani tea. But he didn't have the nerve to do that, he waited until the Pakistanis kidnapped me with guns and tazers, and then he came along after I was handcuffed and shackled.

'This is the reality of who you are. You all know what you did to me. But despite all that, I've gone all out of my way to come here to speak to you. You need to be a little bit ashamed of yourselves.'

Lucy's reaction was defensive. She talked about how it was all just policy, and she herself didn't know how to imagine what I'd gone through, though of course she couldn't speak for other members of the organization. What she did not say was that she was sorry for what had happened to me. I could feel that she was looking for some way of saving face without making an apology.

I wanted to know about Ian. I wanted them to arrange for me to meet him. I wanted to speak to him, face to face, now that we were both free men. I wanted to know how he felt about all that had happened, how he felt then and afterwards about not getting me a lawyer, nor access to the British Consul, nor some assurance that my family, British citizens, were OK. Had I been white, an ex-pat living in Pakistan, my sense is that things would probably have been very different.

I had one more question. It was for Lucy's colleague. 'Are you recording this conversation?'

She hesitated for a second. She looked to the side, and then looked me straight in the eye, and said no. I didn't believe her.

MI5 were no different in Birmingham in 2005 than they had been all those other times we had met. They wanted something from me, but they didn't know what it was. I had nothing to give them. I never had. I don't know who al-Qa'idah are. I don't know how al-Qa'idah plan their operations, or get their intelligence. I don't know their structure. If I did . . . I would be a different person.

Epilogue

Within three weeks, while I was in London, working on this book, I turned on the news to learn that another bombing had been attempted, but failed. The tragic murder of the Brazilian Jean Charles de Menezes soon followed. One of the alleged bombers was arrested within days, only a mile or so from where I live in Birmingham. All those arrested and charged were Muslims.

A couple of months later film clips were shown, allegedly Mohammad Siddique Khan's last message, before the fateful act. He said he did it because of the war in Iraq and Afghanistan. He was a Muslim.

Like many of us, I wanted to believe the conspiracy theories; that someone else was behind it, but I was not going to fool myself. My heart sank again, fearing for our future in this country.

I avoided travelling to London to work on the book at Victoria's house as much as possible. Sensing my anxiety, she often arranged for us to work at her friend's house out in the country, closer to Birmingham, which was fine with me. When I did eventually restart my regular train journeys it was with double the apprehension. People might think me a terrorist because of how I looked, if I wasn't wearing the right sort of jacket, if I walked too fast or slow. I was afraid of being shot, and I was afraid of being bombed.

On 19 November 2005, and for the three days that followed, there was a conference hosted by Amnesty International and Reprieve, Clive's organization. It was entitled 'The Global Struggle Against Torture: Guantánamo Bay, Bagram and Beyond'. The conference was based on an idea that Clive had mentioned back in Camp Echo, although I'd had my doubts about its eventual fruition. How, as Clive had proposed, would we expect the UK to allow the entry of all those former Guantánamo and Bagram detainees, when so many British residents still remained? And yet that is what happened.

The first day was a press conference and my call was simple, inspired by my father. 'We are not begging for clemency, we are not pleading for mercy. We are simply demanding justice. If someone has committed a crime, charge him and put him through a transparent system of justice. But since it is my experience that that will never happen, return them all to their loved ones, compensate them, close Guantánamo and all the other black holes of detention.'

Later that day, Manfred Nowak, UN Special Rapporteur on Torture, and Paul Hunt, UN Special Rapporteur on the Right to Health, individually interviewed all the former detainees who attended the conference, after the US had denied them access to meet with detainees held at Guantánamo – already described by Amnesty as 'the gulag of our times'.

That evening I met lawyers, human-rights activists, and journalists from Japan to Argentina, from Uganda to the USA. Guantánamo had consumed much of their lives, even more than mine (after my release). I met one student who 'knew everything about me' because I was the subject of her law thesis.

The next day, all the former UK detainees attended and spoke, either on stage, via microphone or recorded video interview. First Gareth reminded us all about the US Supreme Court decision in *Rasul versus Bush* and, despite its negligible tangible effect for detainees, the record will always show that Rasul won. Then, for the first time in public, the Tipton lads, Shafiq Rasul and Asif Iqbal, in their Black

Country accents, described their ordeal and how, when US intelligence had claimed they were seen in a video with bin Ladin, they had in fact been working in Currys – a fact that was made available by MI5.

When someone asked me how I was able to express myself so well, I answered, 'Well, before my incarceration I was not a very confident public speaker, so I would like to thank the CIA, MI5, FBI and the US military for giving me the confidence, and experience, after over three hundred interrogations, to perfect my style.' The audience roared with laughter.

Martin Mubanga rapped his 'Listen to Dem Bombs Drop' to huge rounds of applause and calls for an encore. The last time I heard that I was in Papa Block. I still didn't understand the lyrics.

And the last time I saw one particular Russian I had just been taken captive by the US military in Kandahar, Afghanistan. Airat Vakhitov had been my companion in the barn for several weeks. We embraced like old friends, and spoke about when we last met. It was so uplifting to see this man free, even though I'd never really known him. I also met Rasul, another Russian, who I'd never met, but who embraced me like a long-lost brother. I met Mohammad Sagheer, a Pakistani, one of the first to be released from Guantánamo. His house had been destroyed in the earthquake. Airat began a collection for him.

I met Abdullah Almalki, the Canadian Syrian who'd been tortured in Syria, allegedly with Canadian complicity. I told Abdullah that I now believed it was him (or his friend Maher Arar)* Nathan from US military intelligence had been referring to when I had been told, in Bagram, that I was going to Egypt.

'One of the things that helped me survive my ordeal, Abdullah,

---

* A Canadian national detained by US authorities and 'rendered' to Syria in October 2001, where he was held in a 'grave-like' cell and brutally tortured. He was released in October 2003. The Canadian government has launched an inquiry into the actions of its officials relating to his detention.

was the knowledge of people like you. I knew that no matter how bad I had it, there were always people who had it worse.'

The hardest part of the conference was listening to the heart-wrenching speeches of the relatives of those left behind. I met the brother of Sami al-Haj, the Al Jazeera cameraman detained in Guantánamo. Most people agreed that he was only there because of the US's vendetta against the Arabic television channel. I met Rabiye Kurnaz, mother of Murat Kurnaz, the Turkish detainee who was born and bred in Germany, but is denied representation by either government. Rabiye had gone to the very doors of the White House, with my father, to ask for justice for her son, when I was still captive. She hugged me like her own son. I met Nadia Dizderovic, wife of El Hadj Boudella, one of five Bosnian Algerians abducted by CIA agents outside the court where they were cleared of all charges in a terror plot, and sent to Guantánamo. She had taken photographs of the kidnap to prove it. I met the brother of Ahmed Arrachidi, who spoke so movingly and eloquently in Arabic about how his brother, a British resident from Morocco, once a cook, had now become 'the General', as the Americans had named him. I met the Brighton family of Omar Deghayes, the British resident whose father had been murdered by Gaddafi's regime. It broke my heart to tell them that the only time I saw their brother was in photographs presented by MI5 and CIA, in which his face looked terribly bruised and gaunt.

When Victoria read out two very emotional messages from Mrs el-Banna and from the mother of Bisher al-Rawi, and the children of Jamil el-Banna got up on stage and read out letters they'd written to their dad, there wasn't a dry eye in the audience.

Finally, my biggest surprise was from Shaker's family. I knew his father-in-law was due to speak, but I had no idea his wife was going to as well. She had suffered from terrible bouts of depression and spent time in hospital as a result. But she spoke so clearly and from the heart that I wished I could exchange places with Shaker in Guantánamo, so that he could come home.

I have read that in July 2003, Tony Blair was quite content to say, 'We have got very good information out of Guantánamo,' when asked what was to be done about me and the other British nationals still in Guantánamo. On 22 November 2005, however, coincidentally the last day of the conference, Blair conceded to a Commons committee, 'Guantánamo Bay is an anomaly' that has 'got to be brought to an end'. I was not as euphoric to hear this as some when I spoke for the first time to a few MPs about it in the House of Commons two days later. Blair's track record on the issue speaks for itself.

Still I must credit the Blair government for successfully negotiating my eventual repatriation to England, although that is true even of countries like Pakistan and Afghanistan for some of their own nationals. But one of the hardest truths I've had to face since my return has been the complicity of my own government in what happened.

For me the questions remain. Who provided false information to the US, and allowed my detention in the first place? Who exploited my situation to the maximum at every stage of my ordeal in Islamabad, in Kandahar, in Bagram, and in Guantánamo? Who was then, as now, the closest ally of the US? I have read Foreign Office letters to my father that maintain the Americans denied access to UK officials in Afghanistan, and yet I was interrogated by British intelligence in these very places – places where people, in the same situation as me, were tortured to death.

The sad fact is they have acted duplicitously, immorally and unlawfully. It is not just their uncritical acceptance of and obedience to torturous conditions, regimes, and physical restraint or worse. They were there by choice. These are the lessons of Nuremberg. You cannot simply be present in these circumstances and escape your own role.

The definition of torture under the UN convention is the application of extreme mental or physical pressure by a state on an individual for the purpose of obtaining information. Any complicity in that, as well as direct application, is in breach of international law and is criminal by definition. The paradox is that whilst the government is unperturbed in using that information and depending upon it as reliable, it acknowledges too that information obtained through torture and duress is abhorrent to the British way of life.

After 7 July, Tony Blair said, 'We shall not allow the terrorists to change our way of life,' but that is precisely what is happening. The knee-jerk approach to tackling terrorism pretends somehow that it is a new phenomenon in Britain because the war is an ideological one. The time allowed for detention without charge has already doubled to twenty-eight days, but Blair tried for ninety; plans for the closure of religious places (meaning mosques) deemed 'suspect' are in motion; new extradition agreements with countries that have torture as part of their unwritten convention, if not written constitution, have been signed; and, probably the most alarming of all: the accepted shoot-to-kill policy. I pray there are no more bombings, or our way of life will change, again.

Despite all of this I have learned much and developed since my incarceration, and even more after my return. One of the biggest lessons has been that there are so many people in this country who care and stand up for justice, and they are by no means all Muslim. When I heard from US guards in Guantánamo that there had been mass anti-war protests in London, in their millions, I was proud that it happened on the streets of the country I call home. Perhaps this is what Paxman really meant about never underestimating the Englishman's capacity to back the underdog. If that is the case, I'd like to say, 'I'm proud to be British, the same way I say I'm proud to be Muslim.' But only time can be the true judge of that.

Homeward Bound

Written by Moazzam Begg whilst in solitary confinement

> Begins this journey without reins,
> Ends in capture without aims;
> Now lying in the cell awake,
> With merriment and smiles all fake:
>
> Freedom is spent, time is up –
> Tears have rent my sorrow's cup;
> Home is cage, and cage is steel,
> Thus manifest reality's unreal
>
> Dreams are shattered, hopes are battered,
> Yet with new status one is flattered!
> The irony of it – detention, and all:
> Be so small, and stand so tall
>
> Years of tears and days of toil
> Are now but fears and tyrants' spoil;
> Ordainment has surely come to pass,
> But endure alone one must this farce

Now 'patience is of virtue' taught,
And virtue is of iron wrought;
So poetry is in motion set
(Perhaps, with appreciation met)

Still the paper do I pen,
Knowing what, but never when –
As dreams begin, and nightmares end –
I'm homeward bound to beloved tend